STUDIES IN IMPERIALISM

General editor: Andrew S. Thompson
Founding editor: John M. MacKenzie

When the 'Studies in Imperialism' series was founded more than twenty-five years ago, emphasis was laid upon the conviction that 'imperialism as a cultural phenomenon had as significant an effect on the dominant as on the subordinate societies'. With well over a hundred titles now published, this remains the prime concern of the series. Cross-disciplinary work has indeed appeared covering the full spectrum of cultural phenomena, as well as examining aspects of gender and sex, frontiers and law, science and the environment, language and literature, migration and patriotic societies, and much else. Moreover, the series has always wished to present comparative work on European and American imperialism, and particularly welcomes the submission of books in these areas. The fascination with imperialism, in all its aspects, shows no sign of abating, and this series will continue to lead the way in encouraging the widest possible range of studies in the field. 'Studies in Imperialism' is fully organic in its development, always seeking to be at the cutting edge, responding to the latest interests of scholars and the needs of this ever-expanding area of scholarship.

Gendered transactions

MANCHESTER
1824

Manchester University Press

Gendered transactions

THE WHITE WOMAN IN COLONIAL INDIA, *c.* 1820–1930

Indrani Sen

MANCHESTER
UNIVERSITY PRESS

Published by Manchester University Press
Altrincham Street, Manchester M1 7JA, UK
www.manchesteruniversitypress.co.uk

British Library Cataloguing-in-Publication Data is available

ISBN 978 0 7190 8962 6 *hardback*
ISBN 978 1 5261 4348 8 *paperback*

First published by Manchester University Press in hardback 2017

This edition first published 2019

Typeset by Servis Filmsetting Ltd, Stockport, Cheshire

For Chandan

CONTENTS

[vii]

ACKNOWLEDGEMENTS

In many ways, this book is the outcome of years of researching and writing on the subject of the white woman in colonial India. However, this particular book was completed in a specifically challenging context of setbacks, heavy teaching schedule and onerous administrative responsibilities, which all seemed to come together. It is all the more so that while completing it, I have incurred innumerable debts of goodwill, help and support from friends and well-wishers.

My young friends, Manu, Samiksha and Saurabh, former students who are young teachers themselves today, tracked down electronic journals and read earlier drafts of chapters in the midst of their own busy schedules. Without them this book just would not have fructified. To Waltraud, a warm thank you for her encouragement over the years and especially for her support for this book. Thanks to Ranjana for sharing rare research materials, and to Amar, Lata, Menka, Parimala, Partho, Prasun, Shashank and Shilpi for sustaining me with their friendship, help and interest in my work at different stages.

The genesis of this book lay in a Research Award Fellowship awarded by the University Grants Commission which gave me the opportunity to research and mull over fresh dimensions of gender and colonial India, besides giving me leave from Sri Venkateswara College, Delhi University. Various fellowships and grants at different junctures over the years cumulatively contributed towards the shaping of this book. They were crucial in enabling me to access primary materials at that amazing repository, the British Library in London. I gratefully acknowledge here a British Academy Visiting Fellowship, a Visiting Fellowship at Oxford Brookes University, travel grants from the Wellcome Trust and the Indian Council of Historical Research, as well as two academic grants from the Charles Wallace India Trust. In addition, I wish to thank the staff of Sri Venkateswara College Library and the Nehru Memorial Museum and Library at New Delhi, the National Library at Kolkata, the University Library, Cambridge University, the School of Oriental and African Studies library, as well as the Wellcome Library at London.

At Manchester University Press, I am thankful to the series editors for including this book in their Studies in Imperialism Series. I must also express my gratitude to them and also to the anonymous readers of the manuscript for their constructive suggestions and comments. This book has turned out to be the better for them. I wish to extend my sincerest thanks to Emma Brennan for the sustained good-humour, co-operation and patience that she has shown during the finalisation of my book.

Finally, as always, my family members – my sister Nandini, brother Jayanta (Dada), Bhaskar, Chiru, Shubhalaxmi, Alexus – were always there for me. And not to forget little Siddhu and Francis who provided such joy and carefree laughter on their occasional visits from half way across the globe. But of course, as always, it has been Chandan, my dear partner of three decades who has had to bear the brunt of the challenges of this particularly rocky journey. This book is therefore dedicated to him.

INTRODUCTION

The idea behind this book is to explore colonial gendered interactions, with a special focus on the white woman in colonial India. It examines a wide range of both literary and non-literary colonial narratives which offer a rich site for studying constructions of inter-racial interactions as well as gender representations against a grid of colonial transactions. My primary aim is to capture the multiple facets, the contradictions as well as the complexities in white women's experience in colonial India in the course of the nineteenth and early twentieth centuries. The three groups of white women whom I seek to focus upon are memsahibs, missionaries and, to a certain extent, ordinary soldiers' wives. In order to do this, I examine a diverse range of writings – memoirs, letters, personal accounts, literary narratives, housekeeping manuals and medical guide books – authored largely by white women, but also by western-educated Indian women and by white, colonising men as well.

As is by now well recognised, throughout the colonial period, the dominant category of the white woman (that is to say, the middle-class memsahib) occupied an ambivalent position, enjoying both power and privilege by virtue of her race, while simultaneously suffering gender disadvantage with regard to men of her own community. This book tries to explore in its two parts these ambivalences, examining the spheres in which she ostensibly exercised power as well as the areas in which she was disadvantaged, while at the same time noting the ambiguities, overlaps, slippages and fluidities that sometimes blurred the distinctions between the two situations. Part I broadly explores areas of white women's 'power': their participation in the 'civilising mission' (specifically, female education), their encounters with 'native' women, their 'imperial gaze' – but also a return of the gaze. In Part II the focus is on the white woman's gendered disadvantage in the colony, her anxieties and insecurities about the colonial home, her health problems as well as the colonial misogyny that undergirded writings by white men, such as powerful colonial physicians.

The memsahib in colonial India: historiography

The subject of the middle-class white woman in British India has been the focus of a great deal of research during the last two decades of the previous century. Nevertheless, it still continues to be a topic that needs to be unpacked in many of its dimensions, such as the representation of white women in medical texts, or the recovery of the virtually forgotten 'native' writings of the memsahib-novelist, Flora Annie Steel, who was praised in her time as a female Rudyard Kipling, in her close knowledge of 'native' life.

Research on the white woman (specifically the middle-class memsahib or administrator's wife) began in all seriousness with Pat Barr's *The Memsahibs: The Women of Victorian India* (1976), which projected the memsahib as the victim of a male-centric colonial enterprise.[1] To a large extent, this perspective continued through the 1980s, epitomised by Margaret Macmillan's *Women of the Raj* (1988).[2] However, from the 1990s onwards the research on gender and empire became more sophisticated and nuanced, beginning with the path-breaking *Western Women and Imperialism: Complicity and Resistance* (1992), a collection of wide-ranging and incisive essays edited by Nupur Chaudhuri and Margaret Strobel, followed by Clare Midgley's edited study, *Gender and Imperialism* (1998).[3] Both these important collections of essays presented the European woman in India in a nuanced manner, as *both* victim *as well as* beneficiary of colonialism. While the white woman was shown to be a beneficiary of imperialism, enjoying the race and class privileges of belonging to the ruling elite group, she was shown to also undoubtedly suffer marginalisation and gender disadvantages with regard to the men of her own community. In addition, these two latter studies opened up the category of 'white woman' further and subjected to critical scrutiny other groups such as missionaries. Around the same time, studies such as Anne McClintock's path-breaking *Imperial Leather* (1995), followed by Anne Laura Stoler's *Carnal Knowledge and Imperial Power* (2002) unpacked the issue of female sexuality as it played out in imperial discourses.[4] Both these studies focused on the intertwining of colonialism, race, sexuality, gender and power.

In her *Women Travellers in Colonial India* (1998) Indira Ghose explored the colonial, 'female gaze' in the specific context of white women's travel writing in colonial India. Underlining their heterogeneity, she argued that these narratives display a 'wide spectrum of gazes' which are 'frequently mutually contradictory and shifting'.[5] Rosemary Raza's *In Their Own Words* (2006) importantly scrutinised white women's writings of the earlier part of the nineteenth century, while Nancy Paxton has looked at literary narratives of the late nineteenth century in *Writing under the Raj* (1999).[6] However, the two works that have scrutinised the category of the white woman through a study of literary representations, historical documents, newspaper reports as well as archival materials have been two studies which focused on the white woman in India, namely, Mary Procida's *Married to the Empire*

(2002) and my own *Woman and Empire* (2002).[7] Procida's comprehensive, landmark study essentially argued that British women in colonial India were active masculinist imperialists, rather than the stereotypical frivolous party-goers that had become, since Kipling's time, a part of the mythology of empire.

In *Woman and Empire* (2002) I focused on the heterogeneity of the white woman living in colonial India, by probing the tensions, contradictions and diversities in the construction of the white woman in colonial discourse. I unravelled how she was perceived as both the 'tragic exile' in a faraway land, but also, at the same time, as the 'disorderly memsahib' who enjoyed freedom from the ideas about 'acceptable' feminine conduct prevailing in the metropole. I demonstrated how colonial discourse was undergirded by submerged colonial anxieties about the memsahib's sexual power being exercised in society, thereby threatening to destabilise sexual power equations within the white community in India. Hence, colonial discourse was rife with hostile constructions of the white woman as a shallow, frivolous social butterfly who was busy enjoying the power of her sexuality and neglectful of her domestic responsibilities.

Furthermore, in collating primary texts for my anthology, *Memsahibs' Writings* (2008) I sought to capture in the words of white women the interactions that they had with Indian women – in their diverse roles: as memsahibs, missionaries, travellers, novelists, journalists, physicians and even as converts to Hinduism.[8] I tried to present through these white women's narratives, the fascinating nuances in their gendered encounters which took place against a complex backdrop of caste/class, religious and regional diversities. I also sought to present how these enormous diversities inflected their inter-racial encounters and perceptions of nautch girls (dancing girls), ayahs (female domestic servants), wet-nurses, middle-class zenana women (women living in seclusion), princely women and western-educated women graduates (college educated).

Themes and concerns of this book: white women in colonial India

The three groups of white women whom I address in this book are memsahibs, missionaries and, to a certain extent, ordinary soldiers' wives. While the middle-class European women's experience is presented through their own writings, poorer class white women (notably soldiers' wives), who have left behind barely any written records, can only be represented at second hand. Indeed, one of the points that I aim to underline in this book is that the category of the white woman in colonial India was never a socially homogeneous one. Instead, it was constituted of diverse social classes – including middle-class and upper-middle-class memsahibs (wives of civil administrators or military officers), missionaries of largely lower-middle-class origins, and lower-class soldiers' wives, besides other poor whites, 'European marginals', including vagabonds and prostitutes.[9] Moreover, these women came from various regions of Britain, and included Irishwomen, Scotswomen, as well as Englishwomen, although they all went by the generic title of 'Englishwoman' or 'European' woman.[10]

In order to widen the scope of the enquiry, I foreground not only the middle-class memsahibs (which is of course the category of European women most widely discussed in studies on the subject), but also include other categories of white women in the colony, such as female evangelicals and barrack wives. In fact, one of my efforts in this study is to bring out the heterogeneity of the 'white woman in India' in terms of class contradictions, and also probe the internal divisions and disentangle the various strands that constituted this gendered community.

The 1820s is set as the starting date of this study since it was from around this period that more and more European women started coming out to India and writing about their Indian experience.[11] The majority came out as brides, accompanying husbands who were colonial administrators, military officers, judges, doctors, planters or other non-officials. During the next two decades, which were dominated by Utilitarianism and Evangelicalism, Indian society came to be perceived as decadent and in urgent need of reform, with the abolition of social evils as well as the introduction of English education being seen as key objectives.[12] Nevertheless, such attitudes co-existed with East India Company officials and their wives being encouraged to keep *munshis* (clerks) to learn Indian languages. Besides, there was vibrant cross-cultural mixing across race, with social life including visits to the homes of wealthy Indian zamindars (landowners) where they were entertained with music and dance in the form of nautch.

Following the Rebellion of 1857 and the takeover by the Crown, the policy adopted by the imperial government was that of social distance and imperial aloofness.[13] Government policy also encouraged the larger presence of resident wives and the setting up of British style homes for a new generation of administrators, with the objective of furthering an 'imperial identity'. For the first time, middle-class English women came out in large numbers from around the 1860s and formed an important segment of the colonial community.[14] The term 'memsahib' (i.e. 'madam sahib'), which came into greater usage during this time, signified colonial power, privilege and status, and wives were ranked according to their husband's official status and rank in a highly hierarchical colonial society.[15] However, as this book seeks to show, memsahibs simultaneously suffered gender disadvantage, being subjected to enforced idleness, limited sources of recreation, and most of all, separation from their children who were sent away to study in Britain.

By the early decades of the twentieth century, the domestic lifestyle of the white memsahib remained more or less the same. However, growing anti-imperialist sentiments as well as nationalist politics alienated them further from the colonised.[16] The early years of the twentieth century was a period of anti-imperialist struggle, and the nationalist politics of this period strengthened memsahibs' co-opted entry into an imperialist discourse.[17]

Colonial gender constructs and the memsahib

Colonial society was never a cohesive, harmonious entity, but a fractured space undercut by a web of race, class and gender ambivalences and contradictions.[18] In a colonial enterprise that was often perceived as a 'manly' activity rooted in aggression, control, competition and power, the white woman was negatively viewed as some sort of obstruction to this enterprise. Indeed, an important issue that underpins this study is that the middle-class memsahib was constructed in colonial discourse in three principal ways: first, that of the pleasure-loving, social butterfly immersed in a hectic social life; second, that of the tragic exile separated from her children; and third, the construct of the co-opted imperialist.[19] Of course, these constructions varied in their emphases and in their negativity. For instance, while the construct of the social butterfly was rooted in colonial misogyny (examined in Chapter 5), the construct of the tragic exile which ostensibly sympathised with the white woman, was actually undergirded by the idea of the colony as 'no place for a woman' (seen in Chapter 6). And the construct of the memsahib as imperialist and as reformer, sought to co-opt her into the imperial project (seen in Chapters 1, 2 and 4). Thus, in this book we get a glimpse of all three types of constructions.[20]

As I have discussed in *Woman and Empire*, the construct of the 'disorderly' memsahib was an overwhelming one in colonial discourse.[21] It was consistently buttressed by newspaper reports, periodical articles, memoirs, prescriptive manuals and literary writings – and indeed, by the bulk of colonial medical writings as well, as I argue in Chapter 5 of this book. Gender prejudices clearly underlay the construction of the memsahib as an irresponsible, 'disorderly' socialite, betraying anxieties and insecurities about European female sexuality and the threat it posed to the male colonial order.[22] The fears about female sexuality were further reinforced by the numerical sex imbalance in colonial India, where, at the highest point, men outnumbered women 3:1, a situation that created a critical stress in society.[23] This also resulted in considerable stresses in colonial Indian marriages, given the frequent separations that were unavoidable, as well as the problem of adulterous liaisons between married women and single men. Indeed, anxieties about this problem of adultery were frequently voiced in colonial discourse and the preoccupation with a woman's 'morality' took the form of exhortatory writings in Anglo-Indian journals, newspapers and books.[24] These focused on the moral responsibilities of the English woman in India, in both her gender relationships and her imperial duty as wife and a member of the ruling class – all of which informs my discussion of colonial medical discourse in Chapter 5 of this book.

Memsahibs and the colonial home

In recent years there has been a growing scholarly interest in the colonial family and in the role of the white woman as mother in the colonial home. Increasingly, the family is being identified as an important analytical unit for probing the cultural history of colonialism. Following upon Anne Laura Stoler's *Carnal Knowledge and Imperial Power* (2002) and Elizabeth Buettner's *Empire Families: Britons and Late Imperial India* (2004), there has emerged a new thrust on the family, on colonial motherhood as well as on colonial childhood and child-rearing.[25] More recently, in studies such as Esme Cleall's *Missionary Discourses of Difference* (2012), and Emily Manktelow's *Missionary Families* (2013), this interest has been expanded and extended to include the complexities entangling missionary family lives in colonial India.[26] Stoler's path-breaking work on colonial domesticity essentially focused on lower-class colonials, co-habitation with 'native' female servants as well as the problem of the mixed-race household in the Dutch East Indies. By far the most incisive as well as comprehensive exploration of memsahibs and the colonial home in the context of India has been made by Alison Blunt in her article, 'Imperial Geographies of Home: British Domesticity in India, 1886–1925', where she focused on the colonial home in India and the power relations between the memsahib and her domestic servants.[27]

By the late nineteenth century, child-bearing was presented in colonial discourse as a woman's 'main function in life' and women were increasingly projected as progenitors of future generations for the sake of empire and the job of nation-building.[28] Indeed, the importance of the colonial home led to the appearance, from the second half of the nineteenth century onwards, to housekeeping manuals authored by memsahibs which gave advice on the running of the colonial home, on bringing up children, handling 'native' servants and providing recipes for daily meals based on 'Anglo-Indian' food. Then again, there were medical handbooks written by male colonial physicians which gave stern advice on subjects such as mothering, reproductive and maternal health as well as children's diseases. I shall be examining aspects of the white woman as mother in Chapters 4 and 5 – extending the discussion to analyse memsahibs and the colonial home, as well as medical exhortations by male physicians in medical handbooks about responsible mothering.

Female missionaries in India

Missionaries form an important part of this book as a whole. In the initial years evangelical activity was perceived to be a male activity and female missionaries were generally the wives of missionaries.[29] From the 1860s, however, following a shift in evangelical policies, unmarried female missionaries from the more educated middle classes started to be sent out to India primarily on zenana work. From this period onwards, evangelical activities in India became feminised; so much so, that by the end of the century, there was a predominance of female over male evangelicals in India.[30] In addition, towards the end of the century, as part of a new evangelical strategy, missionaries who were trained physicians started to be sent out to provide medical care to purdah women (women in seclusion) who refused to be treated by foreign, male doctors. Healing thus came to be intermeshed with proselytisation, as 'Clinical Christianity' was deployed to gain access to the most orthodox zenanas.[31]

In this rigidly hierarchical colonial society, class distinctions were sharp within the white community. A wide gap, for instance, separated missionaries from memsahibs primarily due to the latter's social superiority based on their husbands' official status. Female evangelicals consequently tended to be markedly deferential towards white administrator's wives. Moreover, their practice of mixing closely with 'natives' and 'living as nearly as possible on the same lines' as the local populace was frowned upon because it was considered damaging to British prestige.[32]

Barrack wives

One rather neglected section of the white colonial community whom we shall briefly discuss in this book is the common soldiers' wives

– a subject that has been rather marginal in the histories of the colonial armies. Besides Myna Trustram's classic study, *Women of the Regiment* (1984), Douglas Peers' *Between Mars and Mammon* (1995), and very recently, Erica Wald's *Vice in the Barracks* (2014) have highlighted the plight of soldiers' wives in the barracks.[33] Building on their work, I shall examine in Chapter 6, the problem of addiction and the mental condition of 'barrack wives' (as they were called), seeking to draw connections between their mental health and the degree of degradation to which their lives were reduced. A wide class gap separated memsahibs from soldier's wives, and virtually no connection existed between them – except when the latter worked as a mid-wife for officer's wives, or carried out some other chore in the cantonment.

There was no clear government policy on soldiers' wives; marriage for British 'other ranks' was discouraged as a rule and soldiers tended to live with 'native' women and Eurasians. Although inter-racial marriage was taboo for officers, it was encouraged for soldiers, and 'unofficial marriages' frequently took place between them and local women.[34] In cases where the wives were European, they were given higher amounts in matters such as pension for widows. Only wives of British birth became eligible for widows' pensions, which automatically ruled out Eurasian wives.[35] Moreover, while soldiers' wives in Britain were usually required to cook, sew and launder for the entire regiment, in India, 'native' servants did many of these tasks, since it was considered harmful to British prestige. Nevertheless, inside the barracks the conditions for the women were utter degradation, consisting of alcoholism, wife-beating, desertion by husbands, poverty and squalor, along with high female and child mortality. Commenting on the 'misery and degradation' of soldiers' wives in the colonies, one young soldier remarked in Burma during the 1840s that 'of all the lives of misery in this world a married soldier's is the worst' and warned his 'poor deluded countrywomen who are continually marrying soldiers' against taking 'such a step'.[36] Barrack wives had little contact with memsahibs and interactions with officers' wives were primarily confined to their role as seamstresses or as midwives. Midwifery was, according to Myna Trustram, 'an important function which a few wives performed in a regiment'. Some regiments had a regular midwife who was paid out of the regimental fund.[37] Some of these women were trained by army medical officers in midwifery at various army hospitals, where they 'attended the wives of both officers and men'.[38]

White women's writings

Much of this monograph (although not all of it), examines white women's writings authored by two categories of European women: missionaries and memsahibs. For middle-class memsahibs, writing was a very important activity in colonial India. As demonstrated by Rosemary Raza's *In Their Own Words* (2006), long hours of female leisure and enforced inactivity in a colonial set-up, especially in the earlier years of the nineteenth century, resulted in them writing long letters to friends and family members back in Britain. These women penned memoirs, maintained diaries and wrote letters which they subsequently published in the form of books.[39] Most of them wrote on topics pertaining to their lives, such as their domestic and social experiences. One important subject which preoccupied these women was the daily difficulty that they faced in the course of running their homes and in negotiating colonial domesticities. They voiced their anxieties in rearing their small children in India, handling tropical diseases and 'controlling' their domestic servants, including female servants, such as the ayah and the wet-nurse.[40] Thus, in these personal writings the average memsahib turned a critical 'colonial gaze' upon low caste/class women with whom they were the most closely associated.

In addition, from the second half of the nineteenth century onwards, experienced middle-class memsahibs started to write housekeeping manuals and handbooks, which sought to address the difficulties of young brides who were arriving in India and to guide them on household matters. They outlined the duties of the ayahs, gave advice on how to run the colonial home, raise small children, and especially on how to control and administer their huge retinue of servants.

However, it was missionaries who were the most prolific writers – of newsletters, periodical articles, biographies, personal accounts and sometimes novels. Considered most knowledgeable on the subject of the zenana, female evangelicals took upon themselves the task of disseminating information about it to the wider, western public. They wrote authoritatively on it, generally constructing it negatively as a prison, a site of disease, idleness, ignorance and sensuality. They also sometimes wrote novels specifically meant to be read aloud to women inside the zenana to bring about a cultural transformation among them, recasting them along exemplary western lines.

By late nineteenth century, colonial administrators' wives had also emerged as popular novelists and writers of short stories. While the overwhelming majority of them wrote 'station romances', delineating only the British community in India, there was a handful of memsahib-writers who delineated Indian life, locales and characters in their fiction.[41] Flora Annie Steel (1847–1929) was one such leading writer. Her writings, as we see in Chapter 2 of this book, focused on 'native' women from both urban and rural Punjab and delineated encounters with school-going Muslim girls as well as the sufferings of peasant women.

White women's narratives thus not only became an important source of information on Indian women but revealed much about their own perceptions and prejudices. Indeed, sometimes their writings displayed a cultural superiority, overt as well as unspoken, especially during the period of social reform and at the height of the 'civilising mission'. In other words, these female writers' narratives contributed to circulating stereotypes about the abject condition of 'native' women and producing colonial knowledge about the 'Other'.

Gendered encounters

As the title indicates, one of this book's central tropes is gendered encounters across race. This is something that I examine in a number of the book's chapters. As noted earlier, it was women missionaries who mixed most closely with 'natives' of various classes, their greatest advantage being their ability to speak the local languages fluently.

However, as far as memsahibs are concerned, in contrast to the inter-racial socialising of the earlier decades, most contacts with Indian women dwindled after the gap between the races widened following the establishment of empire and the adoption of an imperial policy of aloofness. Thereafter, this inter-mixing dwindled down to day-to-day encounters with female domestic servants, such as ayahs (and sometimes the wet-nurse), as we see in Chapter 4. Occasionally they also made formal, mutually disliked 'purdah visits', with their ayahs acting as interpreters since they were ignorant of the language; or they would catch a glimpse of 'native' school-going girls when invited to be the chief guest at some school function (as we see in Chapter 2).[42] Or sometimes, a memsahib in a big city would invite school girls to her house to tea, as we see in a Mumbai-based novel in Chapter 3. Obviously these kinds of interactions (purdah visits, as well as school functions) were a mere formality, almost a social ritual precluding any genuine interaction.

By the turn of the century there were further shifts in the relationship between European and Indian women, especially those belonging to the middle classes. One was the emergence from purdah of the educated *bhadramahila*, the genteel, middle-class Bengali woman. During this period European women also interacted with the 'New Indian Woman', a new generation of middle-class Indian women, educated and westernised, some of them educationists themselves.[43] Moreover, the early twentieth century was also the period of the Indian National movement.[44] Cross-cultural encounters too began to change in society, and the old type of purdah visits came to be increasingly replaced by 'purdah parties': all-female social gatherings organised by white women for their secluded, elite female guests.[45]

With regard to gendered encounters, it is also important to unpack the colonial category of the 'native' woman, as this study seeks to do. I seek to scrutinise how these cross-racial gendered interactions were inflected by regional diversities, and wish to bring across the complexity of the category of the 'native woman'. Far from being a monolithic category, it was inflected with variations of class, caste, religion and cultural practices, involving regions as culturally distinct and geographically separate as Bengal in the east, Bombay in the west or Punjab in the north.

Social reform in the nineteenth century

The nineteenth century was an age of gendered social reform; the 'Native Female Social Amelioration' programme focused on eradicating 'native' patriarchal practices such as sati (widow immolation), female infanticide, child marriage, polygamy, the oppression of high caste widows, enforced female illiteracy and the practice of purdah (female seclusion). While in the first half of the century, reform had been sought through legislation with the help of male Indian reformers, there was a shift in strategy following the Rebellion of 1857.[46] Reform measures thereafter assumed the form of gradual change – especially through female education and the gradual eradication of purdah. For this purpose, there was a widespread induction of white women into the reform agenda. The vast majority involved in reform activities in the second half of the nineteenth century – notably female education – were female evangelists. As noted earlier, they established schools for girls from the early part of the century and taught both in the regular schools as well as in the zenana classes held for grown women inside Indian homes.

Very rarely, however, did memsahibs or wives of British colonial administrators show any interest in this subject of social reform.[47] One striking exception was Flora Annie Steel whose writings we examine in Chapter 2. Steel, the wife of an administrator, not only wrote on topics related to gendered social reform, but was actively associated with female education, starting schools for girls in remote parts of Punjab and later, taking up the government post of Inspectress of girls' schools in the province. Besides, she also revealed in her short fiction a reformist's preoccupation with the abject condition of Indian women and an interest in female education.

More indirectly, the English woman was incorporated into the process of cultural imperialism by being projected as a role model for the Indian woman who was emerging from the veil. Underlining the grave imperial responsibilities of all middle-class white women, *The Calcutta Review* intoned in 1886 that 'the future of India's women' was tied with 'the unsuspected influence of the lives and characters of their more privileged English sisters'.[48] Such an exhortation simultaneously served a double purpose. On the one hand it urged a western model for the 'New Indian Woman' to follow. On the other hand it deployed notions such as 'British prestige' and the 'white woman's burden' to control the *white* woman's morality and any possible disorderliness or deviations from the norm.

Part I: The white woman and the 'civilising mission'

As noted earlier, the first three chapters which make up Part I of this book focus on aspects of the white woman's role as imperialist and as participant in the 'civilising mission'. Narratives authored by European female missionaries, memsahibs, as well as Indian women, such as memoirs, short stories, novels, newspaper and periodical articles are examined in order to probe their representations of gendered interactions with the 'native' female across race and class. This section is informed by the intertwined themes of the female 'colonial gaze' and the 'civilising mission'. By focusing specifically on issues related to gendered social reform, such as female education and 'colonial modernity', I seek to explore how diverse categories of women (both white and Indian) participated both as proponents and as targets of the colonial 'civilising mission'.

One way in which different groups of white women – social reformers, educationists, evangelists or even incorporated wives – participated in this 'civilising mission' was by writing about Indian women and turning a critical 'colonial gaze' upon the 'abject', 'native' woman. Indeed, the concept of the colonial 'female gaze' suggests that women were complicit in colonialism and its structures of power.[49] In other words, by circulating stereotypes about the abject condition of 'native' women and producing colonial knowledge about the 'Other', these female writers effectively performed the role of colluders in the colonial enterprise.[50]

In Chapter 1, 'The missionary "gaze" and the "civilising mission"': zenana encounters in nineteenth-century Bengal', I examine missionary writings (both personal accounts by female evangelicals, as well as missionary novels), their delineation of zenana education visitations, their construction of the oppressed purdah woman, as well as their projection of the zenana as a site of disease, ignorance and idleness. Simultaneously, while presenting themselves as rescuers of Indian women, they also projected the figure of the Victorian genteel woman as a female paradigm to be emulated.

The theme of education and the criticism of 'native' patriarchies provides an interface between the first chapter and Chapter 2, 'Flora Annie Steel, social reform and female education in late nineteenth-century Punjab', which focuses on gender problems in colonial Punjab. Flora Annie Steel (1847–1929), who was a major figure of her time, exercised considerable influence over her generation. While she resembled the missionaries in attacking patriarchal practices in Indian society (e.g. female infanticide, child marriage and polygamy), she sharply critiqued evangelical methods of schooling as well as their objective of culturally transforming Indian women on a western model. Thus, her critical gaze on the missionaries and on 'native' patriarchal practices presents an intertwining of seemingly oppositional strands: while echoing female evangelicals (in their shared critical gaze directed at gendered social evils in Indian society), she is simultaneously positioned in critical opposition to the missionaries.

Giving a voice to the educated 'native' female and presenting her perspective on issues of female education and westernised role models, is Chapter 3, 'Returning the "gaze": colonial encounters in Indian women's English writings in late nineteenth-century western India'. This chapter discusses two literary narratives authored by the earliest generation of educated Indian women who wrote in English. These two Indian female authors, who also happened to be Christian converts, focused in their writings on 'native' female schooling, besides offering a critique of missionary schooling. In their responses to 'colonial modernity', we study the interface between the missionary agendas of education, reform, conversion to Christianity and the manner in which reformist programmes were received by Indian female converts. Thus, this chapter serves to provide a counterpoint to the writings by colonising women, and is in an important sense, a case of 'reversing the gaze', providing a counter-viewpoint, a critical 'native' perspective on European women in the colony.

Part II: Colonial domesticity, white women's health and gender disadvantage

The chapters in Part II of this book focus on narratives which underline the disadvantaged position of the white woman in India. At the same time, one notes the fluidities and overlaps that exist between Parts I and II. For instance, while the colonial gaze defined and united the chapters in Part I, it was simultaneously shown to be subverted by the 'native' female gaze. In Part II, the colonial gaze is undermined and subverted by the context of domesticity in colonial India. Memsahibs, in turn, are subjected to the gendered medical gaze.[51]

Chapter 4, 'The ambivalences of power inside the colonial home: memsahibs, ayahs and wet- nurses', introduces the theme of the white woman's disadvantaged position in the colony. This chapter scrutinises memsahibs' writings and their constructions of 'native' female domestic servants as dishonest, sensual and unhygienic – revealing thereby profound anxieties and insecurities. The colonial nursery emerges as a contested site where the memsahib's authority was constantly undermined by these 'native' females in a daily power-struggle over emotional authority over the white children. At the same time, this chapter takes forward the theme of the 'colonial gaze' from the earlier three chapters – in this case, both the memsahib's gaze as well as the return of the gaze by the ayah.

The remaining two chapters of this book further develop the theme of the disadvantaged position of the white woman in colonial discourse through the lens of women's health issues. Chapter 5, 'Marginalising the memsahib: the white woman's health issues in colonial medical writings', seeks to unravel the gender politics that undergirded colonial medical handbooks which were authored mostly by male colonial physicians. These handbooks subjected the memsahib to a critical 'medical gaze', and sternly set out the agenda of gender control under the guise of medical advice. Admonishing the memsahib and critiquing her mothering skills, these handbooks also laid stress upon the vulnerabilities affecting her health and critiqued her as an 'irresponsible' imperial mother. While examining the medical advice on white women's health, we shall unravel the race/class/gender ideologies which underlay colonial medical discourse.

The themes of the white woman's medical vulnerability and the colonies being perceived as 'no place for a woman' are further developed in Chapter 6, 'The colonial "female malady": European women's mental health and addiction in the late nineteenth century'. This final chapter focuses on yet another aspect of female health in the colony, namely mental health. Taken up for discussion is the perceived occurrence among middle-class memsahibs of the fashionable ailment known as 'tropical neurasthenia'. In addition, we probe, in the case of the lower-class soldier's wife, the problem of 'delirium tremens'. The projection of white women's 'mental unfitness' and vulnerability to the tropical climate, the conditions of middle-class domestic and social life as well as economic hardships in the case of poorer white women will be examined. Both colonial realities as well as perceptions are examined in this chapter.

Regarding the historical time-frame of this book, the period c.1820–1930 is a broad framework within which this study is set. While it follows a thematic structure, historical chronology is also largely maintained. Thus the earlier three chapters broadly focus on the second half of the nineteenth century while the later three chapters go down to the early decades of the twentieth century. At the same time, we note that periods in history are not watertight divisions – but consist instead of overlaps, shifts, changes, fluidities as well as continuities. I have therefore deliberately avoided adopting a mechanical, linear, straight-line time-frame. Instead, the idea is to capture the tensions and contradictions, shifts and continuities that marked perceptions, attitudes and perspectives. Hence, in some instances the time span is wide and extends to almost a hundred year period. For instance, my discussion of memsahibs' writings on ayahs (in Chapter 4) reveals an almost seamless continuity in their race/class prejudices towards domestic servants for almost a hundred years. Similarly, in Chapters 5 and 6, we see how colonial medical writings displayed a continuing gender prejudice among the medical fraternity towards both white colonial maternities and female mental health in the colony, prejudices that were visible well into the early decades of the twentieth century. This also suggests that in many instances, despite all the historical shifts and changes, certain perceptions and constructions lingered on for decades, and there was often a curious sameness to be found in the position of the white woman in India and in the attitudes to her throughout the colonial period.

Notes

1 Pat Barr, *The Memsahibs: The Women of Victorian India* (London, Secker and Warburg, 1976).
2 Margaret Macmillan, *Women of the Raj* (London, Thames and Hudson, 1988).
3 Nupur Chaudhuri and Margaret Strobel (eds), *Western Women and Imperialism: Complicity and Resistance* (Bloomington and Indianapolis, Indiana University Press, 1992), Clare Midgley (ed.), *Gender and Imperialism* (Manchester, Manchester University Press, 1998).
4 Anne McClintock, *Imperial Leather: Race, Gender and Sexuality in the Colonial Contest* (London and New York, Routledge, 1995); Ann Laura Stoler, *Carnal Knowledge and Imperial Power: Race and the Intimate in Colonial Rule* (Berkeley, University of California Press, 2002).
5 Indira Ghose, *Women Travellers in Colonial India: The Power of the Female Gaze* (Delhi, Oxford University Press, 1998), p. 158. For a recent, generalised discussion see Susmita Roye and Rajeshwar Mittapalli (eds), *The Male Empire under the Female Gaze: The British Raj and the Memsahib* (Amherst, Cambria, 2013).
6 Rosemary Raza, *In Their Own Words: British Women Writers and India, 1740–1857*

(New Delhi, Oxford University Press, 2006); Nancy Paxton, *Writing under the Raj: Gender, Race and Rape in the British Colonial Imagination, 1830–1947* (New Brunswick, NJ, Rutgers University Press, 1999).

7   Mary Procida, *Married to the Empire: Gender, Politics and Imperialism in India, 1883–1947* (Manchester, Manchester University Press, 2002), and Indrani Sen, *Woman and Empire: Representations in the Writings of British India, 1858–1900* (New Delhi, Orient Longman, 2002).

8   Indrani Sen (ed.), *Memsahibs' Writings: Colonial Narratives on Indian Women* (New Delhi, Orient BlackSwan, 2008). During the anti-colonial movement around the early twentieth century, there were 'Indianised' European women who embraced Hinduism, such as Margaret Noble or 'Sister Nivedita' (1867–1911), and Madeline Slade or 'Mira Behn' (1892–1982), a follower of Gandhi.

9   Wives of civil administrators occupied the highest social position, followed by wives of military officers, with the wives of non-official British, such as planters, located much lower in the hierarchy. For a discussion of the different classes of white women in India, see Macmillan, *Women of the Raj* and especially Indrani Sen, 'Between Power and "Purdah": The White Woman in British India, 1858–1900', *The Indian Economic and Social History Review*, 34:3 (1997), pp. 355–376. For a discussion of vagabond and destitute whites see Sarmistha De, *Marginal Europeans in Colonial India: 1860–1920* (Kolkata, Thema, 2008), and Harald Fischer-Tine, *Low and Licentious Europeans: Race, Class and 'White Subalternity' in Colonial India* (New Delhi, Orient BlackSwan, 2009).

10   In colonial India the terms 'European', 'English', or 'British' were generic terms loosely used for white colonialists, including people of Scottish, Irish or Welsh origins (in some cases, Canadian, Australian or American origins as well). In keeping with this usage, I use these terms interchangeably throughout this book. In addition, I use the term 'white woman' to refer to colonising women across diverse social classes. Moreover, I use the term 'Anglo-Indian' in its original sense of a British colonial residing in India.

11   Prior to that, a handful of Englishwomen did come out to India as early as the seventeenth and eighteenth centuries but they were very few in numbers because of the rigours and hardships of the seven-month long sea voyage around the Cape of Good Hope. For details see Dennis Kincaid, *British Social Life in India 1608–1937* ([1938], London, Routledge and Kegan Paul, 1973) and Ketaki Kushari Dyson, *A Various Universe: A Study of the Journals and Memoirs of British Men and Women in the Indian Sub-Continent, 1765–1856* ([1978], New Delhi, Oxford University Press, 2002). For a more recent account written for a general readership, see Joan Mickelson Gaughan, *The 'Incumberances': British Women in India 1615–1856* (New Delhi, Oxford University Press, 2013).

12   The Utilitarian, James Mill, harshly condemned Indian culture as inferior, in *History of British India* (London, Baldwin, Cradock and Joy, 1817) , while T. B. Macaulay's 'Minute on Education dated 2 February, 1835', in *Bureau of Education. Selections from Educational Records, Part I (1781-1839), edited by H. Sharp, Calcutta: Superintendent, Government Printing, 1920* (Delhi, National Archives of India, 1965), pp. 107–117, talked about the inferiority of Asian culture, and the need to bring in English education. During this period many East India Company officials took an interest in evangelical activities. Julia Maitland and her husband who lived in Madras in this period set up schools for 'heathen' children in the hope that they would embrace Christianity. However, they also mixed closely with Indian elites.

13   See Kenneth Ballhatchet, *Race, Sex and Class Under the Raj: Imperial Attitudes and Policies and their Critics, 1793–1905* (New York, St. Martin's Press, 1980).

14   This increased presence was further encouraged by the reduced journey-time from England, following the opening of the Suez Canal in 1869 and the introduction of the steamship.

15   The word 'memsahib' (i.e. 'madam sahib'), used to denote a married European lady, came into popular usage from around the 1850s onwards. See *The Oxford English Dictionary*, Vol. VI ([1933], Oxford, Oxford University Press, 1961), p. 332. For a

discussion of this term see also my article, 'Memsahib', in Bonnie G. Smith (ed.), *The Oxford Encyclopaedia of Women in World History*, Vol. 1 (New York, Oxford University Press, 2008), pp. 206–207.

16 Anti-imperialist sentiments in the early twentieth century, such as the swadeshi movement following the partition of Bengal in 1905 as well as the outcry after the Jallianwallah Bagh massacre at Amritsar in 1919 (firing on an unarmed crowd and killing many by General Dwyer) all added to tensions.

17 Mary Procida notes how, 'By the inter-war years, Anglo-Indian women could no longer be depicted as ... helpless creatures ... In order to be fully integrated onto British imperialism in India, Anglo-Indian official wives had to reject notions of women's helplessness and dependence ... Anglo-Indian wives met the perceived challenge of violence to the Raj by integrating themselves into the culture of imperial violence, not as passive victims but as active, assertive, and assured defenders of the Empire', in Mary Procida, 'Married to the Empire: British Wives and British Imperialism in India, 1883–1947', PhD thesis, University of Pennsylvania, 1997, p. 267.

18 See Sen, *Woman and Empire*.

19 For a more detailed discussion, see Sen, 'Between Power and "Purdah"'; and Sen, *Woman and Empire*.

20 The memsahib as imperialist is discussed in Chapters 2 and 4 of this book, the memsahib as a social butterfly is addressed in Chapter 5 and the construction as the tragic exile can be seen in Chapter 6.

21 See Sen, *Woman and Empire*.

22 For details see Sen, 'Between Power and "Purdah"', pp. 364–369. In colonial fiction the 'disorderly memsahib' is epitomised by the ubiquitous figure of the married flirt who poses a threat to lonely males. See also Sen, *Woman and Empire*, Chapters 1 and 3.

23 While, at its highest point, the male:female ratio among Europeans in colonial India stood at 3:1, women in Britain demographically outnumbered men 1,050 to 1,000. For population figure for India, see Macmillan, *Women of the Raj*, p. 16; for population figures for England see Patricia Hollis (ed.), *Women in Public, 1850–1900: Documents of the Victorian Women's Movement* (London, George Allen & Unwin, 1979), p. 33.

24 Two newspapers can be cited here. While *The Madras Mail*, 29 April (1869), critiqued the commonly found 'penchant for another man's wife', the Calcutta-based *The Friend of India* (12 June 1875), p. 551, censured the '"flirtations" ... between married men and married women' which all too often ended 'in separation and the Divorce Court'.

25 Stoler, *Carnal Knowledge and Imperial Power*, Elizabeth Buettner, *Empire Families: Britons and Late Imperial India* (Oxford and New York, Oxford University Press, 2004).

26 Esme Cleall, *Missionary Discourses of Difference: Negotiating Otherness in the British Empire* (Basingstoke, Palgrave Macmillan, 2012), and Emily J. Manktelow, *Missionary Families: Race, Gender and Generation on the Spiritual Frontier* (Manchester, Manchester University Press, 2013). Another recent study, Dianne Lawrence's *Genteel Women: Empire and Domestic Material Culture, 1840–1910* (Manchester, Manchester University Press, 2012), explores the setting up of homes and genteel housekeeping values in the empire.

27 Alison Blunt, 'Imperial Geographies of Home: British Domesticity in India, 1886–1925', *Transactions of the Institute of British Geographers*, New Series, 24:4 (1999), pp. 421–440.

28 See Anna Davin, 'Imperialism and Motherhood', *History Workshop Journal*, 5:1 (1978), pp. 9–66.

29 Initially, the East India Company did not allow evangelical activity in the country but finally, under growing pressure at home, missionaries were allowed into India from 1813 onwards.

30 Jane Haggis, 'Professional Ladies and Working Wives: Female Missionaries in the

London Missionary Society and Its South Travancore District, South India in the Nineteenth Century', PhD thesis, University of Manchester, 1991, p. 157.

31   For details see Patricia and Peter Sherlock, 'Women and Cultural Exchanges' in Norman Etherington (ed.), *Missions and Empire* (New York, Oxford University Press, 2005), p. 184; and especially Rosemary Fitzgerald, '"Clinical Christianity": The Emergence of Medical Work as a Missionary Strategy in Colonial India, 1800–1914', in Biswamoy Pati and Mark Harrison (eds), *Health, Medicine and Empire: Perspectives on Colonial India* (New Delhi, Orient Longman, 2001), pp. 88–136. See also Antoinette Burton, 'Contesting the Zenana: The Mission to Make "Lady Doctors for India", 1874–1885', *Journal of British Studies*, 35 (July, 1996), pp. 368–397.

32   Maud Diver, *The Englishwoman in India* (Edinburgh and London, William Blackwood & Sons, 1909).

33   Myna Trustram, *Women of the Regiment: Marriage and the Victorian Army* (Cambridge, Cambridge University Press, 1984); Douglas Peers, *Between Mars and Mammon: Colonial Armies and the Garrison State in Nineteenth Century India* (London, I. B. Tauris, 1995), and Erica Wald, *Vice in the Barracks: Medicine, the Military and the Making of Colonial India, 1780–1868* (London, Palgrave Macmillan, 2014).

34   Douglas Peers, 'Imperial Vice: Sex, Drink, and the Health of the British Troops in North Indian Cantonments, 1800–1858', in David Killingray and David Omissi (eds), *Guardians of Empire: The Armed Forces of the Colonial Powers, 1700–1964* (Manchester, Manchester University Press, 1999), p. 34. Peers also quotes an army officer: 'Half caste women are frequently chosen by the British soldiers for their wives and I believe they make extremely good ones', *ibid.*, p. 35. For the condition of barrack wives, see 'Englishwomen in Hindustan', *The Calcutta Review*, 4:7 (1845), pp. 96–127. For a discussion on Indian companions of soldiers see Durba Ghosh, *Sex and the Family in Colonial India: The Making of Empire* (Cambridge, Cambridge University Press, 2006), pp. 206–245.

35   Douglas Peers, 'Privates Off Parade: Regimenting in the Nineteenth-century Indian Empire', *The International History Review*, 20:4 (December 1998), p. 846.

36   Letter of Lance-Corporal David Banham of the 94th Regiment of Foot, Moulmein, Burma, to a friend in England, dated 1 August, 1845, from the National Army Museum, London, www.nam.ac.uk/exhibitions/online-exhibitions/wives-sweet-hearts/women-regiment/lives-misery-transcript-1 (accessed 26 August 2016).

37   Trustram, *Women of the Regiment*, p. 114. Trustram further points out that in 1868 a scheme was begun in Dublin 'to train wives as midwives so that each regiment would have a trained woman ... The Army Medical Dept urged medical officers to use wives who had completed the Dublin course to attend childbirth and general sickness amongst women in preference to untrained women. By 1881 500 wives had been trained: many had been posted to India with their husbands where they attended the wives of both officers and men', in Trustram, *Women of the Regiment*, p. 114.

38   *Ibid.*

39   For details see Raza, *In Their Own Words*. Julia Maitland's *Letters from Madras during the years 1836–39, by a Lady* ([1843], London, John Murray, 1846) were based on letters to her mother; Emily Eden's *Up the Country:Letters Written to her Sister from the Upper Provinces of India* ([1866], London, Oxford University Press, 1930) were based on letters to her sister, and Anne Wilson's *Letters from India* ([1911], London, Century, 1984) were originally written as personal correspondence. Emma Roberts' *Scenes and Characteristics of Hindostan, with Sketches of Anglo-Indian Society*, vol. 1 (London, W. H. Allen, 1835) originally appeared as separate papers published in the *Asiatic Journal*. Mary Frances Billington's *Women in India* (London, Chapman & Hall, 1895) was based on articles she wrote for the *Daily Graphic*; Maud Diver's *The Englishwoman in India* (1909) was based on her articles that had appeared in the periodical *Womanhood*.

40   Of course, returning 'home' was fraught with mixed feelings, regrets and nostalgia

as they turned from 'somebodies' into 'nobodies' – a transition skilfully delineated in Buettner, *Empire Families*.

41 The few other memsahib-writers who occasionally delineated Indian characters and themes include, Maud Diver (1867–1945), Alice Perrin (1867–1934), and to a lesser degree, Sara Jeannette Duncan (1862–1922). For a discussion on nineteenth-century colonial fiction, including the station romances, see Sen, *Woman and Empire*, Chapter 3, pp. 71–103.

42 For discussions on the zenana see Janaki Nair, 'Uncovering the Zenana: Visions of Indian Womanhood in Englishwomen's Writings, 1813–1940', *Journal of Women's History*, 2:1 (Spring 1990), pp. 8–34.

43 Some of the Indian universities too, such as the Universities of Bombay and Calcutta, had been opened up to women – in fact, soon after London University.

44 As the anti-colonial movement gathered momentum, it saw the involvement of highly educated, intelligent and articulate Indian women such as Sarojini Naidu, as well as 'Indianised' European women, such as Margaret Noble or 'Sister Nivedita' (1867– 1911), Annie Besant (1847–1933) and Madeline Slade or 'Mira Behn' (1892–1982), a follower of Gandhi.

45 Seclusion from males would be maintained and upper-class women from both races would mix on a footing of some degree of equality.

46 These legislations included the Act banning sati in 1829, and Hindu Widows' Remarriage Act of 1856. Indian reformers like Raja Rammohan Roy and Ishwarchandra Vidyasagar spearheaded these reforms respectively.

47 An unusual reformist memsahib was Annette Akroyd (1842–1929), who started schools for girls in Calcutta in 1873. However, her involvement in female education came to an end with her marriage to Henry Beveridge, an ICS officer.

48 J. E. Dawson, 'The Englishwoman in India: Her Influence and Responsibilities' (Part II), *The Calcutta Review*, 83:165 (1886), p. 362.

49 As Indira Ghose mentions, the female colonial gaze, which at some level shows 'their collusion in colonialist structures of power', also serves to 'circulate stereotypes and images of the other and actively participates in the production of knowledge and the disseminsation of the effects of power', Ghose, *Women Travellers in Colonial India*, pp. 160, 2.

50 The concept of the 'imperial gaze' has been theorised by several, including Mary Louise Pratt, *Imperial Eyes: Travel Writing and Transculturation* (London and New York, Routledge, 1992).

51 Chapters 5 and 6 refer to the 'medical gaze' which is based on Michel Foucault's concept of the depersonalising 'medical gaze' or 'clinical gaze', whereby the physician exercises power/knowledge over the patient. However, it is given a more gendered colouring in my work. See Michel Foucault, *The Birth of the Clinic: An Archaeology of Medical Perception*, trans. A.M. Sheridan Smith (London, Tavistock, 1973).

PART I

The white woman and the 'civilising mission'

CHAPTER ONE

The missionary 'gaze' and the 'civilising mission': zenana encounters in nineteenth-century Bengal

Among white women in colonial India, it was the female missionaries who undoubtedly participated most closely in the colonial 'civilising mission'. They established schools for girls and taught both in the regular schools as well as in the zenana classes that were held for grown women inside Indian homes.[1] Women missionaries also wrote prolifically about the zenana, an area that was not accessible to their male counterparts. In this chapter I propose to examine the role of European female evangelicals in their zenana encounters in colonial Bengal, as well as their representations of these interactions in their writings. The texts we shall examine include both personal accounts as well as specifically two 'missionary novels', a category of missionary writing which has largely eluded critical scrutiny. The role of English women missionaries has been widely discussed, notably by Geraldine Forbes, Jane Haggis, Clare Midgley and Rhonda Semple, among others, while Anna Johnston has studied different types of missionary writings over various parts of the British empire.[2] More recently, Esme Cleall and Emily Manktelow have examined missionary homes and family lives.[3] What I propose to do in this chapter is to focus not so much on missionary work as a means of enhancing female agency and creating female employment in Britain as much as on the female missionary 'gaze' and the constructions of Indian women in missionary writings and finally to assess the contribution of these writings to the discourse of empire. I look first at representations of zenana visitation in missionary writings as a cross-cultural encounter, examining the type of female education and proselytising that was adopted. I then go on to study delineations of such encounters in missionary memoirs and other first-person accounts by female evangelicals working in zenanas in Bengal and conclude with a scrutiny of two 'missionary novels' written by female missionaries for a high-caste Bengali zenana audience.

[23]

Focus on the 'native' female

By the middle of the nineteenth century, gender had come to be foregrounded in evangelical Protestant discourse, with women being viewed as an important source of a culture's morality. In the colonial context, the education of the 'native' female was perceived as essential for transforming the character of the community as a whole. In fact, the improvement of the 'female mind' inside the zenana was advocated by early missionaries in Bengal, such as Alexander Duff, who believed that it would impart a long-term beneficial impact on the family as a whole.[4] And since Hinduism was frequently identified as the cause of the Indian woman's degradation, conversion, along with education, became a part of the strategy for their social, cultural and moral uplift. The guiding principle behind this Protestant missionary project was the Victorian belief that women were the moral guardians of the home, and this notion fed into the 'civilising mission's' foundational belief that the spiritual regeneration of a society could be brought about only by re-shaping 'native' mothers and wives.

Thus, by around the mid-nineteenth century there was a distinct shift in evangelical strategy, with a new focus on the zenana. Moreover, following the failure of missionary attempts at upper-caste conversion (in contrast to the success of mass, large-scale lower-caste conversion), womenfolk belonging to the upper castes/classes who maintained purdah gradually came to be identified by European missionaries as the most effective site for making a religious as well as reformist break-through. By targeting the heart of 'native' domesticity, it was hoped that western missionaries would gain access to the upper strata of Indian society. As missionary efforts from the 1860s onwards resulted in what Geraldine Forbes terms, 'the penetration of foreign ideas into the zenana, the very nerve centre of family life', the zenana came to assume greater importance as a site for female missionary (and colonial) intervention, with missionary agendas and colonial policies often colluding and intersecting with one another.[5]

This new focus on the zenana resulted in female missionaries gaining greater importance, given their ability to enter this female space and communicate with 'native' women in their own language.[6] From the 1860s onwards, a number of mission organisations meant solely for female work came to be established, marking the entry of a new generation of professional, unmarried white women into evangelism.[7] Quite unlike the missionary wives who had preceded them, for whom missionary work had been a 'labour of love', these unmarried female evangelicals were paid for their work. There was also a class component in their selection: many of them came from middle-class missionary families, being daughters, nieces or sisters of clergymen, and emphasis was laid on their possessing the qualities of a 'lady', such as 'culture, civility and manners'.[8] The induction of professional female missionaries into colonial missions did indeed mark a welcome advancement in terms of female employment and financial independence. However, this does bring into sharp contrast the labours of the 'missionary wife', whose work has largely gone unrecognised. Geraldine Forbes points out that these wives, whose names were associated with 'the schools they set up for girls', were never 'recognised as missionaries in their own right' and 'were neither paid, nor listed on missionary rolls nor eligible for pensions'.[9] Terming the missionary wife 'a pillar of the missionary movement', Jeffrey Cox concludes that her 'extensive missionary work' has gone 'largely unacknowledged in missionary literature'.[10]

Female education and zenana instruction

Among upper-caste/class families in Bengal, enforced female illiteracy had come to be the norm by the late eighteenth century. What underlay prejudices against female literacy were fears of losing control over women's sexuality; hence, reading and writing were not only derided as the art of the courtesan but also feared as instruments of female immorality, resulting in adulterous liaisons, and the writing of erotic missives to lovers. Most important, literacy was said to draw the curse of widowhood. Subsequently, from the early nineteenth century onwards, popularly known as the 'age of reform', thanks to European missionaries, Indian reformers, philanthropists and the colonial government, female education was promoted, and the first schools for girls were established in Bengal.[11] However, these preliminary missionary efforts at female schooling did not meet with much success among upper-caste/class families due to caste restrictions and the prevalence of child marriage. Hence, what followed was a shift in evangelical strategy from around the mid-nineteenth century, with the adoption of the method of zenana instruction. This system involved 'house-to-house visiting' by female missionaries who would teach married women inside the women's quarters of elite homes, under the watchful eye of their husbands, thereby carrying both literacy and evangelism into the zenanas.[12]

The zenana visitation system, which continued alongside schools for girls, had its beginnings in Bengal, although it spread to other parts of India as well, reaching its height of popularity around the 1860s to 1890s.[13] Started by the individual efforts of missionary wives in the mid-nineteenth century, it became a professionalised system by the later decades. Early tentative beginnings can be traced to the 1850s when a Mrs Sale of the Baptist Zenana Mission 'gained access to the inner compartments of a gentleman's home in Jessore' and conducted her first zenana visitation on her own initiative, an experience that she later recalled:[14]

> I was shown into a small room with two small barred windows near the roof ... A lady covered with jewels came in, but drew back when I approached her. When, however, she found that I could talk to her in Bengali, she became very Communicative and told me that she was the second wife and had two sons ... She said she had heard that European ladies excelled in needlework, and I replied that I would bring some and some books. 'Oh ! no,' she did not want books, 'learning amongst women brought down the anger of the gods.' On my next visit, I took canvas, needles and wool, also 'The Peep of Day' in Bengali and read several pages to her. After some time and much persuasion she learned to read.[15]

Gradually, around the 1860s, zenana visitation came to be systematised on a large scale in Calcutta by Mrs Hannah Catherine Mullens, who is often hailed in evangelical hagiographies as 'the Apostle of the *Zenanas*' who opened up zenanas with the 'tip of her embroidery needle'.[16] She (along with Mrs Murray) began by working in the neighbourhood of Bhowanipore, where the male heads of the households were eager to have their womenfolk taught; from there it later spread to other Calcutta neighbourhoods such as Entally, Behala and Chettlah.[17] At first, instruction was free and was supported through collections from charity and donations and also by government grants-in-aid, but gradually, after zenana visitation increased in acceptability, fees were collected from the families being visited, in addition to the funds raised through donations and subscriptions.[18] Of course, although 'pioneered by ... married women', notes Esme Cleall, 'the development of zenana work in the 1860s coincided with the entry of single women into LMS [London Missionary Society] as missionaries. Newly employed single women were able to use their privileged access to the zenana to forge a specifically female missionary role in India.'[19]

With Bengal being the first region in the country to be colonised by the East India Company as far back as the 1750s, it is not surprising that the zenana system of education should have begun in Calcutta, with its distinctive socio-historical environment, including the emergent *bhadralok* class. Although by no means interested in gendered social reform, the *bhadraloks*, the new western-influenced elite, educated in English-medium schools, encouraged female education as an important element in the 'modernising' scheme.[20] 'Many of these men', observes Geraldine Forbes, 'expressed a direct concern that their womenfolk learn the manners and occupations of English ladies'.[21]

[26]

Indeed, male initiative formed the bedrock of this education system, since it was the male heads of households, eager to have their women-folk taught, who invited zenana visitation.[22] However, the question of Bengali zenana women showing any female agency at all is something that we shall look at briefly later in this chapter.

By the 1880s zenana work had become stable, and the visitations, which took place on a daily or a weekly basis, consisted of missionar-ies reading aloud from the Bible or from printed tracts, pamphlets or readers which were printed in large numbers by missionary society printing presses. Often, European female missionaries would be accom-panied by 'Bible-women', or 'native' female converts (described rather condescendingly in a contemporary missionary text as 'the simple, half-educated, but honest-hearted, native Bible-woman').[23] These lower-class 'native' assistants, notes Jane Haggis, who were useful in communicating – possibly even more effectively in the zenana than were white missionary women – were 'overwhelmingly drawn from the ranks of the lowest communities in the Indian caste hierarchy' and 'actually did most of the teaching, nursing and training being carried out'.[24] However, even when they 'came to resemble the lady mission-ary in qualification, effort and dedication', points out Haggis, they were 'never accorded the title, "lady"', but always occupied a lower status than the European missionary.[25]

Inside the zenana, the evangelists would raise and answer questions, while their students knitted, sewed or embroidered as they listened. Gradually, a distinct curriculum emerged which incorporated teach-ing of the letters as well as training in plain sewing, fancy embroidery, knitting and lace-work. The practical usefulness of plain sewing in par-ticular made it an immense success with pupils when they found 'they could do many things without the help of a tailor'.[26] Thus the evangeli-cal programme astutely wove together 'femininity' and 'Christianity', strategically deploying the teaching of needlework for furthering their conversion programmes. A young female missionary, writing in the 1890s, described this covert intermeshing of needlework and teaching of the letters with evangelical agendas of conversion:

> We teach them plain and fancy sewing, reading or music, all the time talking to them and watching for every opportunity of sowing the seed. Before leaving, we read and explain a few verses from the Gospel, and sing some hymns which they dearly love.[27]

What is more, the ideology behind the zenana mission was not only evangelical but also gendered, the idea being not only to convert upper-class/caste women to Christianity but also to impose 'colonial moder-nity' upon them, and shape them into suitable wives and mothers.

Consequently, the two main components of the zenana mission curriculum (namely, reading and needlework), drew upon what Eliza Kent terms 'a long-standing European association between needlework and femininity', the objective being to 'inculcate in Indian women a particular style of genteel femininity', and shape them into 'better wives and mothers'.[28] After all, as Jane Haggis points out, the missionary endeavour was not merely to convert, educate or enlighten but also to very clearly impose a westernised gender role model, 'a very specific set of gender roles and models belonging to Victorian middle-class culture ... transforming Indian women into good wives and mothers as well as active Christian workers, much in the image of their missionary teachers'.[29] Thus these zenana missions closely interlinked their conversion programme with the agenda of 'civilising' and 'elevating' 'native' women into companionate wives and enlightened mothers, along the lines of a western model of womanhood – a point that Mrs Emma Raymond Pitman drew attention to in *Indian Zenana Missions* (1910):

> The civilisation of their heathen sisters is another object also ardently sought by lady-workers. In the dreary, monotonous life of the Zenana, one sees no books, writing materials, fancy-work nothing in fact of the innumerable traces of civilisation which are scattered around the boudoirs of English ladies.[30]

Of course, this process of 'recasting women' essentially entailed a reconstitution, rather than a rejection, of patriarchies. After all, similar patriarchal elements linked together European female paradigms, such as meekness, self-sacrifice and submissiveness, with the ideal of the 'Sati-Savitri' (faithful wives from Hindu mythology) traditionally enjoined upon high-caste Hindu women.[31] In addition, the Victorian, middle-class gender model also envisaged the companionate wife and educated helpmate.

With this objective of westernisation and 'modernisation', western evangelicals also sought to remodel the zenana along the lines of middle-class British social structures. They attacked the Hindu joint-family system, which consisted of all the sons living together over generations, along with wives and children. Evangelicals maintained that this system adversely affected husband–wife relations, rendering them subordinate to the husband's relations with his natal kin. Hence, they actively encouraged the installing of a nuclear family system, in the firm belief that Christianisation, westernisation or 'modernisation' were not possible without a change to a British-style nuclear-family system.[32] Although the larger objective was 'the spread of Christian knowledge', it was felt that even in those homes where direct teaching of the scriptures was not permitted, the system of visitation at least 'helped to remove prejudices and superstitions'.[33]

Constructing the zenana in missionary writings

Missionary women were often prolific writers and many of them also carried out their educational and conversion work through their writings, which ranged from tracts, articles in periodicals, Sunday school texts for children, to books and serious treatises. As Anna Johnston points out, the early setting up of missionary printing presses in Bengal gave a spurt to the missionary publication programme, with texts including 'autobiographies; biographies of individual missionaries, missionary wives, or Indian converts; local, regional, and colonial histories; and non-fictional ... accounts of Indian life and customs, education, women's place in society'.[34] These latter carried descriptions of zenana visitations, female education and 'historical' accounts of missionary achievements. In addition, a great number of missionary periodicals appeared regularly, carrying topical articles.[35] In many instances, popular articles from Christian magazines and periodicals were later collected together and published as a book in order to reach a wider readership.[36] Finally, there was the colonial 'missionary novel' which focused on Indian life and domesticities – a category of writing upon which we shall focus later, taking up two evangelical novels for discussion.

From mid-century onwards, there was an enhanced curiosity about life behind the purdah; 'What is a zenana?' was being 'constantly asked by those who are being aroused to sympathy for their Hindu sisters', pointed out Mrs Mary Weitbrecht of the Church Missionary Society who worked in Burdwan during the 1840s to 1870s.[37] Missionary women assumed the task of disseminating detailed and purportedly authentic information to the public on the interiors of zenanas and the nuances of 'native' domestic life. In many cases, their writings were publicised as being privy to the secrets of purdah life, with the promise of disclosing authentic details about it.[38] Not only did they serve to reinforce images of the *antahpur* ('zenana' in Bengali) as a 'benighted' space but also aided in the continual circulation of stereotypical representations about the 'Self' and the 'Other' – thereby feeding into broader imperial discourses.

Missionary writings turned a critical eye on the zenana and its inhabitants, endlessly reiterating some broadly distinctive themes and tropes throughout the century, 'othering' the purdah woman – with descriptions of the dark interiors of women's quarters, their ill-ventilated and unhygienic living conditions, their idle sensuality. In fact, even before zenana visitation was initiated, Priscilla Chapman, who came out to work in the Central Female School at Calcutta in the 1830s, termed the courtyards of the 'Zenanah' a 'receptacle of the worst filth and rubbish' – a view that was echoed forty years later by the Burdwan-based Mrs Mary Weitbrecht who described Bengali zenanas as consisting of 'dirty courtyards, dark corners, break-neck staircases, filthy outhouses and entries, overlaid with rubbish'.[39] Mrs Weitbrecht further pointed out that in Bengal, women always had 'the worst part of the house assigned them' so that, 'Even in the large residences of the rich Babus, one can always tell when getting near the rooms allotted to the women, by the dirty miserable appearance of the walls, staircases, and courts.'[40] This kind of architectural description continued to be echoed in reports filed by unmarried female professionals in later years: for instance, Miss Pepper of the Bengal Auxiliary Mission, noted in 1898, how, only 'After making our way to the back of a house, and climbing many narrow, winding steps, we find ourselves in the apartments of the women.'[41]

One persistent colonial construction throughout the period was that of 'native' women's abject enslavement. Indeed, the prison metaphor which abounded in female missionary writings actually began to emerge in early nineteenth-century missionary reports. For instance, as far back as 1822, William Ward had described the windows of the zenanas in Bengal as 'mere air-holes, through which the women may be seen peeping as through the gratings of a jail'.[42] A few years later, a female missionary commented that 'the gratings or shutters with small air holes' served 'not simply as a protection from the heat, but rather as prison security, through which none can penetrate'.[43] Echoing this, Mrs Weitbrecht observed in a missionary pamphlet, that 'Hindu ladies' are 'prisoners, for what is the Zenana ... but a place of confinement'.[44] In her widely circulated study, *Women of India and Christian Work in the Zenana* (1875) she further elaborated that 'native' women were kept deliberately imprisoned inside the zenana because of the sexual anxieties and insecurities of their men-folk: 'Everywhere it *means* the same thing, namely, that women are not to be trusted, but must be shut up as birds in a cage – must be hidden from the sight of all but their own husbands.'[45]

In addition, there was the persistent trope of 'native' female idleness and sensuality. Priscilla Chapman lamented in the 1830s about the moral coarseness that she had witnessed while visiting the zenana of a 'Baboo of high caste':

We were pained beyond expression with the frivolousness and impurity of their minds and conversation: their better feelings being roused, the

Bebees one and all confessed that they had never been taught otherwise; but that they were willing to learn to read, or work like English ladies: ... it was their custom to be idle and to talk about foolish things.[46]

Most importantly perhaps, the zenana was constructed as a site of ailments and disease, both psychological and physiological, ranging from fatal diseases such as consumption, to hysteria and depression. Mrs Weitbrecht mentioned how there were 'repeated allusion to sickness in the journals of the zenana teachers', a view echoed as late as the early twentieth century by western missionaries in Bengal, and by female medical missionaries who entered the zenanas with western medicine from around the 1880s onwards.[47]

Zenana visitation and gendered interactions

The mode of regular zenana visits, of course, resulted in close, everyday interactions between 'native' and missionary women. Clearly, embedded in these colonial interactions were elements of 'maternal imperialism' in the situation of missionary women 'mothering' their 'native' protégés.[48] Several narratives constructed zenana women as imprisoned and eagerly waiting to be 'rescued' from their benighted existence. By doing this of course, they effectively delineated purdah women as *not desiring* the practice of seclusion to continue. They thereby contradicted an existing strand in colonial discourse, which was the widely circulated charge that zenana women, in fact, *liked* their seclusion: they considered the practice genteel, and wished it to continue.

In the earlier years of zenana work, missionary visits had the character of 'friendly calls', with 'both parties asking curious questions about each other's society and practice'.[49] Indeed, one aspect of missionary writing that has not been much addressed by scholars is their construction of the relationship between *purdahnashins* (women who observe purdah or seclusion) and missionary women, especially in the narratives of missionary wives in the early phase of zenana visitation. Many narratives underlined the closeness of these relationships: they highlighted the zenana women's immense joy at visitations by white evangelicals and the opportunity these offered of interacting with strangers.[50] Missionary personal accounts stressed these women's eagerness for visits, and the warm emotional bonds that were forged between women of the two races, the thrust of this discourse being to underline the profound desire for colonial intervention from *within* the zenana – thereby reifying the 'rescue narrative' of colonial discourse. At the same time, it is indeed striking that these Bengali women, as described in missionary accounts, seemed to be exercising their own will and even agency, inviting and calling upon the white evangelicals – without the intervention (or even knowledge, perhaps) of their husbands, who were reportedly the organisers of such zenana visits made by foreign missionaries.

The warmth of these female relationships (and perhaps even friendships) were mentioned even prior to the establishment of the system of zenana instruction. In the 1830s, Priscilla Chapman mentioned how, 'On taking leave of them', the women 'begged that we would come again, and bring them books, pictures, and dolls'.[51] Elaborating on this point, Mrs Wylie a prominent Bengal-based missionary wife, mentioned in the 1850s how, 'It was very affecting to see the poor women and their children, so thankful for the least instruction given them, so eager for the visits of their teachers', while Mary Weitbrecht noted that Bengali purdah women would eagerly grasp at every available opportunity and would call out – from roof tops, from behind walls or windows – to the 'mems' (missionary-memsahibs), imploring them to come and visit them. Quoting Mrs Wylie, she elaborated:

> One day I was walking, gazing with longing eyes at the zenanas I passed on the way, when I heard a window opened above me, and an entreating voice in Bengali, 'Mem, Mem, won't you come and see us?' ... I found myself eagerly welcomed by seven or eight women, all wanting to catch hold of me at once. They dragged me into a room, took off my hat, and put me into a chair before I could say a word. They then seated themselves round me, and began asking questions as to where I lived. Would not I always come to see them?[52]

In fact, Mrs Weitbrecht quoted innumerable such instances of purdah women calling out and asking missionary women to 'Come to us', invariably receiving them warmly and displaying eager curiosity about white women:

> 'Is the Mem here? Open, that we may see her!'
> The shutters were soon opened, and then three bright faces gazed at me through the bars; it was so amusing to hear their remarks to one another on my appearance ... I go and talk to them; and it is so cheering to see how they look for me, and how anxious they are to keep me with them, sometimes holding my hat that I may not go away.[53]

Some of the later reports by unmarried professional female missionaries further echo this idea of mutual emotional attachment: one Miss Daniell of the Auxiliary Mission Society mentioned in her report in the 1880s, how she used to visit eighteen houses in the neighbourhood of Bhowanipore in Calcutta, and once when she was unable to visit them for four months due to illness, all her pupils were greatly worried: some sent their servants, children or husbands to ask after her, and some even came to see her themselves by night: 'After nearly four months leave, when I came back again to my work, all the ladies were quite pleased to see me looking well. Many of them had left off learning for some reason or the other, but as soon as I returned, they all recommended [sic].'[54]

While the non-literary writings focused primarily upon the pathetic condition of the purdah women, they also sought to construct implicitly, what Jane Haggis has called, 'a mission of sisterhood' whereby British women were cast as 'saviours of Indian women, liberating them from the degradation of a vindictive Hindu culture and religion'. Thus, British women were projected as 'having virtues and responsibilities of their free-born and independent situation'.[55] Indeed, while these personal accounts focus on the abject condition of the 'Other' (namely the zenana woman), the construction of the 'Self' in these visitation narratives is that of the hard-working, self-sacrificing female evangelicals who carry on 'day after day', toiling 'under a tropical sun, in the midst of foul ditches, open sewers, and defective drains, and surrounded by a moral degradation'.[56] Mrs Weitbrecht too pointed out the 'stern reality' behind the 'very fascinating' words 'Zenana visitation':

> There is something very fascinating in the sound of these two words, 'Zenana Visitation,' ... yet in its practical details the romance is soon forgotten in the stern reality of the work. Going forth in the hottest part of the day, in a burning sun, and making your way through narrow lanes – walking is a necessity, for no wheeled conveyance can proceed.[57]

A part of the rescue narrative was the thematic about the more fruitful occupation inside those zenanas where missionary visitation was allowed. Evangelical accounts repeatedly remarked upon the cheerful and busy air that pervaded homes where women had learned the letters, and contrasted it with the idle and bored atmosphere in unlettered homes, where 'you see the ladies sitting in the sun, with their knees drawn up to the chin, *absolutely* idle' or sitting all day long, 'counting their jewels or combing their hair':

> [Y]ou go in and find the whole female part of the family with their books and work ... some learning their lessons, mothers and daughters together; some working; others, it may be reading... but you seldom find them idle, and they are so much more cheerful and happy ... than they were in their days of indolence.[58]

Evangelical fiction and the female colonial gaze

Besides personal accounts which formed the bulk of missionary writings, evangelicals also sometimes wrote novels meant to be read aloud to women during zenana visitation, with the purpose of converting, 'westernising' or 'civilising' them. This category of writing, which has been neglected and is yet to be fully documented, offers an exciting and potentially rich site of excavation, in order to gain an insight into the colonial missionary archive.[59]

While evangelical stories had indeed been written earlier (for instance, Mrs Sherwood's stories for children), the missionary-authored fiction that was used in zenanas was distinct in specifically targeting grown women.[60] This type of writing essentially aimed at doing three things: to reveal the evils of the purdah; to try and convert zenana women to Christianity; and to attempt to bring about a cultural transformation among zenana women and recast them along the lines of an exemplary female paradigm based on a western model. The colonial missionary novel which appears to have been written by a few female evangelists, was specifically addressed to 'native' females and employed for the purposes of westernising and converting zenana woman, if possible. This fascinating category of writing has not been much discussed by scholars – with the conspicuous exception of Anna Johnston, who in her study, *Missionary Writings and Empire* (2003) has examined the writing of evangelicals in British colonies. However, while Johnston has studied missionary writings across the British empire in colonies as diverse as India, Polynesia and Australia, she has not specifically looked at the writings of *female* evangelicals.

The usual practice among missionaries was to read aloud from various texts during visitations, including from story books, 'Readers' and the Bible. Novels, in particular, were extremely popular with the inhabitants of these elite female quarters, especially with those 'of mature years' who were 'reluctant and even unable to go through the drudgery of learning reading and writing and arithmetic', but were fond of hearing fiction and 'loved to hear stories'.[61] In fact, in instances where elderly zenana women objected to overtly evangelical scriptures being read out, story books were considered acceptable. While the bulk of the evangelical fiction was written in the metropole, a few novels specifically written by colonial female evangelicals for a zenana audience were deployed as reading materials inside the women's quarters.[62] In other words, these novels written by missionaries possibly played a key part in the mission strategy of carrying the civilising/westernising mission into the interiors of the zenana and disseminating evangelical as well as cultural ideologies.

It may not be an exaggeration, in fact, to suggest that this type of fiction could probably penetrate the interiors of the zenana more effectively than other kinds of evangelical writing, such as Bible stories, since 'native' women could identify themselves with the fictional characters and situations. One of the greatest strengths of this type of writing was their familiarity with the intricacies of Bengali domestic life, which made them recognisable to the zenana women who were its targeted audience. In a number of cases the texts were translated into Bengali and other vernacular languages. But even when written in simple English, they displayed their close acquaintance with colloquial Bengali, being liberally sprinkled with Bengali terms – thereby adopting a discursive strategy, which would no doubt have further strengthened the sense of a close and comforting familiarity with the nuances of upper-caste Calcutta life. In this section we examine the 'civilising mission' in two such novels, probing the strategies they deployed in promoting conversion, female education, western cultural practices as well as European paradigms of womanhood. The emergent concept of the Bengali *bhadramahila* (genteel or respectable lady) which came into prominence around this time (i.e. the 1860s and 1870s), was a product of the westernised aspirations of *bhadraloks* and Bengali male reformers. Meredith Borthwick has noted in her classic study on the Bengali *bhadramahila*, that this concept coalesced the Hindu female's ideal of self-sacrifice with the Victorian lady's ability to be a housewife, companion and helpmeet to her husband, with her basic education and social presence.[63]

Hannah Catherine Mullens' Faith and Victory *(1865)*

One of the most popular missionary novels which came to be widely used by female evangelicals as instructive reading material inside zenanas was *Faith and Victory: A Story of the Progress of Christianity in Bengal* (1865), the posthumously published novel written by Hannah Catherine Mullens, a second-generation, Calcutta-born missionary who was fluent in Bengali and who, we may recall, systematised the zenana mode of instruction in Calcutta in the 1860s.[64] Mrs Mullens, who wrote her first hugely popular novel, *Phulmoni O Karunar Bibaran* (1852) in Bengali, wrote *Faith and Victory* in English. The latter novel too enjoyed enduring popularity over several decades, going into numerous reprints, revised editions and translations into several Indian languages (including Bengali) and in fact, even found mention in missionary personal accounts as well as in evangelical fiction.[65] For instance, Weitbrecht's *Women of India* described how 'native' women could be found 'reading a story book, such as "Faith and Victory", "The Dairyman's Daughter", and other little books which have been translated into their language'.[66]

The larger objective of Mrs Mullens' novel was to demonstrate how Christianity helped in transforming the quality of life through the conversion of its highly educated, young Brahmin hero.[67] It targeted two sets of readership simultaneously: one, the general audience back 'home' in the metropolis who were curious to know about the zenana; and second, and more importantly, the zenana women who would hear the book read aloud by missionaries during their visitations. In the book's Preface she mentions her original intention of writing it 'only in the Bengalee language' and her current plans of translating it later into Bengali. She spelled out her aim of demystifying fantasies about the zenana created by 'Eastern Tales and Indian Romances' and noted that 'In penetrating into the secret recesses of a Hindu home, and lifting the veil of the Zenana, the writer is aware she is treading on dangerous ground.' Nevertheless she felt humbly confident that her 'little work contains no glaring errors respecting Hindu life and manners' and hoped that it would 'promote the lasting welfare of ... the gentle, the loving HINDU WOMAN'. Hence, although her aim was to provide western readers with authentic information based on her 'direct intercourse with native families' about the 'real position of social life in the East', her larger, more important objective was to reach out to Zenana women themselves, and to 'send [the novel] forth on its humble mission of love to the native ladies of India'. The idea was to present these colonised 'native' women with a 'faithful picture of Indian life, which they should recognise' and thus help to open their eyes to their oppressed condition and make them welcome change.[68] Indeed, it is this latter, 'native' female audience that distinguishes this missionary novel and sets it apart from non-literary missionary writings which were meant for a metropolitan British or an Anglo-Indian audience.

Mrs Mullens' absorbingly written novel, with its dramatic plot, full of twists and turns, its intimate knowledge of the customs and conventions governing a high-caste, traditional Bengali household, was a tremendous success.[69] Not specifically woman-related, for the greater part it focused upon the religious dilemmas of the male protagonist, Prosonno Kumar Chatterjee, a young Brahmin, educated at Calcutta's Presidency College, who embraces Christianity in the teeth of fierce opposition from his joint-family. It has been well documented how missionaries considered Brahmin converts as prized trophies – thereby, effectively betraying a covert reverence for caste.[70] While low-caste/ class Hindus tended to convert in masses, high-caste Hindus converted only as individuals, and that too after much reflection, thought and deliberation over the matter. Moreover, high-caste converts had much to lose, since the individual (generally male) was ostracised by his community and considered to be dead, and *shraddha* or the ritual death rite was performed for him. We see this happening in Mullens' novel: when the upper-caste hero, Prosonno, embraces Christianity, he is expelled by his family; his orthodox old father burns a Bengali Bible and ritually pronounces him 'dead' by performing his *shraddha*, while his young wife, Kaminee, dons a widow's garb, and accuses him of having rendered her 'a widow in the bloom of my youth'.[71] The young Brahmin, however, sticks to his resolution and it is finally towards the very end that his estranged wife – who is different from the other zenana women in being educated – follows him in a manner befitting a dutiful wife, by accepting his religion. After she has been reunited with her husband, both of them embark on an exemplary life of companionate domesticity.

Padma Anagol has argued in her study of conversion in the Bombay presidency that writings on conversion reveal a gendered dimension, in the sense that they show the husband accepting Christianity only after intellectual debate and grappling with its religious and philosophical questions, while the wife's reasons for converting are primarily that of wifely fidelity of a dutiful spouse.[72] In other words, while the husband displays a 'male', rational approach to questions of belief, the wife is constructed stereotypically as female and emotional – thereby upholding the ideal of the 'faithful wife', a paradigm at which both Indian and British Victorian patriarchies intersected.

Although the central focus in this narrative is not specifically on women, several 'native' gendered social practices which were on the social reform agenda – such as child marriage, female illiteracy, infanticide and purdah – are censured along the way. Presented here are the staple missionary tropes of the inferior social position of the Hindu woman and the benighted state of the *antohpur* (women's quarters) with its illiterate inhabitants (the only exception being the hero's wife, who had been educated by her parents). In the novel, there are six women in the zenana of this large joint-family, consisting of Prosonno's mother, his widowed old grandmother, his wife and his two brothers' wives, besides a little sister who is just a child. This female space is constructed stereotypically, as a site of boredom, quarrelsomeness, 'ignorance and degradation', where everything 'noble in their nature is crushed, almost destroyed', where women take 'recourse to mean methods in obtaining favour', and 'every-day dealings' are ridden with 'petty jealousies' and intrigues:[73]

> their total want of education deprives them of the pleasures of reading and writing ... therefore time hangs heavy on their hands and they have the leisure afforded them for carrying on at will the most perfect system of domestic warfare.[74]

Additionally, Mullens draws attention to the zenana women's lowly position in society, their economic dependence on men, their absolute lack of skills at needlework, and especially their poor mothering skills which makes them incapable of providing any guidance to their children.

Moreover, the joint-family system is attacked and projected as antithetical to a western-style companionate marriage and effective motherhood. The 'plan of having several branches of the same family to reside together in one house' is critiqued as leading to 'discord'.[75] It lacks the close emotional ties that are nurtured in the nuclear family, and is the cause of human alienation: instead of the warm, western-style family conversations and interactions during meal-times, eating a meal in a Hindu home is shown to be a solitary, aloof, a-social activity. Moreover, it is only in the western-style nuclear family that a sober companionship between husband and wife – the kind to be emulated – can to be found.

In this novel missionary women make no zenana visitation. In fact, there is no gendered encounter between women of the two races at all. Instead, the European evangelical is represented here by a missionary's wife, who carries out lengthy discussions with Prosonno, the young Brahmin convert, on the subject of western domestic ideology and women's position in society. In her essay on female evangelical work in India, Geraldine Forbes has noted that from mid-century onwards, a class angle entered this discourse after the induction of unmarried, middle-class women into missionary work, and that it was imperative for these missionaries to be 'lady-like':

> Above all, she had to be a 'lady' by birth and education. A 'lady' had the following characteristics: the virtues of tact, patience and good temper, a pleasing exterior and conciliatory manner, and a good education which included music, needlework and drawing. Daughters of clergymen were particularly well-suited.[76]

And indeed, Mullens takes care to present the English missionary's wife as a refined 'lady', in terms of class. Jane Haggis has incisively argued that the stereotype of the zenana woman that was presented in female evangelical accounts was, in effect, a textual strategy adopted to give 'the agency of the missionary woman … its feasibility'; hence, rather than being the subjects of these narratives, Indian women are actually 'the textual device around which the missionary story turns'.[77] This would indeed appear to be apposite in this case, where the missionary's wife exemplifies the exalted status of women in English/Christian families. Although, as Anna Johnston points out, this missionary wife remains anonymous in the text, there is no doubt that she represents not only refined class attributes, but is also the exemplary female role model around which the 'civilising mission' cohered.[78]

Valorising western domestic ideology, the missionary wife argues that European women, who marry not in childhood but at a mature age, are educated and industrious and make better wives and mothers. They possess 'ladylike' accomplishments, such as the ability to converse intelligently and graciously on a range of topics, while their active industriousness contrasts with zenana women's Oriental indolence and weak will-power – evident in their inability to finish even their needlework. In fact, at one point in the novel, the English missionary's wife even remarks in a superior tone (verging on the racist) that there is a fundamental difference in the energy levels and strength of character between women of both the races:

> I confess I am often amused at your Hindu ladies in their Zenanas. I go one day and set one of them a small piece of needlework to be finished in a week: I go again; only a few stitches have been done, and the excuse always is, 'I had so much house-work to do;' whereas, if the truth were known, they have had many hours to spend in gossip, sleep, and plaiting their hair. A Hindu lady would hardly believe what an English woman gets through in the course of the day.[79]

However, unlike most missionary writings, Mrs Mullens' novel does, at the same time, admit to certain positive features of zenana life inside joint-families. Thus, in the 'woman's world' of the *antohpur*, the inhabitants enjoy the companionship of other women in the household, and alongside the female intrigues and quarrels, there is also space for chatting, playing popular Bengali board games like *Mogul-Pathan* and forming female friendships.[80] During such happy moments, the women sit together, while Prosonno's wife, Kaminee (being the only lettered one among the women), reads aloud to them from books, especially to little Hemlota (her husband's sister) and to *Thakur ma*, her husband's affectionate old grandmother.

Later, the narrative also presents a 'native' convert who leads an exemplary Christian married life with his wife. This further crystallises the issue about women's exalted status within western-style (that is to say, Christian) domesticity – which is a marker of cultural superiority. Towards the novel's close, both Kaminee and her recently widowed, eldest sister-in-law, Shoudaminee, secretly slip out of the house and opt for conversion; after which they are able to joyfully experience for themselves the elevated status that Christianity bestowed on women: 'One thing that struck them both was the treatment of the women.'[81]

Mary Leslie's The Dawn of Light *(1868)*

Far more directly foregrounded are gender issues and zenana visitation in another evangelical novel: *The Dawn of Light: A Story of the Zenana*

Mission (1868), written by Mary E. Leslie, which appeared a few years later. Although Leslie, who was the daughter of a Baptist missionary, may not have been a missionary herself, she always remained closely associated with the Baptist Zenana Mission, participating in many of their activities, including in female schooling.[82] While it is not clear whether Leslie's novel was actually used inside zenanas or not – as Mrs Mullens' two novels, *Phulmoni O Karunar Bibaran* and *Faith and Victory*, clearly were – one may speculate that, keeping in mind its huge popularity and the number of editions that it seems to have gone through, it too perhaps formed a part of the evangelical literary archive.[83] Indeed, the gender encounter paradigms are so central to this text that it would be fruitful to examine it.

More than in *Faith and Victory*, gender issues are foregrounded in this absorbingly written work which focuses on 'native' characters, and directly addresses the subject of zenana visitation and its emancipatory benefits. Revealing an intimate knowledge of gendered social and familial practices, it delineates intricate details about 'native' female daily habits, customs and inter-personal female equations within upper-caste, Calcutta-based Bengali joint-families, besides demonstrating a close knowledge of the vernacular in its liberal sprinkling of colloquial Bengali words drawn from female daily life – such as *chhoto bow* (youngest daughter-in-law), *toktopose* (hard, wooden cot), *kokil* (cuckoo), *chik* (necklace), *alta* (red paint used to decorate feet), *sari*, *Thakoor* (god), *boshonto* (spring season) – all of which its zenana audience would no doubt have recognised and delightedly identified with.

It is today of special interest to us because of its woman-centredness, as it specifically mobilises reform issues such as Hindu widowhood, female education, child marriage, polygamy, widow remarriage and infant mortality within its larger focus on conversion. Seeking to target the *purdahnashin* inside the very heart of elite indigenous domesticity, the story revolves around issues of widowhood and the death of a child, raw emotions which it addresses by focusing on the figure of Boshonto, a young Brahmin widow. This young female protagonist who was pregnant at the time of her husband's death, gives birth after a few months to a male infant who becomes her greatest solace and comfort. But tragically enough, when he is two years old, the baby is shown to fall ill during the rainy season and die of the 'terrible epidemic fever of Bengal' – leaving her distraught and inconsolable.[84]

However, the heart-broken Boshonto who continues to live with her in-laws, is well treated and spared the oppression that widows were usually subjected to – something that was highlighted in missionary and reformist discourse. The household is headed by her eldest brother-in-law, Babu Rajkumar Bhattacharya, a learned Sanskrit scholar, who teaches in a Calcutta-based college. This *chhoto bow* (youngest daughter-in-law) peacefully co-inhabits the female quarters with the other female family members, namely the wives of her two older brothers-in-law (Kumari and Prosonno), and a kindly old widowed aunt (*piseema* or father's sister) named Taramoni.[85] In keeping with evangelical discourse, however, the novel does project the zenana as a 'dull, colourless, and unintellectual' prison house, where women only 'slept, looked over their jewels, and oiled and tied up their long hair':[86]

> Monotonous is the life of a bird in its cage. Yet it is scarcely more monotonous than the life of a Hindu woman in her husband's house ... [where] she is kept a perfect prisoner.[87]

It is purely by chance that the women in this family come to learn one day about the regular zenana visitation that is being carried out in a neighbour's house, where the daughter-in-law ('Bungshi Babu's Bow') is learning to read and write. When they come to hear that 'an English lady goes twice a week to teach them, and a native teacher, a learned woman, goes every day', the neighbourhood women are at first scandalised – all the more so because this English lady 'is about twenty and not married'.[88] At the same time, their curiosity is aroused when they hear that this attractive young white woman is 'fair, with brown eyes and brown hair ... has such a pleasant laugh, and says such winning words'.[89] Reflecting the missionary policy of employing younger, unmarried, professional women for zenana work from around the 1860s onwards, the young English missionary is shown to be unmarried – in contrast to the missionary wife of Mrs Mullens' novel – although in both instances it is stressed that they are polished and educated English 'ladies'. As we have noted earlier, there was a deliberate emphasis on class in the mid-century recruitment policy for single missionary women: these recruits had to be 'ladies' 'by birth and education' and possess lady-like qualities such as a pleasant personality and a tactful, agreeable manner. Besides, they had to have a 'good education' which included music, needlework and drawing.[90]

At first, the zenana women in the novel find the concept of female literacy shocking – but the head of their household, the learned Brahmin pundit and 'Sanscrit scholar', presumably gives his consent, for one day, the white female missionary finally visits them. The text underlines that it is only with the consent of male family members that zenana visitation could take place: 'Had they made any opposition, all would have gone wrong, for in the hands of men lie the destinies of the women of India' – thereby constructing the zenana women as passive and raising questions about how far female agency is shown to be imbricated in the sphere of female education and social reform.[91]

On the day of the first visit, there is great excitement, and the neighbourhood women come thronging through back-ways, to see the young white woman, as, 'Twenty eager faces crowded round the fair English girl'. What follows is a highly glowing account of gendered interaction during a zenana visitation. As the women cluster around her, listening eagerly, the friendly missionary girl talks to each one of them kindly, sings a simple Bengali hymn, and enthrals them by showing fine pieces of needlework: slippers, caps, comforters, rugs and hookah-carpets, beautifully embroidered with roses and cherries. She also displays photos of Queen Victoria (symbol of a powerful western female monarch who is also a wife and mother), along with pictures of the royal family, and soon enough, the white girl 'had won all their hearts'.[92]

As sincere as she is pretty, the 'brave English girl' keeps her promise of visiting them every fortnight, despite having to undertake this journey from Calcutta to the outskirts of Gopalpore, where they live. With the regular visitation of this kind and loving 'lady teacher', the zenana is soon transformed by the needlework and teaching of the letters which constituted the twin parts of the zenana curriculum.[93] The women from neighbouring houses also throng there for the 'spelling books and pieces of work' that she distributes.[94] Thus, the pretty English evangelical shows them how to sew and to knit useful items such as comforters, caps and slippers; and most importantly, she teaches them to read – using evangelical novels like *Gopal Kaminee* and later on, Mrs Mullens' famed Bengali novel, *Phulmoni O Karuna*, for this purpose. Indeed, in all likelihood, *Gopal Kaminee* refers to Mrs Mullens' *Faith and Victory* (possibly to the Bengali version), since titles of evangelical writings often underwent change in course of translation.[95]

Soon, the women in this family take to habitually sitting together on a mat in the verandha with their books and needlework, engaged in reading aloud and stitching. 'They always read aloud, and Boshonto being the best reader, Kumari and Prosonno would work and listen while she was reading.'[96] Gradually, the young widow, who is much more intelligent than the other women, feels happier in her new, constructive zenana life: 'the life that had once been so dim and colourless brightened for these poor women. The gay coloured wools threw a gleam upon their daily paths; the books with their characters peopled the realms of their imagination.'[97]

The larger evangelical textual strategy deployed by Mary Leslie's novel is to foreground specific gendered problems which directly affected the lives of nineteenth-century zenana woman, something with which the book's targeted female audience would no doubt have identified immediately, perhaps even more directly than they did with Mullens' novel. Many of these were commonly feared occurrences including the loss of an infant – an all too frequent occurrence in a period that was marked by a very high infant mortality rate – as well as the danger of polygamy (a common feature in cases where a wife was childless), or the dread of becoming a widow. Boshonto has not only lost her only child but she is also doomed to life-long widowhood and the denial of motherhood, since despite legislation sanctioning it, the remarriage of upper-caste widows hardly ever occurred in actual practice. Indeed, in nineteenth-century Bengal the cause of widows and their remarriage was supported mainly by the Brahmo Samaj, the reformist group, which also set up Widows' Homes for abandoned widows and imparted vocational training to them. In fact, upper-caste widow remarriage is shown in this novel to be bitterly opposed by Hindu society. In one instance, when a youth belonging to the Brahmo Samaj is inspired by the 'sentiments of the Pundit Bidyasagor' and decides to marry a young widow, there is widespread outrage and 'a terrible commotion throughout the little town' for days.[98]

Polygamy, the common social practice, where a barren woman's husband married again for the sake of progeny, is censured as 'a heavy sorrow ... the heaviest a Hindu woman has to bear, short of losing her husband'. This fear of polygamy comes true for one of the sisters-in-law, named Prosonno, who has remained childless even after eight years of marriage. She now has to helplessly watch her husband get married again – this time to a pretty little child of 9 years. The child-bride's plight and the institution of child marriage, in their turn, come to be critiqued through the trauma of separation that is suffered by this child. When an old aunt lifts the little bride's veil in the customary manner, in order to see the 'new bow's [daughter-in-law's] face', the frightened little girl bursts into tears, sobbing inconsolably and begs to go home – finally falling asleep 'in the arms of the female servant who had come with her'.[99]

For the grieving Boshonto, an important moment comes when she hears from the English lady missionary about a heaven where little children go after they die, where they live happily: 'Our Holy Book teaches us that all little children, when they die, go at once to heaven.' Christianity thus offers great solace through the idea of the 'Good Shepherd' who 'has gathered our lambs in His loving arms', and Boshonto is overjoyed at the thought of this 'beautiful place' where she will be reunited with her child some day.[100]

There is no low-class 'Bible-woman' in this novel; instead, there is a dignified Christian female school teacher, 'a comely native woman', whom they meet in Calcutta – a meeting which marks the turning point in Boshonto's conversion.[101] The English lady has since returned to her country, and it is this Indian Christian teacher, who speaks as a bereaved mother herself, disclosing how she too had lost three of her children in the past – two infants and one daughter aged seven – but after the initial grief had been 'comforted too in thinking that she [her daughter] had gone to heaven'.[102] Deriving peace from these words, Boshonto is strongly attracted to Christianity for its profound compassion, and after covertly procuring a Bengali New Testament, she secretly embraces Christianity. Conversion, in her case, is therefore shown to be a considered, rational, agential choice – quite in contrast to the passive, emotional acceptance of a husband's choice that Padma Anagol had noted was often a feature of women's conversion.

Like Mullens' text, this novel too ends on a note of happy domesticity, reiterating the western ideal of a companionate marriage, and also valorising Christianity. Indeed, conversion along with a nuclear-style family, is shown to facilitate western-style domesticity, as Boshonto, the young widow gets married to a reformist-minded young Brahmin widower named Bishonauth Mukarjee. Thanks to the influence of 'Pandit Bidyasagor' and other social reformers, this young man categorically rejects the idea of marrying a child-bride. Recalling how in his previous marriage he had shaped his late wife into 'a companion for himself by teaching her to read and write', he once again seeks 'an educated young woman'.[103] After the initial reactions of shocked outrage, her in-laws grudgingly give their consent and the couple embark upon a model, Victorian-style, companionate married life where the wife is the husband's helpmeet. Besides, Boshonto's maternal instincts are fulfilled by the widower's small daughter who is of the same age as her own dead son. Subsequently, her joy knows no bounds when she discovers that her husband too is a secret Christian convert, just like herself. The novel ends therefore with husband and wife embarking on a new life together of happy and sober Christian domesticity, culminating eventually in the birth of their male child, Anondo Chondro.

Two features are particularly striking in these two missionary novels which set them apart from the non-literary missionary discourse. First, the focus is equally divided between images of the oppressed 'Other' and images of the exemplary gendered 'Self'. As a counterpoint to the oppressed and backward Brahmin woman who suffers silently in the zenana as wife, or as widow, and is the victim of an unfeeling, patriarchal joint-family, there is presented the exemplary female paradigm of the white missionary woman. It is not the memsahib but the missionary woman – be it the missionary wife of Mullens' novel, or the unmarried evangelical English girl of Leslie's novel. These texts are thus equally about the *purdahnashin* as they are about the white woman.

Moreover, in both instances, the novels end with conversion and sober Christian domesticity. They present a marital relationship which is a *Christian* model of companionship, rooted in a nuclear family system, and based on mutual respect and equality.

Conclusion

In pursuit of their 'civilising mission', missionaries entered the zenanas and turned a critical 'colonial gaze' upon their inhabitants, representing them in their prolific writings as abject and oppressed, and reinforcing negative colonial constructions about them. Female missionaries entered the exclusive female spaces of the zenanas, focused on teaching, domestic training and, most importantly, promoted paradigms of womanhood based on Victorian and Edwardian models.

Within missionary discourse there were both similarities as well as fine distinctions between non-literary and literary writings. Both kinds of narratives presented a critique of the zenana as a prison-house of boredom, idleness and petty quarrels. Non-literary writings projected *purdahnashins* as oppressed inhabitants who themselves called out to missionaries and begged them to visit them and rescue them from boredom – gesturing at a 'female friendship' that was forged between missionaries and secluded Indian woman. Clearly, these encounters were rooted in the discourse of 'Self' and the 'Other', of western superiority and 'native' abjectness. Hence the colonial transactions between women of both the races were complicated by the element of 'sisterly', racial superiority. Nevertheless, what is particularly striking in this discourse is how these requests for visitations were made directly by Bengali women, which is suggestive of female volition and agency on their part – contesting thereby the conventional construct of the 'passive' zenana woman who is dependent on male initiatives in such matters.

The missionary novel had direct access to the zenana audience that it targeted, and could therefore focus its efforts at 'civilising' and 'modernising' more effectively. Speaking more openly about issues such as conversion, companionate domesticity and Christian marriage, it projected conversion to Christianity as the sole means of achieving 'modernity' and female emancipation. A prominent figure in this discourse was that of the white female evangelical (who was overtly absent in the non-literary writings). This figure served both as an exemplary western gender-model to be emulated by the 'native' purdah woman, and also as a catalytic agent of change through conversion. Besides, this representation of the 'Self' by the female missionary also introduced a distinctive strand of social class – with the female missionary anxious to project herself as a 'lady'. This discourse thus helped give shape to the evangelical agenda of 'civilising' *purdah-nashins*, recasting them in the mould of 'colonial modernity' through conversion.

Notes

1 Prior to that, reform had been sought through legislation, with the help of Indian reformers (e.g. the law banning sati in 1829 and the Hindu Widows' Remarriage Act of 1856), such as Raja Rammohan Roy and Ishwarchandra Vidyasagar, who spearheaded these reforms respectively. In the 1860s female education came to be actively promoted in Bengal by the Brahmo leader Keshub Chandra Sen.

2 See Geraldine H. Forbes, 'In Search of the "Pure Heathen": Missionary Women in Nineteenth Century India', *Economic and Political Weekly*, 21:17, Review of Women's Studies, April 26 (1986), pp. WS2–WS8; Jane Haggis, '"A Heart that Has Felt the Love of God and Longs for Others to Know It": Conventions of Gender, Tensions of Self and Constructions of Difference in Offering to Be a Lady Missionary', *Women's History Review*, 7:2 (1998), pp. 171–193; Jane Haggis, 'Ironies of Emancipation: Changing Configurations of "Women's Work" in the "Mission of Sisterhood" to Indian Women', in *Feminist Review*, 65 (2000), pp. 108–126; Clare Midgley, 'Can Women Be Missionaries? Envisioning Female Agency in the Early Nineteenth-century British Empire', *Journal of British Studies*, 45 (2006), pp. 335–358; Rhonda Semple, *Missionary Women: Gender, Professionalism and the Victorian Idea of Christian Mission* (Suffolk, Boydell Press, 2003). For a discussion of the key features of missionary writings, see Anna Johnston, *Missionary Writing and Empire, 1800–1860* (Cambridge, Cambridge University Press, 2003), pp. 82–83.

3 Esme Cleall, *Missionary Discourses of Difference: Negotiating Otherness in the British Empire, 1840–1900* (Basingstoke, Palgrave Macmillan, 2012), and Emily J. Manktelow, *Missionary Families: Race, Gender and Generation on the Spiritual Frontier* (Manchester, Manchester University Press, 2013). See also Rhonda Semple, 'Christian Model, Mission Realities: The Business of Regularising Family in Mission Communities in Late Nineteenth-century North India', *Journal of Colonialism and Colonial History*, 14:1 (2013), DOI: 10.1353/cch.2013.0003.

4 Alexander Duff, *Female Education in India* (Edinburgh, John Johnstone, 1837), p. 18, cited in David Savage, 'Missionaries and the Development of a Colonial Ideology of Female Education in India', *Gender and History*, 9:2 (1997), p. 209. Duff believed in the 'top down' form of education.

5 Forbes, 'In Search of the "Pure Heathen"', p. WS3.

6 For a detailed discussion of zenana visitation, see among others, Jane Haggis, 'White Women and Colonialism: Towards a Non-recuperative History', in Clare Midgley (ed.), *Gender and Imperialism* (Manchester, Manchester University Press, 1998), pp. 45–75; Judith Rowbotham, '"Hear an Indian Sister's Plea": Reporting the Work of 19th-century British Female Missionaries', *Women's Studies International Forum*, 21:3 (1998), pp. 247–261; and Eliza F. Kent, *Converting Women: Gender and Protestant Christianity in Colonial South India* (New York, Oxford University Press, 2004).

7 These included the Baptist Church's Zenana Missionary Society (1867) and the Church of England Zenana Missionary Society (1880).

8 Haggis, 'White Women and Colonialism', p. 56.

9 Forbes, 'In Search of the "Pure Heathen"', p. WS3.

10 Jeffrey Cox, *The British Missionary Enterprise since 1700* (London and New York, Routledge, 2008), p. 111.

11 The years 1817–1837 marked the opening of schools for Bengali girls by missionaries. The Serampore Baptist missionaries were the first to open a school for

girls in 1818, with fourteen students, while Miss Mary Anne Cook (later Mrs Wilson), who came out to Bengal in 1821 under the auspices of the Calcutta School Society, set up schools for girls there. The syllabus in these early years included needlework, Bengali reading and writing, arithmetic, other 'useful knowledge' and Christian religious teaching. The leading Protestant missions to work in Bengal in the early nineteenth century were the Baptist Missionary Society (BMS), the London Missionary Society (LMS) and the Church Missionary Society (CMS).

12 Forbes, 'In Search of the "Pure Heathen"', p. WS2.

13 Zenana missions spread to other parts of the country in the later decades of the nineteenth century; for colonial Punjab see Jeffrey Cox, *Imperial Fault Lines: Christianity and Colonial Power in India, 1818–1940* (Stanford, Stanford University Press, 2002), pp. 159–161; for South India, see Kent, *Converting Women*, p. 141; for a general discussion, see Haggis, 'White Women and Colonialism', pp. 45–75.

14 For details about the first attempt at zenana instruction in 1854 by Mrs Elizabeth (Geale) Sale (1818–1898) of the Baptist Zenana Mission, see *JUBILEE, 1867–1917: Fifty Years' Work among Women in the Far East* (London, Carey Press, 1917), p. 12. Forbes locates the 1850s as the date of origin of zenana instruction, 'In Search of the "Pure Heathen"', p. WS3. However, other dates too have been suggested; Eliza Kent notes that 'the Scottish Free Church mission started the first zenana mission in Calcutta in 1855, with the assistance of a single lady English missionary named Miss Toogood'; see Kent, *Converting Women*, p. 141; while Emma Pitman notes that it was 'About 1830' that 'Miss Bird gained access to several Zenanas in Calcutta', in Mrs Emma Raymond Pitman, *Indian Zenana Missions: Their Needs, Origin, Objects, Agents, Modes of Working and Results* (London, John Snow and Co., 1903), p. 2.

15 Mrs Elizabeth Sale quoted in *JUBILEE, 1867–1917*, p. 12.

16 Forbes, 'In Search of the "Pure Heathen"', p. WS3. See also Kent, *Converting Women*, p. 141. According to Baptist mission records, after Mrs Sale had shifted to Calcutta in 1858, 'she received permission to visit regularly with the object of teaching the women', and 'this was the commencement of systematic work in Calcutta, for the opening of this one door led to the opening of others; and when Mrs. Sale left for England in 1861, she was able to transfer the work she had begun to Mrs. Mullens of the London Missionary Society'. See *JUBILEE, 1867–1917*, p. 13.

17 Benoy Bhushan Roy and Pranati Roy, *Zenana Mission: The Role of Christian Missionaries for the Education of Women in Nineteenth Century Bengal* (Delhi, Indian Society for Promoting Christian Knowledge, 1998), p. 162. Mrs Mullens, accompanied by another female missionary, began by working in six houses in Calcutta, with a total of forty-nine zenana-pupils, ranging in age from four to fifty.

18 By the 1880s fees were charged for regular visitations (average monthly fees: Rs 23; annual fees: Rs 317); while some zenanas took lessons once or twice a week, others took lessons almost daily. See Roy and Roy, *Zenana Mission*, p. 114.

19 Cleall, *Missionary Discourses of Difference*, p. 41.

20 Savage, 'Missionaries and the Development of a Colonial Ideology of Female Education', pp. 204–205. See also Kent, *Converting Women*, p. 128. The colonial takeover of Bengal is usually set at 1757 when Robert Clive and his British forces defeated Siraj-ud-daulah, the Nawab of Bengal at the Battle of Plassey.

21 Forbes, 'In Search of the "Pure Heathen"', p. WS6.

22 A Bengali *bhadralok* complained about the gap between husbands and wives that prevailed in most household in terms of colonial 'modernity': 'We go one way, our old relatives another, and our women yet another … Our educated young men discuss their projects of reform in debating clubs; but as soon as they get home … they carefully put their progressive ideas in their pockets and bend their necks beneath the yoke of custom. … They belong to the nineteenth century, but their homes to the first century', cited in L. S. S. O'Malley (ed.), *Modern India and the West: A Study of the Interactions of Civilizations* ([1941], London, Oxford University Press, 1968), p. 789.

23 Pitman, *Indian Zenana Missions*, p. 28.
24 Haggis, 'White Women and Colonialism', p. 57.
25 *Ibid.*, p. 58. See also Kent, *Converting Women.*
26 Roy and Roy, *Zenana Mission*, p. 101.
27 Miss Pepper, 80th Report of the Bengal Auxiliary Mission Society, 1898, cited in Roy and Roy, *Zenana Mission*, p. 127.
28 Kent, *Converting Women*, p. 143
29 Haggis, 'White Women and Colonialism', p. 60.
30 Pitman, *Indian Zenana Missions*, pp. 26–27.
31 Sati and Savitri are faithful, self-sacrificing wives from Hindu mythology, and were traditionally held up as exemplary wives to be emulated.
32 Kent, *Converting Women*, pp. 139–140; Johnston, *Missionary Writing and Empire*, p. 53.
33 Roy and Roy, *Zenana Mission*, p. 102
34 Johnston, *Missionary Writing and Empire*, p. 81.
35 Missionary periodicals included, among others, the quarterly *The Indian Female Evangelist* and the monthly publication *The Female Missionary Intelligence*. The wide range of missionary journals ranged from serious periodicals (e.g. the *Church Missionary Intelligencer*, the *Missionary Magazine and Chronicle*, the *Missionary Herald*), to immensely popular short tracts known as 'quarterly papers', such as the CMS quarterly, *Missionary Papers*, with its 'page-sized illustration and three pages of printed text … couched in simple, direct language'; for details, see Geoffrey A. Oddie, *Imagined Hinduism: British Protestant Missionary Constructions of Hinduism, 1793–1900* (New Delhi, Sage, 2006), p. 206.
36 Two examples of such books are Mrs Mary Weitbrecht, *Women of India and Christian Work in the Zenana* (London, James Nisbet & Co., 1875) and Mrs Marcus Fuller, *The Wrongs of Indian Womanhood* (Edinburgh and London, Oliphant Anderson and Ferrier, 1900). While the former consisted of articles taken from a 'monthly scientific review of missions' in German, the latter was based on articles from *The Bombay Guardian*. For details see the Preface in each book.
37 Weitbrecht, *Women of India*, pp. 93–94. Mrs Mary Martha Weitbrecht (1808–1888), wife of Reverend John Weitbrecht of the Church Missionary Society, was a prolific missionary writer and was actively involved in zenana work and female education in Bengal.
38 Even Saleni Armstrong-Hopkins, an American medical missionary attached to the Methodist Episcopal Church, who worked in north India in the late nineteenth century, gave her memoir the tantalising title, *Within the Purdah: In the Zenana and Homes of Indian Princes and Heroes and Heroines of Zion* (New York, Eaton & Mains, 1898).
39 Priscilla Chapman, *Hindoo Female Education* (London, R. B. Seeley and G. Seely, 1839), p. 2; Weitbrecht, *Women of India*, p. 105. Mrs Priscilla Chapman (formerly Miss Priscilla Wakefield), came to work with Mrs Wilson at the Central Female School in Calcutta; after marriage she resigned from this school and repaid her passage money to the Ladies' Native Female Education Society. She became honorary secretary to the Ladies' Society. See *Missionary Register for 1838*, pp. 140–141, cited in Savage, 'Missionaries and the Development of a Colonial Ideology of Female Education' p. 217, fn 21.
40 Weitbrecht, *Women of India*, p. 106.
41 Miss Pepper, 80th Report of the Bengal Auxiliary Mission, 1898, quoted in Roy and Roy, *Zenana Mission*, p. 127.
42 William Ward, *A View of the History, Literature, and Mythology of the Hindoos* (Serampore, 1822), p. 192.
43 Chapman, *Hindoo Female Education*, p. 3.
44 Mrs Mary Weitbrecht, *The Christian Women's Ministry to Her Heathen Sisters in India* (London, J. Nisbet & Co., nd), p. 4.
45 Weitbrecht, *Women of India*, p. 104.
46 Chapman, *Hindoo Female Education*, p. 30.

47 Weitbrecht, *Women of India*, p. 129. Around the turn of the century, the Bombay-based missionary Mrs Marcus Fuller remarked that 'a large percentage of *Zenana* women die of consumption', in Fuller, *The Wrongs of Indian Womanhood*, p. 70. Later still, the Bengal-based missionary, Mrs Margaret Urquahart, mentioned how, 'The heavy mortality from respiratory diseases and tuberculosis amongst women is clear proof of the deadly effect of depriving them of fresh air and light by confining them in the zenana', in Mrs Margaret Urquahart, *Women of Bengal: A Study of the Hindu Purdahnashins of Calcutta* ([1925], Calcutta: Association Press, YMCA, 1927), p. 20.

48 The by now well-known term 'maternal imperialism' was originally used by Barbara N. Ramusack, 'Cultural Missionaries, Maternal Imperialists, Feminist Allies: British Women Activists in India, 1865–1945', in Nupur Chaudhuri and Margaret Strobel (eds), *Western Women and Imperialism: Complicity and Resistance* (Bloomington and Indianapolis, Indiana University Press, 1992), pp. 119–136.

49 Roy and Roy, *Zenana Mission*, p. 114.

50 For details see Indrani Sen (ed.), *Memsahibs' Writings: Colonial Narratives on Indian Women* (New Delhi, Orient BlackSwan, 2008), pp. 94–124.

51 Chapman, *Hindoo Female Education*, p. 30.

52 Weitbrecht, *Women of India*, pp. 101–102.

53 *Ibid.*

54 Miss Daniell, 63rd Report of the Auxiliary Mission Society, 1881, cited in Roy and Roy, *Zenana Mission*, p. 115.

55 Haggis, 'White Women and Colonialism', p. 59.

56 Mrs Wylie, quoted in Weitbrecht, *Women of India*, p. 96.

57 Mrs M. Weitbrecht, quoted in Pitman, *Indian Zenana Missions*, p. 30. In this anniversary volume, Pitman reiterated this point, noting that 'The work of these Zenana visitors is not always pleasant or easy; it is oftener difficult, arduous, and trying', p. 30.

58 Weitbrecht, *Women of India*, pp. 113–114.

59 Anna Johnston's discussion of Mrs Mullens' *Faith and Victory* focuses on high-caste conversion, and not so much on gender; see Johnston, *Missionary Writings and Empire*, pp. 96–105.

60 Mrs Mary Martha Sherwood (1775–1851), famous for her well-known evangelical-minded children's stories set in India, was not a professional missionary but a military officer's wife in Bengal. Her highly popular evangelical children's stories include *The History of Little Henry and His Bearer* (London, Houlston and Son, 1814) and *The History of Little Lucy and Her Dhaye* (London, Houlston and Stoneman, 1823). For details see Supriya Goswami, *Colonial India in Children's Literature* (London and New York, Routledge, 2012); see also Joyce Grossman, 'Ayahs, Dhayes, and Bearers: Mary Sherwood's Indian Experience and "Constructions of Subordinated Others"', *South Atlantic Review*, 66:2 (Spring, 2001), pp. 14–44. For a discussion of Sherwood's views on child-rearing and Indian servants, see Chapter 4 of this book.

61 Roy and Roy, *Zenana Mission*, p. 114.

62 Metropolitan evangelical fiction included the highly popular religious tract (later published as a booklet), *The Dairyman's Daughter* (1814) by Rev. Legh Richmond, which narrated the real-life religious transformation of Elizabeth Wallbridge, a resident of the Isle of Wight; and *The Peep of Day* (1836), an immensely popular book of religious instruction and scriptural stories for children by the British evangelical author, Favell Lee Mortimer. Both texts were translated into several languages.

63 Meredith Borthwick, *The Changing Role of Women in Bengal, 1849–1905* (Princeton, Princeton University Press, 1984), p. 56. Although Borthwick specifically deals with the Bengali lady belonging to the reformist Brahmo Samaj community, many of her observations can be applied to the Bengali lady in advanced families as well.

64 Hannah Catherine Mullens (1826–1861) was born in Calcutta to Alphonse

Francois Lacroix of the London Missionary Society, a prominent Calcutta-based missionary. As prominent stalwarts of the LMS, she and her husband Joseph Mullens established and developed several 'native' female schools. At the time of her early death, she had published several books. Her earliest novel, written in Bengali, *Phulmoni O Karunar Bibaran* (translated into English as *Phulmani and Karuna: A Book for Native Christian Women*), met with immediate success, being translated into several Indian languages, including Hindi, Telugu and Oriya. Set in a Bengali village, it focused on two female characters, one an idyllic Christian and the other a benighted Hindu, with contrasting characters, personalities, family life, personal relationships and destiny. For details see Meenakshi Mukherjee, 'Mrs Mullens and Mrs Collins: Christianity's Gift to Indian Fiction', *The Journal of Commonwealth Literature*, 16:65 (1981), pp. 65–75; and Meenakshi Mukherjee, *Realism and Reality: The Novel and Society in India* (New Delhi, Oxford University Press, 2010), pp. 21–27; see also Weitbrecht, *Women of India*, p. 191.

65 Weitbrecht, *Women of India*, pp. 113–114; Mary Leslie's novel *The Dawn of Light: A Story of the Zenana Mission*, with an Introduction by Rev. E. Storrow (London, John Snow, 1868), which is discussed later in this chapter, also mentions this novel as being read inside zenanas.

66 Weitbrecht, *Women of India*, pp. 113–114.

67 This evangelical novel traces how its young, intellectually oriented Brahmin protagonist is drawn to the principles of Christianity, and opts for secret conversion after undergoing agonising moral dilemmas and conflicts. His public acknowledgment of conversion is followed by rejection by his family and ostracism by Hindu society. Eventually, happiness is found in reunion with his wife (who follows her husband into conversion) – projecting thereby an exemplary 'Christian' companionate marriage, centred around a nuclear family, and based on mutual respect and enlightened parenting.

68 Mullens, *Faith and Victory*, pp. v–vi.

69 The novel displays a close knowledge of the intricacies of upper-caste Bengali family life, through the large joint-family of Mohendro Kumar Chatterjee, an orthodox Bengali Brahmin, who lives in Calcutta, along with his wife, four grownup sons, and his youngest child, a daughter. The sons are: Surjo Kumar (married to Shoudaminee), Chondro Kumar (married to Nishtarinee), Prosonno Kumar (married to Kaminee) and Nobo Kumar, an unmarried college student. Besides his six-year-old daughter, Hemlota, there is his widowed old mother and a younger brother, Rajen, who is a widower with two children.

70 Elizabeth Kent notes that high-caste converts, who were the 'pride and joy' of missionaries, 'suffered enormously' because of their 'contact with *mleccha* foreign missionaries and low-caste converts' and were 'ostracised from Hindu civil society', Kent, *Converting Women*, p. 32.

71 Mullens, *Faith and Victory*, p. 89. However, Prosonno sticks to his resolution, despite his great sufferings, and in the end, several other family members also embrace Christianity, namely his old *Thakur ma* (grandmother) who converts on her deathbed, Kaminee, his educated young wife who also converts – after initially arguing animatedly against Christianity – and joins her husband, taking along with her Shoudaminee (the wife – and now widow – of Prosonno's eldest brother).

72 Padma Anagol, 'Indian Christian Women and Indigenous Feminism, c. 1850–c.1920', in Clare Midgley (ed.), *Gender and Imperialism* (Manchester, Manchester University Press, 1998), p. 82.

73 Mullens, *Faith and Victory*, pp. 68–70.

74 *Ibid.*, pp. 69–70.

75 *Ibid.*, p. 70.

76 Forbes, 'In Search of the "Pure Heathen"', p. WS3.

77 Haggis, 'White Women and Colonialism', p. 66.

78 Johnston, *Missionary Writing and Empire*, p. 105

79 Mullens, *Faith and Victory*, pp. 167–168.

80 For instance, zenana intrigue can be seen in the plot jointly hatched against

Kaminee by her mother-in-law and an envious sister-in-law; while a close female friendship exists between Kaminee and another sister-in-law, namely the gentle-natured Shoudaminee, the wife (and later, widow) of her husband's eldest brother.

81 Mullens, *Faith and Victory*, p. 240.

82 Not much is known about the author, Mary Eliza Leslie (c. 1834–1907). By all accounts she was born in Monghyr, the daughter of Rev. Andrew Leslie, a Scottish Baptist missionary. She lived in Calcutta and was closely associated with and later became a member of the Calcutta Missionary Conference for the Protection of Young Girls. According to the Baptist Zenana Mission's Jubilee issue: 'Miss Leslie ... though never a missionary on the staff of our Society, yet gave most valuable help for many years. About the year 1870, Miss Leslie commenced a school for native girls, called the "Sale Institution" ... and the school did a useful work in the training of young Christian girls. It was helped by a yearly grant from the B.Z.M', in *JUBILEE, 1867–1917*, p. 17. For details see Maire ni Fhlathuin (ed.), *The Poetry of British India, 1780–1905*, vol. 2 (London, Pickering and Chatto, 2011), pp. 151–152.

83 Mary Leslie, *The Dawn of Light*. First published in 1868, it had an abridged, illustrated American edition in 1875 and at least two more editions in 1876 and 1900. Leslie's other publications include *Eastern Blossoms: Sketches of Native Christian Life in India* (London, John Snow, 1875) and *A Child of the Day: A Brief Memorial of Mrs H. C. Mukerji* (Calcutta: Baptist Mission Press, 1882). For details see Fhlathuin, *Poetry of British India*, pp. 151–152.

84 Leslie, *The Dawn of Light*, p. 38.

85 Babu Rajkumar Bhattacharya is the eldest brother and head of this high-caste joint-family which resides at Gopalpore, in the outskirts of Calcutta. This large house-hold essentially consists of three brothers and their families: the eldest brother, Babu Rajkumar, his wife Kumari (aged 28), their two sons Premchand (aged 12) and Preonath (aged 8) and daughter Kamini (aged 4), fondly called 'Toki' at home; the second brother, Jodunath and his wife Prosonno; the youngest brother's widow Boshonto (aged 18), along with Taramoni, an old widowed aunt and Herani, an old Brahmin widowed servant-woman

86 Leslie, *The Dawn of Light*, pp. 16, 15.

87 *Ibid.*, p. 16.

88 *Ibid.*, p. 46.

89 *Ibid.*

90 Forbes, 'In Search of the "Pure Heathen"', p. WS3.

91 Leslie, *The Dawn of Light*, p. 52. The role of male family members has been well-documented by historians. In the text too this is stressed in the Introduction written by Rev. E. Storrow, which hails the 'social and moral revolution' taking place among the Bengali youth, who are now teaching 'their wives, sisters, or aunts' to read; in Rev E. Storrow, Introduction, Leslie, *The Dawn of Light*, p. xiv.

92 Leslie, *The Dawn of Light*, pp. 49, 46.

93 *Ibid.*, p. 51.

94 *Ibid.*

95 For example, *Faith and Victory: A Story of the Progress of Christianity in Bengal* (1861) was later also published under the titles, *Life by the Ganges, or Faith and Victory* (1867) and *Prasanna and Kamini: The Story of a Young Hindu* (1885). *Prasanna and Kamini* is said to be the Bengali translation of *Faith and Victory* re-translated into English.

96 *Ibid.*, p. 52.

97 *Ibid.*

98 *Ibid.*, pp. 137, 136. The Brahmo Samaj (originally termed the Brahmo Sabha and established in 1828 in Calcutta by Raja Rammohan Roy) focused on both religious reform of brahminical Hinduism as well as social reform. It actively opposed child marriage, besides promoting widow remarriage and female education. Pandit Ishwar Chandra Vidyasagar (1820–1891), a leading Hindu Bengali social reformer and educationist, championed female education, widow remarriage and

was instrumental in helping push through the Hindu Widows' Remarriage Act of 1856.

99   *Ibid.*, pp. 53, 60. The second wife is a pretty child aged about 9 or 10, named Joggotarini, who is the daughter of a wealthy Brahmin of Calcutta. She brings along with her 500 rupees worth of jewels as dowry.

100   *Ibid.*, pp. 66, 41–42, 69.

101   *Ibid.*, p. 76.

102   *Ibid.*

103   *Ibid.*, pp. 140, 141. The young 25-year-old 'Babu' had lost his beloved wife, aged 18, two years before in childbirth.

CHAPTER TWO

Flora Annie Steel, social reform and female education in late nineteenth-century Punjab

We saw in the last chapter how European women missionaries, interacting with female students inside schools and in zenanas, were among the most active in the colonial 'civilising mission'.[1] This kind of close inter-racial interaction was rarely to be found among memsahibs or the wives of British colonial administrators.[2] However, one unusual memsahib who was concerned with the disadvantaged position of women in the province was the intrepid Flora Annie Steel (1847–1929), the Punjab-based administrator's wife who closely involved herself in the 'civilising mission' and was actively involved in female schooling. Steel, who dominated the ideological landscape of the British Raj in diverse ways, was also a prolific author of numerous works of fiction. While research on her has generally tended to focus only on her 'Mutiny' novel, *On the Face of the Waters* (1896) – although this is slowly changing – she also wrote a number of rather neglected short stories in which she addressed social reform issues with which she was intensely involved.[3] It is some of these short stories that we shall examine in this chapter.

The uplift of the 'enslaved' Indian woman, as we have seen in the previous chapter, was a part of the colonial 'civilising mission'. Steel was concerned with the disadvantaged position of women in colonial Punjab across boundaries of caste, class and religion. She focused in her short stories on gendered problems in rural as well as small-town colonial Punjab, addressing both local as well as broader issues, including polygamy, female infanticide, female illiteracy and widow remarriage.[4] Rather like the missionaries, she too was a pro-active participant in schooling for girls, although she was bitingly critical of missionaries and their educational methods as well as their efforts at westernising Indian women.[5]

Punjab society was essentially agrarian and in this chapter I will focus on Steel's fictional representations of gendered problems in both rural as well as small-town Punjab. I begin by discussing her representations of the devaluation of women among the agricultural community, and then go on to examine her representations of girls' schooling in small-town Punjab, including the role played by European female evangelicals. Through these I hope to explore the ambivalences in Steel's perspective on social reform. By focusing upon her critique of missionaries and their methods, I hope to draw out the complexities within the 'civilising mission' and reveal how, far from being a unified enterprise, it was undercut by internal tensions, divisions and contradictions within the white community in India. In other words, we find rifts and fissures within the colonial 'civilising mission', thereby indicating that it was not a simple or uncomplicated initiative.

Steel and the colonial 'civilising mission'

Flora Anne Steel, who came out to India with her administrator husband in 1867, lived a life full of contradictions: while she enjoyed the typical life of a 'burra memsahib', replete with picnics, amateur theatricals, badminton and tea parties, at the same time, she was involved with 'native' female life and education, unusual for an administrator's wife in those days.[6] Much of her close knowledge of the region was acquired during her early years in the remote town of Kasur in Lahore district where she and her husband were the only Europeans.[7] Her maternalist interest in local gendered issues took the form of conducting reading classes, helping to establish girls' schools in the province, besides giving medical advice to rural women and children.[8] By the second half of the nineteenth century a knowledge of the vernacular was highly unusual for an administrator's wife, with most European women generally being ignorant of the local language or culture. However, in consonance with several other contradictions in her, Steel's sympathetic interest in Punjab village women and learning their language was intertwined with the imperialist agenda of 'learning more or less how to manage them'.[9]

This interest in gender issues, and especially involvement in education, was widely recognised; the metropolitan periodical *The Queen* noted in 1897 how even before Steel had gained fame as a novelist, 'she was known as practically the author of the highly successful system of education for women in India'.[10] Indeed, in this regard Maud Diver, articulate spokeswoman of the British Raj and forceful advocate of an active role for the memsahib in 'native' female social uplift, showered the highest praise on Steel as a model memsahib who had shouldered her 'share of the white man's burden in the East', of civilising her Aryan sisters, and pointed out that 'women like Mrs Steel ... would seem to be as rare as they are admirable'. Diver's imperialist argument was that by participating in this manner, memsahibs would effectively help to buttress 'love and respect for the British Raj among the subject peoples'.[11]

Gendered social evils in rural north India

In her non-fictional writings, Steel romanticised the Punjab peasantry, a section of society that was usually valorised in colonial discourse. She especially praised the village women and drew a binary distinction between what she termed as the sensual, indolent (middle-class) purdah '[w]omen in towns' who were 'inevitably over-obsessed by sex', and the hardy peasant women who, she held, were free from excessive sensuality.[12] The valorisation of the hardy women from the agricultural castes of Punjab was common in colonial discourse, and the Jat woman, for instance, was hailed as an 'economic treasure' by colonial officials.[13] Colonial perceptions of subject peoples often betrayed an intermeshing of race and gender prejudices. Communities which were identified as 'masculine' were privileged over those located as 'effeminate'.[14] Especially privileged and constructed as 'manly' and athletic were the Punjab peasantry and tribes of the North West Frontier. In addition, there was a noticeable colonial emphasis on physical fitness and athleticism in the 1880s and 1890s. Steel's valorisation of rural Punjab needs to be located within this late-century climate of colonial glorification of the 'simple' peasantry, metropolitan privileging of philathleticism and valorisation of 'native' communities which were perceived as 'manly' or 'masculine':

> though the most of them were Hindus, I felt however, that here was a Hinduism which was not enervating, which was worthy of respect and admiration. They were a tall people, men and women, physically fit, and they were excellent cultivators ...[15]

However, while Steel romanticised Punjabi peasant women in her autobiography, her short stories which are set in the villages turn a critical colonial gaze on local patriarchal practices that were rampant in agricultural Punjab, such as female infanticide, polygamy and the levirate system of widow remarriage (common among agricultural castes such as the Jats) according to which a widow was remarried to her dead husband's brother through a simple ceremony.

The annexation of the Punjab took place as late as 1849, considerably later than in other parts of the country. The province, which was extensive in size, stretching from Peshawar in the north to Delhi in the east, with Lahore as the provincial capital, was distinct in being largely agricultural. In fact, unlike in other provinces, the 'accepted social superiority of the Brahmin' was negligible and instead of Brahmins being the dominant caste, the province was dominated by the prominent agriculturist Jat caste.[16] As in most other parts of the country, women suffered acute cultural devaluation in Punjabi society and there was an obsessive desire for male offspring. While certain customs found among the agriculturist castes seemed to suggest a relatively high female status – such as polyandry, bride-price, widow remarriage and women's economic participation in agricultural activities – in reality, daughters were traditionally considered a curse and the mother of female children was regarded as a 'barren' woman. Patriarchal practices, notably female infanticide and polygamy, purdah (seclusion) and the use of the *ghunghat* (veil) were widespread among both agricultural and non-agricultural communities but were especially rampant among the Jats, who were the predominant social group in the region.[17]

Female infanticide especially, a glaring index of a culture's devaluation of women, was widespread in the entire state.[18] Although banned by the colonial government in 1870, it continued to be practised in this province by many caste sub-groups.[19] Steel, who was deeply concerned about this practice, documented in *Punjab Notes and Queries* in 1884 the custom of placing the body of a dead female infant in a sitting position under a tree, to be dragged away by dogs and jackals. If the body was dragged *towards* the mother's house, it portended the unfortunate birth of yet another girl; but if it was dragged *away* from home, it signalled the future birth of a son.[20]

In her short story, 'Gunesh Chand', Steel delineates this macabre custom. A barren village wife, subjected to constant social pressures to bear male children, does finally give birth after several years of marriage, but much to her old mother-in-law's bitter disappointment, only to a female infant. When the infant dies after a brief illness, the old woman assisted by the village crones, performs the grisly ritual of placing *gur* (unrefined sugar) and cotton in the dead infant's hands and leaving its body in a sitting position under a tree, to be dragged away by dogs and jackals – accompanying all this with the ritually chanted words: 'Thus we drive you forth, O daughter! Come not back, but send a brother.'[21]

Polygamy was, historically, a particularly rampant social problem in agricultural Punjab. While it was practised by various castes, it was found to be highest among the agricultural castes of the province.[22] Taking a second wife for the sake of progeny in the event of the first wife failing in her 'duty' of bearing children (specifically male offspring) was a common practice. Besides reflecting the general preference for male children, it was also linked in the case of Punjab to the region's peasant economy, whereby male children (and any additional daughters-in-law) were perceived as potential labour for the family.[23] Moreover, as historian Prem Chowdhry notes, in such polygamous marriages, the husband and 'co-wives' customarily lived together, and quarrels and mutual hostility between the two 'co-wives' were a regular feature. Chowdhry goes on to argue that this domestic arrangement created a 'repressive' social structure for women in which they were denied any outlet for their anger, except as 'quarrelling women', through violence towards each other.[24]

Steel targeted the system of polygamy in a large number of her rural stories, locating it as the outcome of the importance given to bearing a male child.[25] Drawing attention especially to the destructive consequences of such domestic arrangements inside village households, she delineated the first wife's neglect and humiliation by the husband and his younger, second wife. Her stories corroborate Chowdhry's point about such 'co-wives' being reduced to 'quarrelling women' by the system of polygamy. Quarrelling women signify, for Steel, the destructive female sexuality which finds a vent in bitter sexual rivalries and mutual destruction among 'co-wives' in polygamous marriages. This rivalry and hatred manifests itself in a fierce struggle for domestic power between the two women, rooted in a competition between the barren first wife and the fecund second one, with regard to their reproductive role (as the mother of the husband's child), as well as in their sexual roles (as the husband's favoured sexual partner).[26]

During the nineteenth century, various kinds of marriages were taking place in colonial Punjab, where brahminical influence was by and large minimal.[27] In her study of gender, caste and class identity formation in colonial Punjab, Anshu Malhotra has pointed out that this period witnessed shifts and changes with regard to social practices among various castes in this province. It saw the emergence of a middle class whereby certain middle-level castes sought to emulate high-caste practices, including the practice of child marriage and the prohibition of widow remarriage. Notwithstanding all this, the rural communities of Punjab continued to be distinct in a number of ways. Firstly, regarding child marriage, due largely to the region's peasant economy and the value attached to a woman's labour in the fields, actual co-habitation after marriage took place at a much later age – a feature that Steel lauded in her autobiography:

> The work of women in the fields was valuable; thus a father though marrying his daughters off before puberty, after ancient custom, would keep them from their husbands' houses as long as possible. Years would often elapse before the bridegroom could get possession of his bride, with the result that children were seldom born before the mother had attained her

full growth ... The result in the general stamina of the people was quite noticeable.[28]

Similarly, while the social reform issue of high-caste Hindu widow remarriage was a hotly debated topic in the nineteenth century, the gendered customs pertaining to widow remarriage in rural Punjab (present-day Haryana) were very different.[29] Far from being culturally taboo, remarriage was in fact practised by many castes, barring a few, such as the Brahmins (who were, in any case, a marginalised caste in this province). Especially among the agricultural castes, such as the regionally dominant Jats, widow remarriage was widely prevalent through the system of levirate marriage, according to which a widow could be married off to her husband's younger brother through a simple ceremony known as *chaddar andazi*.[30]

Strikingly, Steel, despite her supposed interest in the colonial reformist programme, seems to be in fact *against* widow remarriage in the context of colonial Punjab. Projecting remarriage as a potentially explosive unleashing of a widow's destructive sexuality, she *critiques* this practice of levirate marriage in her short story, 'In the House of a Coppersmith' (*The Flower of Forgiveness*), which weaves together the problem of Hindu widowhood, widow remarriage, as well as the havoc caused by uncontrolled female sexuality.[31] In this short story, Durga-dei, a recently widowed woman, faces humiliation, neglect, semi-starvation and shrill abuses from her *dewarani* (younger brother-in-law's wife). Bitter, sexually frustrated and de-sexualised as 'a shapeless bundle of widowhood' in her widow's garb of a 'coarse, whitey-brown veil', she soon starts lusting after her married *dewar's* (younger brother-in-law) virile, muscular body.[32] Confident that he will marry her through the levirate system, especially since his own wife is childless, she starts sleeping with him and soon becomes pregnant. But the young man's marriage is arranged with a nubile young woman – and Durga-dei, betrayed and furious, brings about his death by giving him tamarind water to drink which had deliberately been kept for too long in one of his copper vessels.

It is indeed notable how Steel takes up some of the key arguments voiced by supporters of widow remarriage – such as widowed women's sexual vulnerability, their sexual exploitation by predatory male relatives, unwanted pregnancies and suicides by pregnant widows – and gives them a twist, and an emphasis that is quite distinct. Hence, in Steel's story, the widow does become pregnant – but far from being the victim of a predatory male within the family, it is she who seduces the male relative. Nor does she commit suicide as so many widows did, arranging instead for the death of the man who had betrayed her.

Eventually, it is the bitter sexual rivalry between two women (the widow and the *dewarani* or the younger sister-in-law), exacerbated by the young man's spinelessness, which results in the family's destruction. By the late nineteenth century, debates on the Hindu widow were beginning to shift to the question of remarriage and implicitly to a widow's sexuality. In this regard, Steel, always conservative about female sexuality, lauded widow celibacy in her autobiography, calling it holy and 'comparable to that of a nun'.[33] Thus, the contemporary reformist agenda of remarriage for widows stands complicated by Steel's anxieties about the chaotic potential of a widow's sexual appetite. Moreover, while she did critique rural Punjabi society, Steel did not really seek to pursue any direct form of reformist intervention in the agricultural regions – with the exception of female infanticide.

Steel's involvement in female education in the Punjab

However, it was really in the social reform project of female schooling in small-town north India that Steel actively involved herself, while she also discussed this issue in several of her stories. As we saw in the first chapter, the colonial strategy in the nineteenth century was to bring about changes in traditional social practices and perceptions through the education of 'native' females. Steel's intervention and participation in the social reform and 'modernisation' programme was really through schooling for girls. It is important to point out that, unlike in the case of upper-caste women in Bengal where literacy was strictly forbidden, reading was traditionally acceptable for girls in the Punjab. Sikh, Hindu as well as Muslim girls were taught at home to read the scriptures, although writing was taboo.[34]

As in the rest of the country, female education formed an important plank of colonial gender reform in Punjab in the nineteenth century. From mid-century onwards, female education came to be considered to be the bedrock of social reform in the Punjab, and schools for girls were established by the colonial government. Tim Allender points out that Wood's Education Despatch of 1854 on education for the masses 'helped to cement an important place for the missions in the European-led education endeavour'.[35] By the close of 1857, seventeen schools had been established and the total number of girls attending them was 306 or eighteen per school. In addition, there were also local schools set up and run by 'native' women.[36] Besides mission schools, local schools set up and run by 'native' women where the teachers were 'native' women who observed purdah, were the most numerous of all and thrived well in the Punjab – although, according to Steel, they did not run well.[37]

Steel often accompanied her administrator-husband on his school inspections, besides occasionally teaching at some of the boys' schools, and this, she recalled in her autobiography, led the Chief Native administrator 'to suggest the possibility of a female school'.[38] Describing her first efforts at starting a girls' school, she noted how:

> a convenient little courtyard was found ... two or three dozen little girls from the bazaar, ranging from four to eight, were duly installed as the alphabet class, and from the better houses a scanty few were gathered, who knew parts of the Koran by heart ... Thus the school – a fair example of the State-induced female education – was formed.[39]

Given the prevalence of purdah, women inspectors were always in demand and in 1884 Steel was appointed Inspectress of Girls' Schools at Lahore by the Punjab government (although she was by no means the first woman to be thus appointed), partly because, as she put it, she was 'the only woman in the Punjab, outside the ranks of mission ladies, who could read and write the vernaculars'.[40] During the next five years she was put in charge of schools in the entire northern region, covering the vast state of Punjab which extended at that time from Peshawar and the North West Frontier Provinces in the north to Delhi in the east. As an Inspectress, Steel was deeply disappointed to discover that 'half the schools were really sham. The mission schools were, indeed, the only ones that counted; but there I had to be instantly autocratic and definitely refuse a grant to any school which paid its pupils for attendance...'.[41]

Indeed, the first Indian Education Commission (the Hunter Commission), which had completed in 1882 a vast survey of the condition of western education in India, held that female education in the Punjab was a particularly difficult case.[42] Female schooling was encouraged by both the provincial government as well as by private endowment and grants-in-aid. However, as elsewhere in the country, purdah was strictly maintained and schools had difficulty in attracting high-caste/class girls, with the girl students being drawn mostly from the poorer classes and lower castes (generally poor, Muslim or low-caste girls). As a member of the Education Commission observed a couple of years later: 'Only girls from the lower and middle classes are sent to these schools.'[43] In order to attract and encourage them to attend regularly, the government provided a monthly stipend or 'scholarship', whereby students 'were paid on a graduated scale based on attendance and were provided with accommodation and servants free of charge'.[44] But this 'encouraged some women to attend for years longer than was intended, treating their subsidized education instead as a means of employment' and resulted in the problem of girls staying on for several years.[45]

As an education officer, Steel felt that the provincial Punjab government needed to systematise female education, control expenditure and increase enrolment. She was particularly most critical of the system of student scholarships and firmly refused to give grants to any school – including mission schools – 'which paid its pupils for attendance'.[46] In an Inspection Report submitted in 1884 she officially raised an objection to 'the system of giving stipends to all pupils', ridiculing the idea that 'the parents are so averse to female education that they must be bribed', and argued that 'long practical experience had taught her that to give such stipends is simply ruination to a school'.[47] In another Report submitted later that year, she 'earnestly recommend[ed] the abolishment of the stipendiary or "paisa" system', noting that it also undermined British prestige:

> I have heard a child say to a Mission lady who threatened to withhold the stipend for irregular attendance: 'Then I will leave school altogether.' Such a state of affairs is fatal, and I earnestly hope that Government will put a stop to it by refusing grants-in-aid to schools where the 'paisa' system is maintained.[48]

Regarding the pressing problem of overcrowding in the beginner classes, she pointed out how in 'almost every school there was an alphabet class of two or three dozen', whereas in the 'medium class' there would be only 'half a dozen who could, with difficulty, spell through the first primer'.[49] Steel urged in one of her Inspectress' Report in 1884 that the 'number of pupils in the beginners' class should ... never ... be allowed to be more than one third of the total number of the school'.[50]

Drawing attention to many of these problems is Steel's short story, 'At a Girls' School', which delineates what seems to be a government girls' school set amidst 'the surrounding slums of a big, native city' in the poorer quarter of the town.[51] It has both 'native' and English lady teachers: while the primary department is headed by a fat, Persian epithet-spouting 'Mohammedan' lady with 'betel-stained teeth', whose father had been *munshi* to 'some dead-and-gone Mogul', the English teacher, who, it is hinted, is from Girton or Somerville, is reserved for the more exclusive job of teaching Algebra to the highest classes.[52] The story revolves around Fatma, an impoverished Muslim 'child of about ten, with a sharp, old face', who lives in the 'Cashmiri' quarter of the town with her brother, his wife and their two infant sons.[53] The entire household depends, in different ways, for its livelihood on the school: while Fatma's brother, 'disreputable, good-for-nothing Peru' earns five rupees ferrying 'students to and from the school', his pretty, wasteful wife, Hoshiaribi, gets a 'scholarship of ten rupees' as a student in the highest class, while Fatma shoulders the family's financial burden on 'eight annas a week' which she earns 'for cleaning the writing-boards'.[54] The sister-in-law, who studies in the highest class located in the topmost storey of the school, also has a baby – and Fatma spends her time periodically lugging this infant nephew up and down the stair-case to his mother for feeding.

Like many female schools in Punjab which were housed within grand, decaying old Moghul structures at that time, in this story too, the school is located within an imposing three-storied building, which offers 'three stories of different standards' in what Steel describes as a chaotic 'ladder of learning'.[55] Students sit in an ascending order of seniority – starting with the alphabet class on the lowest floor and going up to the higher classes:

> The Alif Bey-wallahs (alphabet-class) in the first story... was the noisiest story. All day long the inmates chanted letters in high childish voices, while the monitors stood over them like the parent bird, ready to drop a fresh tidbit of knowledge into the clamorous mouths.
>
> Up-stairs, in the primary department, the babel had lost its first bar-barous simplicity; the makers of it did not always understand what they themselves were saying, and the uncertainty of all things had damped their infant light-heartedness. Higher again, in the third story, quite an academic silence prevailed among the girls working away at Euclid, algebra, and all the 'ologies, and they had learned an automatic thrust forward of the arm towards the teacher worthy of a British board school. This never failed to please exotic philanthropy.[56]

Steel critiques the manner in which the younger children learn by rote, while in the higher classes the students 'did not always understand what they themselves were saying'. What is more, many girls seem to be studying mainly for the stipend money, having 'quite understood that learning meant livelihood'. The over-all thrust in this story is to point out the failure of the female education system and to critique European reformers, those 'philanthropic great ones' who naively believed that 'education was really at last beginning to leaven the mass of deplorable female ignorance in India'.[57]

The story draws attention to a number of problems associated with state-sponsored girls' schools in the Punjab, a category of schools which Steel firmly believed did not educate their wards. Always critical of the provincial government's wasteful expenditure, she also critiques the manner in which the government wasted money by unnecessar-ily providing students with female chaperones (a middle-aged widow called Chundoo), besides arranging for all the girl students to be ferried 'back to their homes in decent seclusion' in covered *dhoolies* (roughly made palanquins) carried by bearers who were employed solely for this purpose.[58] Steel, commenting on how pointless and wasteful this arrangement was – since purdah or seclusion was usually strictly observed by genteel women from the elite classes – drily observes that most of the students in this poor locality could not afford the luxury and would hence discard it the moment they reached home:

> many of the claimants to genteel seclusion who were comfortably carried by a paternal Government to their own doors, could, on arrival, set aside the convenient pretence and go about to see their friends with the more simple and less costly protection of a veil.[59]

Similarly, the system of paying female students for attending school for years on end is shown to result in them treating their stipend as an easy means of employment. Thus, Hoshiaribi, the pretty, 'indolent, comfort-loving' married girl with two babies wishes to remain a student all her life because, like many others, she has 'understood that learning meant livelihood ... Ever since she entered the school, nearly sixteen years ago, she had been in receipt of a scholarship of sorts ... If not clever, she was studious. ...'[60]

In 'The Daughters of Aryavarta', her essay on female education in the Punjab, Madhu Kishwar has noted how teaching jobs in colonial Punjab were extremely poorly paid and attracted very few women. There was, as a result, an acute shortage of female teachers available for girls' schools, as well as an absence of adequate teacher-training schools, known as 'Normal schools'. Generally, widowed students were considered the most suitable for the job; in addition, there was the system of 'pupil teachers', whereby senior school students subsequently became teachers after some years of study.[61]

Steel's story shows how, under the new system of 'pupil teacher', Hoshiaribi will have to start working as a teacher after her student stipend has stopped. In earlier times, when the main objective was 'to catch and keep a scholar', her days as a student might have gone on indefinitely; 'but now, under new rules, [her] scholarship would cease in a year, whether she passed or did not pass. Then she must become a teacher, or starve on Peru's five rupees.'[62] Teachers' salaries in colonial Punjab were, as we have noted, pitifully small, and the thought of becoming a teacher generates anxieties in the young woman. The prospect of becoming a poorly-paid teacher 'Was not pleasing ... having to worry over thirty unwilling pupils in a poky little room, spending part of your own pay in bribes so as to get the grant for attendance, and then never knowing from day to day if some neighbourly spite would not result in empty mats on inspection-days.'[63]

While Steel was highly critical of the 'paisa system', her narrative actually (and perhaps unwittingly) contradicts her stand on this subject

– by revealing how the stopping of the old system of student stipend brings about ruination in poor households. The already impoverished household is crushed by the new system; Hoshiaribi's stipend had, after all, been its main source of economic sustenance, and with it gone, the family soon disintegrates: Peru marries a rich, elderly widow and deserts his family, Hoshiaribi herself drifts off to eventually join a bazaar brothel – and Fatma is left to fend for herself and her two small nephews. Struggling now to provide single-handedly for them all, she sets up a school for small girls at the market place, where the pupils sit chanting arithmetic tables all day long. Fatma has barely any other learning to impart, having spent most of her time cleaning blackboards and ferrying her infant nephew up and down the staircase at the old school. However, to the mothers in that 'evil' neighbourhood, this 'market school' where their children stay safe, is a boon. The story ends abruptly, resolving all contradictions, when a cholera epidemic suddenly sweeps through the small town taking away numerous lives, including that of Fatma and her two small nephews.

The narrative therefore delineates precisely those economic stresses and strains that impoverished families, existing on the margins, were subjected to. In such a social and economic context, the much-berated system of granting stipends or school scholarships which used to be provided earlier by the state was often, as is clearly shown, a family's sole financial mainstay. The decision to stop student stipends no doubt helped the government to save on 'wasteful expenditure' – but it also clearly brought about the tragic decimation of many a family living on the margins. Hence, although Steel as an educational officer consistently maintained a hostile stand against the old system of student scholarships, the underlying thrust of her narrative interrogates her own policy, by revealing the tragic consequences and ruination brought upon a family (and, no doubt, on many households) by the cessation of that system.

Missionaries and their schooling methods

As in other parts of the country, in the Punjab too, female evangelicals were among the most active in the 'native' female education programme. They ran schools for girls and also carried out zenana instruction inside 'native' homes.[64] In fact, they were among the first to set up schools for girls, and initially the government too largely relegated female education to them, especially after Wood's Education Despatch of 1854 gave missionary schooling a recognised and integrated role in the Raj.[65] The American Presbyterian Mission was the first to establish a missionary school for girls at Ludhiana and by the 1880s there were eighteen missionary schools in Lahore.[66] Although Steel did always maintain that the mission schools were better-run than government schools, she was, nevertheless, sharply critical of several of their methods, including their system of giving stipends to students for attendance and distributing prizes to everyone on prize-giving day.

Consequently, despite her interest in female education which she shared with female evangelicals, Steel was the sharpest of critics of their ineffectual educational methods. In her famed short story, 'Mussumat Kirpo's Doll' (*Flower of Forgiveness*), which is set in a mission school for girls in the dilapidated quarters of a small town, the narrative ridicules European female evangelicals and their plans. The story opens on school prize-giving day, when the foolishness of the missionary ladies comes to the forefront as they bustle about enthusiastically, naively unaware of the failure of their educational system: 'a few English ladies with eager, kindly faces, trotting up and down, conferring excitedly with portly native Christian Bible-women, and pausing occasionally to encourage some young offshoot of the Tree of Knowledge'.[67]

Cheerfully immersed in the hustle and bustle, they are oblivious to the fact that their education system does not work, their 'paper-pupils' hardly attend, and prizes – consisting of dolls, books or sussi (sic) trouser or Manchester veiling material – are given away to all. In other words, suggests Steel, the average Indian school student is like a 'young offshoot of the Tree of Knowledge, which is uncertain either of its own roots or of the soil it grew in'. As such, the actual acquisition of knowledge in this system remains doubtful.[68] Unaware of the futility of their ill-conceived scheme, 'two or three of the chief Mission ladies' who are 'pale or flushed with sheer good feeling' sit on the dais at a table laden full of prizes for the students.[69] Steel turns an ironic gaze at the 'kindly benevolence' and naivety of the philanthropic guests assembled at the function, as well as at the hollow enthusiasm of Victorian philanthropy:

> Behind these tables sat in a semicircle more of those eager, kindly foreign faces, not confined here to one sex, but in fair proportion male and female; yet, bearded like the pard or feminine to a fault, all with the same expression, the same universal kindly benevolence towards the horticultural exhibition spread out before their eyes.[70]

Studying in the school are the daughters and daughters-in-law of slum-dwellers, sent there not for instruction, but for the yearly prize of a doll, a book, or 'a suit of clothes, or a new veil at least'. Steel was highly critical of the missionary schools' system of having 'every year ... a general prize-giving, at which every pupil received something quite indiscriminately; a sort of reward for coming to school at all, which did not suit my ideas of the dignity and honour of education.'[71]

These evangelicals' naivety is further underlined in this story through the mission policy of forbidding dolls as prizes for little girls who are married – in a ridiculous and ineffectual protest against 'the child marriage question'.[72] As one of them explains:

> Of course, as a rule, we always draw the line about dolls when a girl is married. Sometimes it seems a little hard, for they are so small, you know; still it is best to have a rule; all these tiny trifles help to emphasise our views on the child-marriage question.[73]

Among the assembled students is fifteen-year-old Kirpo, a crippled, 'sickly, stupid-looking girl', who 'had been learning the alphabet for five years' in the same class. By an oversight on prize-giving day, she is given 'a Japanese baby-doll with a large bald head', instead of the book meant for older, married students.[74] At that point she displays no emotion, merely walking 'dully, stolidly back to her place' after collecting the doll. Later, however, when the school missionary-lady goes to her in-law's house to rectify the error, she discerns in Kirpo's 'child-like, yet un-childlike face' a child's desire for the doll – and allows the child-wife to keep it.[75] Steel observes:

> Perhaps Kirpo got up at night to play with it; perhaps she never played with it at all, but, having wrapped it in a napkin and buried it away somewhere, was content in its possession.[76]

Besides the issue of education, this story also raises questions about child marriage. Married for four years, Kirpo has not yet performed 'her duty' of bearing a male child, and is thus subjected to hardships at her mother-in-law's hands. A year later, when she gives birth to a male child (thereby saving her in-laws 'the expenses of another bride'), she returns the doll to the missionary lady, saying, 'Miss ... might give it to a little girl this time'. The precious male infant is soon removed from her, however, and becomes the prized possession of the mother-in-law. When Kirpo falls mortally ill soon after, she is laid out on 'the bare ground of the courtyard ... to die', and in her death throes, keeps 'turning her head restlessly from side to side'.[77] The newly born infant is quickly placed beside her – but to everyone's surprise, she ignores it and cries out, like a child, for the cherished doll, as 'the restless head went on turning restlessly from side to side. "My doll! my doll! I like my doll best."'[78]

This story clearly touches upon a range of gender issues that extend beyond the question of female education – such as child marriage, the girl's inferior position in her in-law's house, the onus on her of presenting them with a male child, as well as the tyranny of the mother-in-law. The young mother, virtually a child herself, longs on her death-bed not for her infant, but for the bald, baby doll she used to play with.[79] The narrative therefore critiques the traditionally inferior position of the young wife inside the home, the cruelty of the mother-in-law as well as the practice of child marriage which was on the social reform agenda.

Gazing upon the colonising self: female missionaries

Besides her critique of missionary educational schooling methods, Steel displayed ambivalences towards missionaries and their 'civilising mission' in other respects as well. We saw in the previous chapter, in the context of mid-century Bengal, how female evangelicals had placed themselves at the forefront of educating and 'civilising' zenana women. They prided themselves on their intimate knowledge of purdah life, and one striking feature of their writing was their projection of a warm and affectionate friendship with secluded women, who would plead with the mission ladies to come and 'rescue' them from boredom in their zenanas. Jeffrey Cox, in his study on missionary activity in colonial Punjab, has similarly observed that such inter-racial transactions inside Punjabi zenanas were 'suffused with considerable sympathy and ... a surprising lack of condescension'.[80]

Steel, however, turns this argument on its head and strongly attacks precisely those inter-racial gendered familiarities in which missionaries prided themselves. Like many of her contemporaries in the late nineteenth century, she shared the widely held view that evangelicals lacked in imperial dignity, and that their undignified conduct threatened to disturb colonial race/class hierarchies.[81] Missionaries occupied an inferior position in colonial society in any case because of their lack of official status, their generally lower-middle-class origins and most importantly, their habit of closely mixing with Indians on a level of equality or familiarity (including with those belonging to low classes/ castes). Steel, who was, among other things, a staunch upholder of British imperial prestige in the colony, complained in her autobiography that her 'chief quarrel with the mission ladies was their lack of dignity in dealing with their clientele'.[82]

The evangelicals in some of the stories are presented as lacking precisely in this kind of imperial dignity, as they work in schools and visit students' homes 'in the slums of the city', threading their way 'through the bye-ways', or pick their way 'along the gutters' to spots never witnessed by any memsahib. At one point, a kindly unmarried evangelical named Julia Smith stands chatting with a student in the slum, 'utterly unmindful of a turgid stream of concentrated filth which at that moment came sweeping along the gutter'.[83] Often such female missionaries are shown getting bullied by predatory 'native' women; Julia Smith, for instance, meekly submits to the shrill harangue of a married student's mother-in-law about the uselessness of the school prizes: 'She wants none of your dolls or your books ... they aren't worth anything, and I expected nothing less than a suit of clothes, or a new veil at least.' In the end, she has to buy peace and 'settle the business with eight annas from her private pocket'.[84]

At the same time, however, Steel's views on female evangelicals were often contradictory, and she sometimes projected them in a positive light. For instance, some of her narratives do present these missionary women as providing a vital mediating point between 'native' and white women, while in others, their kindliness and fluency in local dialects is shown to draw the affection of the Indian girls they interact with. Besides, even if their schools do not impart much education, these institutions are shown to provide the 'native' girls a pleasurable alternative to the daily drudgery of home life. Moreover, Steel's writings also seem to implicitly compare missionaries and memsahibs with regard to their knowledge of Indian culture and languages as well as in modesty in dress – a perspective which went broadly in favour of the evangelicals.

Missionaries versus memsahibs in Steel's narratives

Regarding the role of the administrator's wife in the colony, Steel expected the memsahib who occupied a high position in the colonial hierarchy to display certain imperial responsibilities towards 'natives' of the lower social orders. In this context a total ignorance of the local languages and culture was critiqued as a disqualification – indeed Steel's own views on a knowledge of the vernacular were underwritten by imperialist concerns of control and mastery. While she advocated the white woman's role of 'benevolent maternal imperialism' (to quote Barbara Ramusack's classic definition), she also recommended the 'masculine' qualities of control and masterfulness, exhorting the white mistress to rule the domestic empire with a firm hand in her famous co-authored housekeeping manual, *The Complete Indian Housekeeper and Cook* (1888) – a text that we shall discuss in greater detail in Chapter 4.[85]

By the 1890s, however, most memsahibs were cut off from 'native' life and culture and were almost totally ignorant of the vernacular – a situation Steel briefly satrises in 'Mussumat Kirpo's Doll' where the ignorance of the Commissioner's wife who has been invited to give away the prizes at the missionary school is subjected to irony. The 'half-bewildered look' on her face betrays her ignorance of both 'native' children and the language; 'She neither understands them, nor the fluent scholastic Hindustani' of the 'flushed, excited' mission ladies, as they 'introduce each claimant to her notice. Still she smiles, and says, "*Bohut uchcha*" (very good), and nods as if she did'.[86]

Steel also suggested that female attire was an imperial responsibility, and was rather critical of the ultra feminine or sexually alluring apparel of memsahibs.[87] She cautioned memsahibs that the 'native' female gaze was turned critically upon their behaviour and attire, and their décolleté gowns and ball-room dancing were perceived as shameless, 'dancing like bad ones', with 'bare breasts and arms'.[88] Indeed, with regard to clothing, Steel indicated that evangelical attire was more modest and appropriate in a colonial, purdah-based society. By the late nineteenth century, as we noted in Chapter 1, female evangelicals working in India were young, unmarried professionals coming out alone to the colonies. They seemed to have developed a specific, practical 'missionary attire' suitable for both their hard, outdoors lives and the tropical climate. It consisted of 'a huge pith hat tied round with a blue veil, a gingham dress, a bag of books, white stockings, and tan shoes', as well as a 'white umbrella lined with green'.[89] According to a medical missionary who worked in the northern provinces in the 1890s, the typical garb of the medical missionary who had to drive to the 'home of the sufferer', consisted of a simple, modest dress, a 'pith helmet' which protected the head from the tropical heat and a 'huge umbrella lined with green and covered with white muslin', to offer further protection 'during the intense heat of the midday sun'.[90] Missionary clothing was indeed a sartorial symbol of their active, arduous lives, deliberately designed to be both practical as well as drab. For female evangelicals who constructed themselves in their writings as hard-worked and self-sacrificing (as we saw in the previous chapter), this attire became both a badge of honour and a testimony to their piety and dedication.[91]

Bernard Cohn, in his discussion of the politics of cloth, clothing and colonialism, has noted how the British in India used clothing as well as 'codes of conduct' that constantly 'distanced them – physically, socially, and culturally – from their Indian subjects'.[92] Extending Cohn's argument here, one can speculate that perhaps there was a gendered symbolism of clothing *within* the British colonising community as well, a symbolism which was at play not only along the axis of race (British versus Indian) but also along lines of class and gender (male versus female). As we shall be seeing in Chapter 5, the pith helmet and, to a certain extent, the white umbrella were considered to be 'masculine' pieces of 'protective' tropical attire, signifying hard-work and dedicated service in the colonies.[93] Rather like this 'protective' clothing of male colonialists, then, female missionary attire too becomes in Steel's writing a symbol of hard work, dedication and self-sacrifice.

Moreover, the rationale behind keeping this attire drab and de-sexualised (the 'gingham dress', 'tan shoes') was to stave off possible sexual attention from the supposedly lecherous 'native' males. Anxieties were voiced, for instance, in the Calcutta-based newspaper, *The Friend of India and Statesman*, in 1883 about female evangelicals, 'young, unmarried ladies', being exposed on a daily basis to the danger of 'familiarity or insult from the male members of the household' during the zenana visits which they made 'alone or unprotected' to 'the houses of middle class Hindoos'.[94]

Most importantly, perhaps, the female missionary garb served to bridge the vital gap between 'native' and European notions of cultural acceptability. In contrast, even though Steel shows purdah women finding missionary women's attire ludicrous, and dissolving in 'peals of laughter' over it, nonetheless, 'native' women prefer missionary women, modestly dressed in gingham, because they 'are virtuous and keep their eyes from men ... Not like bold hussies who dance'.[95] Thus, this 'native' female gaze comes to be deployed in Steel's short fiction as a strategic device for containing the public display of white female sexuality in the colony. By serving as a caveat to the memsahib, a reminder of the need to uphold European image and prestige in the colony, the text implicitly enjoins 'Indianised' curbs on her dress and conduct, thereby amply demonstrating the complexities of gendering as well as the fluidities of cultural dynamics in the colonial context.

Zenana visitation, westernisation and the role of missionaries

We saw in the last chapter how zenana visitation was a significant component of the missionary agenda of the 'civilising mission'. Broadly speaking, the Victorian lady was held up as an exemplary female paradigm to be emulated by the new category of western-educated 'New Indian Woman' emerging from the veil. Moreover, this model of womanhood was sought to be imposed upon purdah women largely through the services of female evangelicals in the course of zenana visitations.

Zenana education, which saw 'substantial growth' during the latter nineteenth century, was a popular mode in the Punjab as well, and approved by the government, because it was 'thrifty'.[96] Although Steel was a strong supporter of female education, she was firmly against the anglicisation and westernisation of Indian women. She criticised the role of female evangelicals' in this area and projected them as well-meaning, but feeble-minded women, whose misconceived plans could spell disaster for the 'native' women whom they sought to 'rescue'. Her short story, 'Feroza', brings up the problem of westernisation and the disastrous consequences of this project in a genteel north Indian Muslim household, where Steel critiques as misconceived the intervention by European missionaries and the role they play in the acculturation process. Jeffrey Cox notes in his study of missionary work in colonial Punjab that while zenana work was popular, it also stirred up 'sharp opposition' from Muslim (as well as Arya Samaj) groups who claimed that 'foreign women were challenging the sanctity of marriage and secretly entering homes'.[97] So much so that in 1888 a 'Mohammedan Manifesto' circulated in Lahore, describing zenana visitors as spies and beguilers and declaring that a non-Muslim woman was equivalent to a man in terms of purdah.[98]

In Steel's story, however, this aspect of Muslim hostility is not high-lighted. Instead, the focus is on the folly and failure of the missionar-ies' 'civilising' and westernising agenda. As Feroza, a young Muslim *purdahnashin* awaits the return of her husband, Meer Ahmed Ali, after three years of study at the bar in England, she is troubled by anxieties, since she has heard that it is a country 'where the women go about half naked' and worries that after the enticing charms of the 'mems' he will find her too 'native' and uninteresting. Anxious to please him, she embarks on a secret programme of education and westernisation ('Ah! if she could only learn to read for herself'), taking the help of a female missionary from the Mission House, and asking her to hold zenana classes in her home:[99]

> If she could not go to school, the mems would come and teach her at home. They did such work at Delhi; why not here?[100]

'Miss Julia Smith, spinster of Clapham', who is delighted by this idea which she finds 'most touching', decides to undertake it and enthusiastically plans on doing a write-up on it in a mission maga-zine.[101] Although, as we saw in the last chapter, a request for purdah instruction was generally held to be the prerogative of the men-folk in the household, this story shows the daughter-in-law taking the initiative and inviting the female evangelicals, thereby effectively marginalising the role of the male head of the household and imparting greater agency to the woman. We had also seen in the previous chapter how zenana visitation was often forbidden by 'native' households if it included religious instruction of any kind, including Bible reading and the singing of hymns. In this case too, even though the *Moulvie* sahib, the father-in-law, is determined that 'no singing should be heard in his house', the missionary remains adamant and finally has her way, combining zenana instruction with the singing of Christian hymns.[102]

Julia Smith had sung hymns on the doorstep three days a week. Sometimes she had quite a large audience, and sometimes Feroza herself would listen at the lattice.[103]

Although Feroza resists conversion, she eagerly adopts other forms of westernisation, including western clothing, modes of sitting on a chair instead of on the floor, and keeping the palms of the hands free of elaborate henna designs: 'The palms and nails of those delicate hands were no longer stained with henna.'[104] Gradually, she even picks up some odd bits and pieces of English culture and diet – proudly presenting to Julia Smith an 'afternoon tea tray' of 'a plate of thin bread and butter', brought in by a servant woman, instead of the 'native' snack of 'cinnamon tea and greasy fritters' usually served inside zenanas to visiting evangelicals, and remarks with a happy laugh that her husband 'will think himself back amongst the mems!'[105]

One can read this story as a display of what Jeffrey Cox terms, 'the special bond of sympathy between western and Indian women', which accounts of zenana visits often revealed.[106] On the other hand, Steel sharply blames the missionary woman for being so tragically off the mark in her scheme of turning Feroza into a 'brown mensahib', a scheme which had 'originated in her teacher's sentimental brain'.[107] While the missionary lady is enthusiastic at the thought of presenting the young England-returned barrister with the delightful surprise of a western-educated companionate wife – she is, at the same time, herself troubled by pangs of self-doubt, especially after:

some unkind person had poisoned Julia's peace with remarks of the mixing of unknown chemicals. After all, what did she know of this absent husband ...?[108]

And subsequent events do indeed reveal how tragically off the mark she had been in her westernising enterprise. By the time her husband returns, Feroza is shown to have undergone an uncomfortable transformation. Ill-at-ease now in unfamiliar apparel, 'she sat on a chair now, and her white stockings and patent-leather shoes twisted themselves tortuously about its legs'. She had 'adopted the dress of the advanced Indian lady, which', observes Steel, 'with surprisingly little change, manages to destroy all the grace of the original costume':[109]

The lack of braided hair and clustering jewels degrades the veil to an unnecessary wrap; the propriety of the bodice intensifies its shapelessness; the very face suffers by the unconcealed holes in ears and nose.[110]

Moreover, her room too has been 'travestied into a pitiful caricature of foreign fashions'. Tragically enough, the drab, bookish Feroza soon discovers that her young barrister husband's westernisation is merely skin-deep; it is merely 'a diligent polishing of the surface of things'. He promptly resumes, on his return, the clothes and lifestyle of 'an orthodox Mohammedan', preferring to eat *chuppatties* and *koftas* (unleavened bread and meatball) to tea and toast.[111] What is more, he has eyes only for Kareema, the widow of his younger brother – whose alluring sensuality is further enhanced by her diaphanous garments and Orientalised, 'native' grace:

> Gleams of jeweled hair under the gold – threaded veil; a figure revealed by the net bodice worn over a scantier one of flowered muslin: bare feet tucked away in shells of shoes; long gauze draperies showing a shadow of silk-clad limbs.[112]

Watching with helpless jealousy this strong sexual attraction between the two, Feroza is even more distraught on learning that unknown to her, the *Moulvie* sahib had in the meanwhile, arranged for her husband to take Kareema as a second wife – a polygamous arrangement in keeping with tradition, since the older wife is clearly barren. Torn with 'sheer animal jealousy', Feroza commits suicide by throwing herself into a well. While this is just the kind of polygamous situation which Steel widely censured in her short fiction, in this story, however, it is the missionary who is held responsible for this tragedy – as she herself realises, filled as she is with 'remorseful anxiety':[113]

> 'My dear, my dear!' she whispered through her sobs, 'Surely you need not have gone so far, so very far – for help.'[114]

Clearly, the westernisation experiment here is a failure. Steel sharply critiques as misconceived the intervention by European missionaries and the role that they played in the acculturation process. The story also questions the wisdom of such 'mixing of unknown chemicals', and the point seems to be that no matter how much education is given to Indians, in essentials they don't change; it is only a 'polishing of the surface of things'.[115] The husband's inherent 'Indianness' thus fuels one of the enduring colonial myths of the nineteenth century – that of an 'unchanging India'. Here, Steel seems to draw a distinction between simple female education or literacy on the one hand, and westernisation, on the other. While she commends female education, she seems to suggest that efforts at excessive westernisation are flawed and ill-conceived.

Conclusion

Thus, Steel's relationship to gender problems, social reform and the 'civilising mission' were complex and contradictory. While she critiqued several patriarchal practices among the agricultural community in her short fiction – most notably, polygamy – nevertheless, she remained silent on efforts at reform measures in this community. This ambivalence can possibly be explained by factors such as this region's dominant peasant caste offering men for the colonial army, or the province being the favoured 'granary' of the colonial state, or a racist preference for fair-skinned, 'manly' Punjabis over dark, 'effeminate' Bengalis; quite apart from a British 'softness' towards the province out of gratitude for its loyalty during the 1857 rebellion. Thus, Steel remains silent on the question of gender reform in Punjabi agrarian society, keeping the 'civilising mission' in abeyance as far as Jat peasant women were concerned

At the same time, however, Steel was interested in gendered social reform issues and turned a critical 'colonial' gaze at patriarchal social practices such as female infanticide, child marriage and polygamy. She was especially interventionist in the sphere of female education, setting up schools and later becoming a school Inspectress – although her views on the progress made in female education in the Punjab remained bleak. Regarding European missionaries too, Steel had serious reservations. She found missionaries' friendliness with 'native' women to be servile and lacking in dignity. Missionary educational methods too she faulted as lax and ineffectual, besides critiquing their idea of the westernisation of Indian women.

While one of the objectives of the social reformers of the 1860s was 'modernisation', that is, the westernisation of the Indian woman, Steel's stories, however, often come close to *interrogating* this female role model. 'Modernisation' was premised upon the female paradigm of the Victorian lady, a gender ideal which was at the heart of the 'civilising' and 'modernising' mission. To some extent, Steel did support this paradigm, citing Victoria for instance in one of her stories as 'the great queen' and a symbol of British female emancipation.[116] But far more predominantly, she *attacked* this image of the western woman and instead projected the paradigm of the submissive and sacrificing Indian wife whom she described as the epitome of 'the greatest amount of self-abnegation', as the female role model for western women to emulate.[117]

In other ways too, Steel was critical of western women and their cultural practices. She sometimes used the strategy of looking through 'native' eyes as a means of controlling the Englishwoman's public display of sexuality, and policing her dress and conduct. Her disparagement of European women's 'immodesty' was no doubt meant to serve as a caveat to the memsahib – a reminder of the need to uphold British image and prestige in the colony.

Indeed, Steel often valorised in her non-fictional writing the patri-archal ideal of the submissive and sacrificing wife. She projected this apocryphal 'native' female submissiveness as a prescriptive model to contain the self-assertiveness of European women and – in a curious *volte face* – argued that 'the Western woman has as much to learn from the Eastern woman as the Eastern has from the Western'.[118] For all her suffragette background, she was sharply critical about certain eman-cipatory trends in the west, such as increasing female self-assertion, divorce, the questioning of marriage and so on, and she held up the figure of the dutiful Indian wife as an exemplary picture of marriage, critiquing the west for 'discussing in a thousand ways the dreary old problems of whether marriage is a failure or not'.[119] Thus, the very concept of a European female role model in Steel is ridden with ambi-guity, so that even while she implicitly upholds a Western female paradigm, a good deal of her writing ends up advocating the ideal of the self-sacrificing Indian woman for the Western woman to emulate.[120]

With the female role model of the social reform agenda itself being undermined in this fashion, Steel's discharge of the 'white woman's burden' stands contradicted by ambivalences in the narra-tive. Although many of her stories are concerned with issues of social reform and some criticise certain practices, there is an underlying position in these stories that voices the impossibility of change. What is more, Steel seems to be trapped in an old stereotype associated with colonial discourse, namely the colonial myth of the 'unchanging east', of a stagnant, centuries-old, 'decadent' civilisation that would never change and therefore efforts at social reform become worthless. Displaying unresolved contradictions and ambivalences, many of her stories advocate the need for change while the sub-text simultane-ously *contests* that stand. So that, even while on the surface the need for social change is being urged, the underlying thrust of the narrative subverts the very possibility of reform.

Notes

1 Early nineteenth-century social reform strategy through legislation (e.g. the Acts banning sati (1829), or legalising Hindu widow remarriage (1856)) was later fol-lowed by reform measures, aimed at gradual change in the system of purdah and 'native' female education.

2 Besides missionaries, a small number of 'secular' women too were actively involved in female education, e.g. Annette Akroyd, and philanthropists like Mary Carpenter who came out to India with the purpose of promoting 'native' female education. For details on missionary involvement in female education, see Hayden J. A. Bellenoit, *Missionary Education and Empire in Late Colonial India, 1860–1920* (London, Pickering & Chatto, 2007).

3 Early scholars such as Jenny Sharpe, *Allegories of Empire: The Figure of Woman in*

the Colonial Text (Minneapolis and London, University of Minnesota Press, 1993) and Nancy Paxton, *Writing under the Raj: Gender, Race and Rape in the British Colonial Imagination, 1830–1947* (New Brunswick, NJ, Rutgers University Press, 1999) focus only on Steel's 'Mutiny' novel. Only very recently are her 'Indian' short stories gradually emerging from invisibility and obscurity; see, for instance Rosemary Hennessy and Rajeswari Mohan, 'The Construction of Woman in Three Popular Texts of Empire: Towards a Critique of Materialist Feminism', *Textual Practice*, 3:3 (1989), pp. 323–359; Indrani Sen, 'The White Woman's Burden: The Dilemmas of Social Reform in the Fiction of Flora Annie Steel', *Studies in Humanities and Social Sciences*, 3:1 (Summer, 1996), pp. 89–100; Chapter 5 of Indrani Sen, *Woman and Empire: Representations in the Writings of British India, 1858–1900* (New Delhi, Orient Longman, 2002), pp. 131–159; Ralph Crane and Anna Johnston, 'Flora Annie Steel in the Punjab', in Peter Hulme and Russell Mcdougall (eds), *Writing, Travel, and Empire: In the Margins of Anthropology* (London, I. B. Tauris & Co. Ltd, 2007), pp. 71–95.

4   Steel's 'Indian' short fiction appears in three collections: *From the Five Rivers* (1893), *The Flower of Forgiveness and Other Stories* (1894) and *In the Permanent Way and Other Stories* (1897).

5   Around the 1890s Steel was an important and influential colonial author, comparable to her contemporary, Rudyard Kipling, for her close knowledge of 'native' life. For details on Steel see Sen, *Woman and Empire*, pp. 71–103, 131–159.

6   Flora Annie Steel (1847–1927) who came to India as the wife of Henry Steel, an Indian Civil Service officer, lived mostly in the Punjab region for twenty-two years (1867–1889). Energetic, opinionated and vocal on gender issues, she was known in India as educationist, gatherer of Indian folklore and co-author of an influential housekeeping manual for memsahibs, *The Complete Indian Housekeeper and Cook* (1888). But it was only after her return to England that she gained fame for her prolific India-based short stories and novels, including her 'Mutiny' novel, *On the Face of the Waters* (1896). She joined the suffragette movement subsequently and was elected President of the Women Writer's Suffrage League in 1913, and noted in her autobiography that she had 'always been' a 'vehement Suffragette', and that 'all my life I have been keen not so much on the rights as the wrongs of women'; in Flora Annie Steel, *The Garden of Fidelity* (London, Macmillan & Co. Ltd, 1929), pp. 222, 265. See also Violet Powell, *Flora Annie Steel: Novelist of India* (London, Heinemann, 1981).

7   For details see Powell, *Flora Annie Steel.*

8   For details see *ibid.* See also F. A. Steel, *The Garden of Fidelity* (London, Macmillan & Co. Ltd, 1929), and Daya Patwardhan, *A Star of India: Flora Annie Steel, Her Works and Time* (Pune, Griha Prakashan, 1963).

9   Steel, *Garden of Fidelity*, p. 52.

10   Untitled article, *The Queen* (July 1897), p. 32.

11   Maud Diver, *The Englishwoman in India* (Edinburgh and London, William Blackwood & Sons, 1909), pp. 128, 79–80, 78. The linkages between the social reform programme and colonial ideology have been probed, notably in Antoinette Burton, *Burdens of History: British Feminists, Indian Women and Imperial Culture, 1865–1915* (Chapel Hill, University of North Carolina Press, 1994).

12   Steel, *Garden of Fidelity*, p. 121.

13   Malcolm Lyall Darling, *The Punjab Peasant in Prosperity and Debt* ([1925], New Delhi, Manohar Book Service, 1978), p. 35.

14   The classic work on this is of course, Mrinalini Sinha, *Colonial Masculinity: The 'Manly Englishman' and the 'Effeminate Bengali' in the Late Nineteenth Century* (Manchester and New York: Manchester University Press, 1995).

15   Steel, *Garden of Fidelity*, p. 161.

16   Prem Chowdhry, 'Customs in a Peasant Economy: Women in Colonial Haryana', in Kumkum Sangari and Sudesh Vaid (eds), *Recasting Women: Essays in Colonial History* (New Delhi, Kali for Women, 1989), p. 304. Chowdhry also notes, 'The Brahmin could certainly be sacerdotally superior yet socially he was described as

the "lowest of the low"', and in the 1880s 'there was scarcely a Brahmin there who had even the slightest knowledge of the Hindu law books or was acquainted with their names', in *ibid.*, p. 313.

17 For details see Chowdhry, 'Customs in a Peasant Economy', pp. 302–303.

18 Among the gendered social evils which first attracted the attention of the colonial authorities was the prevalence of female infanticide practised by numerous castes, including Rajputs, Khatris, Aroras, Brahmins, Muslims and especially Jats. See Anshu Malhotra, *Gender, Caste and Religious Identities: Restructuring Class in Colonial Punjab* (New Delhi, Oxford University Press, 2002), p. 49.

19 The Female Infanticide Prevention Act of 1870, passed by the colonial government, focused especially on Awadh, the Punjab and the north-western provinces. In 1911, the lowest sex ratio of 694:1000 in the age group 0–5 was registered among Sikh Jats. See Malhotra, *Gender, Caste and Religious Identities*, p. 49. See also Barbara D. Miller, *The Endangered Sex: Neglect of Female Children in Rural North India* (Ithaca, NY, and London, Cornell University Press, 1981), and Yogesh Snehi, 'Female Infanticide and Gender in Punjab: Imperial Claims and Contemporary Discourse', *Economic and Political Weekly*, 38: 41 (11–17 October 2003), pp. 4302–4305.

20 F. A. Steel, *Punjab Notes and Queries*, 1:5, February (1884), p. 51.

21 F. A. Steel, 'Gunesh Chand', *From the Five Rivers* ([1893], London, William Heinemann, 1897), pp. 31–32. Colonial records do indeed document that when a dead female infant was buried in Punjab, a little *gur* was placed in her mouth and a cotton skein was put in her hands, while a phrase was ritually uttered: 'Eat your *gur* and spin your thread, but go and send a boy instead'; see Malhotra, *Gender, Caste and Religious Identities*, p. 50.

22 Polygamy was not confined to Punjab and could be found across a wide spectrum of other regions and castes as well. For caste variations within Punjab see Malhotra, *Gender, Caste, Religious Identities*, pp. 53–59.

23 Prem Chowdhry points out that polygamy helped to provide free female labour in the labour intensive economy of the region in the colonial period: 'Barrenness invariably led to polygamy … The failure to bear sons was considered a serious misfortune, equated with barrenness … because without sons there are no daughters-in-law to provide labour … so important to the peculiar socio-economic needs of this region'. See Prem Chowdhry, *The Veiled Women: Shifting Gender Equations in Rural Haryana, 1880–1990* (New Delhi, Oxford University Press, 1994), pp. 131–132.

24 Haryana 'folk wisdom' revealed a deeply embedded misogyny in sympathising with the 'pitiable' condition of the husband, caught as he was between his two quarrelling wives. See Chowdhry, *Veiled Women*, p. 368.

25 Occasionally, Steel's stories critically delineate polygamy among other sections of society as well, e.g. town-based Hindus or well-to-do Western-educated, upper-class urban Muslim families (e.g. 'Feroza', a short story, which we discuss later in this chapter).

26 In a short story 'The Sorrowful Hour' located in rural Punjab, Saraswati, a dignified peasant woman of mature age, who has remained childless after years of marriage, feels humiliated when her affectionate husband Gurditta has to take a second wife for the sake of progeny. The husband soon becomes besotted by the alluring, much younger wife, all the more so because she presents him with the much-desired male infant. Torn with sexual jealousy, Saraswati, the neglected older wife, takes a potion to become pregnant – but dies while giving birth to a still-born female infant. See F. A. Steel, 'The Sorrowful Hour', *In the Permanent Way and Other Stories* ([1897], London, William Heinemann, 1898).

27 Steel does castigate child marriage and early childbirth in a few of her minor short stories set outside Punjab, e.g. in F. A. Steel, 'Amor Vincit Omnia', in *In The Permanent Way and Other Stories* ([1897], London, William Heinemann, 1898), where an educated, town-bred youth of sixteen and his thirteen year old bride have a child within a year – only to helplessly watch it die.

28 Steel, *Garden of Fidelity*, p. 161.
29 Despite the Hindu Widows' Remarriage Act of 1856, remarriage was seldom prac-
    tised, and high-caste widows continued to be bound by traditional rules of celi-
    bacy. On the contrary, it was low- caste Hindu widows (among whom remarriage
    used to be customarily practised), who were adversely affected by this legislation.
30 See Chowdhry, 'Customs in a Peasant Economy', p. 312. If there was no younger
    brother-in-law, the widow could be married off to an older brother-in-law or even
    her father-in-law. For details see also Chowdhry, *Veiled Women*, and Malhotra,
    Gender, Caste, Religious Identities.
31 A striking exception is 'On the Second Storey', Steel's short story set in Bengal,
    which *supports* the social reform project of high-caste widow remarriage. A young
    widow and a reformist Bengali youth fall in love but hostile, reactionary family
    members prevent the marriage by having her murdered. See F. A. Steel, 'On the
    Second Storey', in *In The Permanent Way and Other Stories* ([1897], London,
    William Heinemann, 1898).
32 F. A. Steel, 'In the House of a Coppersmith', in *The Flower of Forgiveness* (London,
    Macmillan & Co., 1894). pp. 11, 2. Steel uses the Hindi terms *'dewar'* and
    'dewarani' in the story.
33 Steel, *Garden of Fidelity*, p. 176.
34 Madhu Kishwar observes, 'Among the Muslims and Sikhs, the imperative to
    read the sacred texts made female literacy socially acceptable. Among Hindus of
    the upper castes, girls were taught in the privacy of their own homes. However,
    very rarely were they taught to write, for this was considered an accomplishment
    at which only the superior class of courtesans were supposed to be adept', in
    Madhu Kishwar, 'The Daughters of Aryavarta', in Sumit Sarkar and Tanika Sarkar
    (eds), *Women and Social Reform in Modern India: A Reader*, Vol. I (New Delhi,
    Permanent Black, 2007), p. 306.
35 Tim Allender, 'Anglican Evangelism in North India and the Punjabi Missionary
    Classroom: The Failure to Educate "the Masses," 1860–77', *History of Education:
    Journal of the History of Education Society* 32:3 (2003), p. 274. Sir Charles Wood's
    Despatch of 1854 led to the creation of a separate department for administering
    education in each province and the introduction of a system of grants-in-aid. See
    also Tim Allender, *Ruling through Education: The Politics of Schooling in the
    Colonial Punjab* (New Delhi, New Dawn Press, 2006).
36 Regarding this type of indigenous school, Tim Allender notes that, 'It was esti-
    mated that there were 128 indigenous female schools in Lahore district in 1850.
    When government officials visited them … the teachers retired behind purdahs
    but appeared pleased at the pupils being noticed', in Tim Allender, 'Surrendering
    a Colonial Domain: Educating North India, 1854–1890', *History of Education:
    Journal of the History of Education Society*, 36:1 (2007), p. 52.
37 In the 1890s, Arya Samaj schools were set up in the province. These DAV
    (Dayanand Anglo-Vedic) schools and colleges established by the Arya Samaj grew
    rapidly especially in the last decade of the nineteenth century. For a discussion,
    see Kishwar, 'Daughters of Aryavarta', pp. 316–326. Subsequently, the education
    of Muslim girls was encouraged by the Aligarh educational movement under the
    leadership of Sir Sayid Khan. For details see Allender, 'Surrendering a Colonial
    Domain', p. 62, and Allender, 'Anglican Evangelism in North India', p. 288.
38 Steel, *Garden of Fidelity*, p. 63.
39 *Ibid.*, p. 64.
40 Steel, *Garden of Fidelity*, p. 161. For instance, Allender mentions a Mrs S.
    Mackintosh who was Inspectress of Female Schools in the Lahore Circle, in early
    1875, in Allender 'Anglican Evangelism in North India', p. 285.
41 Steel, *Garden of Fidelity*, p. 164.
42 The first Indian Education Commission (popularly known as the Hunter
    Commission after its chairman, Sir William Hunter) was appointed in 1882 by
    Lord Ripon to examine the state of education throughout the country. For details,
    see the *Report of the Education Commission Appointed by the Resolution of the*

Government of India, 3rd February 1882 (Delhi, Indian Education Department, 1883), pp. 521–549.

43 Hazi Ghulam Shah, Member, Education Commission, in *Appendix to Education Commission Report, Report by the Punjab Provincial Committee and Memorials Addressed to the Education Commission* (Calcutta, Superintendent of Government Printing, 1884), p. 115.

44 Allender, 'Anglican Evangelism in North India', p. 284.

45 *Ibid.* See also Allender, *Ruling through Education*, p. 199.

46 *Ibid.*, p. 164.

47 F. A. Steel, Report to the Director of Public Instruction, Punjab, dated 11th March, 1884, in India, Home Dept, *Proceedings of the Government of the Punjab* (Delhi, Home Department, 1884), p. 160, cited in Rebecca J. Sutcliffe, 'Feminizing the Professional: The Government Reports of Flora Annie Steel', *Technical Communication Quarterly*, 7:2, Spring (1998), p. 165.

48 F. A. Steel, Report to the Officiating Director of Public Instruction, Punjab, dated 11th April, 1884, in India, Home Dept, *Proceedings of the Government of the Punjab* (Delhi, Home Department, 1884), p. 170, cited in Sutcliffe, 'Feminising the Professional', p. 169.

49 Steel, *Garden of Fidelity*, pp. 164, 165.

50 Steel, in Sutcliffe, 'Feminising the Professional', p. 165. Steel once accepted an ingenious solution offered by Dhun Devi, a 'little thin child of ten, with the brightest of eyes', of teaching beginners in a 'market-place' school and bringing them for admission only after they had learned the alphabet (Steel, *Garden of Fidelity*, p. 175); Steel modelled her protagonist, Fatma, on Dhun Devi, in her short story, 'At a Girls' School'.

51 F. A. Steel, 'At a Girls' School', in *From the Five Rivers* ([1893], London, William Heinemann, 1897), p. 143. After Wood's Despatch of 1854, seventeen female government schools were opened during 1856–1857, but gradually most had to be closed down due to a lack of teachers and poor attendance.

52 Steel, 'At a Girls' School', pp. 153, 150.

53 *Ibid.*, p. 147.

54 *Ibid.*, p. 151.

55 *Ibid.*, p. 145.

56 *Ibid.*

57 *Ibid.*, pp. 154–155, 144, 145.

58 *Ibid.*, p. 146.

59 *Ibid.*

60 *Ibid.*, p. 154. For details about this system of scholarship for female students, see Allender, 'Anglican Evangelism in North India', p. 284.

61 For details on this aspect see the comment, 'The teachers worked for miserably low salaries', in Kishwar, 'Daughters of Aryavarta', p. 310.

62 Steel, 'At a Girls' School', pp. 154–155.

63 *Ibid.*, p. 155.

64 For a discussion of zenana missionary visitation work in the Punjab, see Jeffrey Cox, *Imperial Fault Lines: Christianity and Colonial Power in India, 1818–1940* (Stanford, Stanford University Press, 2002), pp. 67, 157–162. See also Bellenoit, *Missionary Education and Empire*, pp. 52–53.

65 Allender, *Ruling Through Education*, p. 185. In 1849 the American Presbytarian Mission was established in Punjab (Lahore and Ludhiana). The two important missions were the two Anglican missions – Christian Missionary Society and Society for the Propagation for the Gospel. See Allender, 'Anglican Evangelism in North India', p. 284.

66 The subjects taught included Urdu, Persian, Gurmukhi and Hindi, and also Arithmetic, History, Geography, sewing and knitting.

67 F. A. Steel, 'Mussumat Kirpo's Doll', in *The Flower of Forgiveness and Other Stories* (London, Macmillan & Co., 1894), Vol. II, p. 117.

68 *Ibid.*, pp. 116–117.

[79]

69 *Ibid.*, p. 117.
70 *Ibid.*
71 Steel, *Garden of Fidelity*, p. 169.
72 Steel, 'Mussumat Kirpo's Doll', p. 119.
73 *Ibid.*
74 *Ibid.*, pp. 119, 118.
75 *Ibid.*, pp. 119, 123.
76 *Ibid.* p. 124.
77 *Ibid.*, pp. 119, 124, 127, 128, 129.
78 *Ibid.*, p. 129.
79 'Mussamat Kirpo's Doll' is one of the few short stories that has attracted scholarly attention. Rosemary Hennessy and Rajeswari Mohan read it as a situation where the only thing in the world that this young wife (who has been dispossessed of her infant by the mother-in-law), can call her own, is her doll. See Hennessy and Mohan, 'The Construction of Woman in Three Popular Texts of Empire', *Textual Practice* 3:3 (1989) pp. 323–359.
80 Cox, *Imperial Fault Lines*, p. 161.
81 See the chapter on Steel in Sen, *Woman and Empire*, pp. 131–159.
82 Steel, *Garden of Fidelity*, p. 165.
83 Steel, 'Mussumat Kirpo's Doll', pp. 120, 121, 127, 123. The missionary woman, Julia Smith, who appears in this story seems to be a different person from the missionary who is called by the same name in the short story, 'Feroza'.
84 *Ibid.*, pp. 122, 122–123.
85 Barbara N. Ramusack, 'British Women Activists in India, 1865–1945', in Nupur Chaudhuri and Margaret Strobel (eds), *Western Women and Imperialism: Complicity and Resistance*, p. 3. Flora Annie Steel and Grace Gardiner, *The Complete Indian Housekeeper and Cook* ([1888], London, William Heinemann, 1909), p. 9.
86 Steel, 'Mussamut Kirpo's Doll', p. 118.
87 For a discussion of the politics of gendered clothing see Chapter 5 of this book, 'Marginalising the Memsahib: The White Woman's Health Issues in Colonial Medical Writings'.
88 F. A. Steel, 'Feroza', in *The Flower of Forgiveness and Other Stories* (London, Macmillan & Co., 1894), Vol. I, pp. 200, 203.
89 Steel, 'Feroza', p. 206.
90 The medical missionary notes, 'She dons her pith helmet, takes a huge umbrella lined with green and covered with white muslin, and drives in her close carriage to the home of the sufferer', in Saleni Armstrong-Hopkins, *Within the Purdah: In the Zenana and Homes of Indian Princes and Heroes and Heroines of Zion* (New York, Eaton & Mains, 1898), p. 242.
91 Female evangelicals' taking pride in their attire ('they were proud of' their clothing), is mentioned in a short story. See Steel, 'Feroza', p. 206.
92 Bernard S. Cohn, *Colonialism and Its Forms of Knowledge: The British in India* (Princeton, New Jersey, Princeton University Press, 1996), p. 111.
93 Male tropical clothing consisted of a sola topi, spinal pad and white umbrella. This, as well as the subject of climate and male European clothing, is further discussed in Chapter 5 of this book.
94 *The Friend of India and Statesman* (9 October 1883), p. 1438, cited in Kenneth Ballhatchet, *Race, Sex and Class under the Raj: Imperial Attitudes and Policies and their Critics, 1793–1905* (New York, St. Martin's Press, 1980), p. 115.
95 *Ibid.*, pp. 206, 206, 203, 203. For details regarding 'native' moral censure of what was perceived as the memsahibs' obscene clothing in colonial India, see Indrani Sen (ed.), *Memsahibs' Writings: Colonial Narratives on Indian Women* (New Delhi, Orient BlackSwan, 2008).
96 Bellenoit, *Missionary Education and Empire*, pp. 52, 53. Jeffrey Cox notes that eventually zenana visitation reached very few Indian women. A government Report of 1873 identified fewer than 2,000 zenana pupils in the entire country

and after 1910, zenana work hardly finds mention. See Cox, *Imperial Fault Lines*, p. 162.

97   Cox, *Imperial Fault Lines*, p. 162.
98   *Ibid.*
99   Steel, 'Feroza', pp. 200, 209.
100   *Ibid.*, pp. 209–210.
101   *Ibid.*, pp. 214, 207.
102   *Ibid.*, p. 210.
103   *Ibid.*, p. 218.
104   Steel, 'Feroza, p. 225. Decorating one's palms and nails with henna dye and elaborate henna designs is the hallmark of a married woman.
105   *Ibid.*, pp. 221, 221, 221.
106   Cox, *Imperial Fault Lines*, p. 67.
107   Steel, 'Feroza', p. 219.
108   *Ibid.*, p. 220.
109   *Ibid.*, pp. 224, 233.
110   *Ibid.*, p. 233.
111   *Ibid.*, pp. 239, 232, 233, 236.
112   *Ibid.*, p. 234.
113   *Ibid.*, pp 225, 242.
114   *Ibid.*, p. 243.
115   *Ibid.*, pp. 220, 232.
116   The educated peasant wife Veeru admiringly makes this reference to Queen Victoria in Steel, 'Gunesh Chand', p. 19.
117   Steel, 'Gunesh Chand', p. 19. F. A. Steel, *India* (London, A. & C. Black Ltd, 1929), p. 159.
118   Steel, *India*, p. 159.
119   F. A. Steel, 'Uma Himavutee', in *In The Permanent Way and Other Stories* ([1897], London, William Heinemann, 1898), p 179. In this portrait of an ideal wife (albeit in a polygamous marriage), Uma, a happily married but barren peasant wife, sacrifices personal emotions and dutifully arranges for her husband's second marriage for the sake of progeny – and receives her husband's grateful appreciation for it. Steel's conservative views on marriage are discussed in Gráinne Goodwin, '"I Was Chosen Out as Oracular": The Fin-de-siècle Journalism of Flora Annie Steel', in *Women's Writing*, 18:4 (November 2011), pp. 505–523. Nancy L. Paxton notes that Steel 'always remained in her perceptions and attitudes first and foremost a memsahib, and only secondarily, if at all, a 'feminist', in 'Feminism Under the Raj: Complicity and Resistance in the Writings of Flora Annie Steel and Annie Besant', in Nupur Chaudhuri and Margaret Strobel (eds), *Western Women and Imperialism: Complicity and Resistance* (Bloomington and Indianapolis, Indiana University Press, 1992), pp. 158–176.
120   Steel, who joined the Suffragette movement after returning to Britain and was elected President of the Women Writer's Suffrage League in 1913, observed in her autobiography that she had 'always been a vehement Suffragette' and expressed her solidarity with women who had 'suffered sadly': 'All my life I have been keen not so much on the rights as the wrongs of women', in Steel, *Garden of Fidelity*, pp. 222, 265.

CHAPTER THREE

Returning the 'gaze': colonial encounters in Indian women's English writings in late nineteenth-century western India

We saw in both the previous chapters the issue of white women and the colonial 'civilising mission' in India. Moreover, we also saw in the first chapter that European missionaries aimed not only to civilise, educate and westernise but also to convert, and that Brahmin converts were specially highly prized. Some questions that arise then are how did educated Indian women who also happened to be Christian converts perceive the issue of conversion, westernisation and female schooling? In what ways were issues such as the 'civilising mission', western models of femininity, companionate marriage and 'colonial modernity' received by educated Indian women? Were they merely passive recipients of the 'fruits' of the 'civilising mission'? Or did they themselves critique the proponents of that civilising endeavour even while drawing upon some of their benefits?

These are some of the issues we shall address in this chapter through a scrutiny of the literary works written in English in the late nineteenth century, by two educated Indian Christian women of Brahmin origin, who may be termed 'New Indian Women', inasmuch as they were both themselves closely involved in girls' education and other gender issues. These literary works were *Ratanbai: A Sketch of a Bombay High Caste Hindu Young Wife* (1895), a slim novella of less than a hundred pages written by Shevantibai Nikambe (1865–1930), an educationist and the principal of a girls' school for young, high-caste Hindu wives in the Bombay presidency; while the second literary text was the complex autobiographical novel, *Saguna: A Story of Native Christian Life* (1895) written by Krupabai Satthianadhan (1862–1894), a second-generation Indian Christian. Both contemporaneous works of fiction which centred around educated female figures and offer an important perspective on social and cultural issues, appeared in the 1890s and were written not in any regional language as most contemporary writings were, but in English. Written against the backdrop of female social reform, both these texts addressed many of the issues which, as we saw in the first chapter, had been raised by missionary novels authored by European evangelicals. Indeed, these Indian women's texts went beyond missionary literature in discussing issues pertaining to the 'native' female social reform project, as well as in raising questions about its internal contradictions. Centring their narratives around a female protagonist, both writers explored the implications of social reform, especially female education along with the manner in which the lives of their protagonists were profoundly impacted – although in vastly different ways – by the shifts brought about by 'modernisation'.

Colonial India in the late nineteenth century saw the gradual emergence of the first generation of western-educated Indian women. Both Shevantibai and Krupabai, who were keenly interested in gender issues, belonged to this generation of literate, middle-class 'New Indian Women' and were the products of a complex 'modernising' process which was constituted of advances in female education, recourse to English-language education, as well as interactions with Christianity and 'western' ideologies.[1] Both of them happened to be located in the Bombay presidency which, along with Bengal, was at the forefront of women's education and activism in the nineteenth century. Moreover, this new generation of Indian women were exposed to ideas about colonial 'modernity', female education as well as western models of 'Victorian womanhood' which – as we saw in the first chapter – were primarily propagated by European missionaries. Indeed, in many cases these 'New Indian Women's' negotiations with 'colonial modernity' were mediated through interactions with white women, in the form of missionaries and school teachers. One outcome of this 'modernising' process was the production of fiction written in English by such pioneering women and their narratives present a fascinating and complex picture of female subjectivities and negotiations with 'colonial modernity' and the 'modernising' process. My discussion of the two works of fiction written by these women will be along the axes of two broad, overarching and intersecting rubrics, namely, 'social reform' and 'interactions with white woman' (that is to say, gendered transactions across race).

Gender reform in nineteenth-century western India

Diverse gendered issues formed an important part of the nineteenth-century social reform debate.[2] While broadly, this was the pattern visible over the three presidencies of Bengal, Bombay and Madras, the specifics of gender reform in the Bombay presidency need to be highlighted, given the fact that both writers discussed in this chapter were from western India. The second half of the nineteenth century was a period of great social ferment, with gender reform debates, including the interrogation of brahminical practices such as child marriage and the prohibition of widow remarriage, forming an important part of the social reform debate in the Bombay presidency.[3] While this period witnessed the rise of brahminical power (including the strengthening of caste hierarchies and enhanced control over women), it also saw the challenge to orthodoxy by Brahmin reformers, as well as the powerful anti-Brahmin movement which fought for greater freedom for women.[4] Indeed, some of the most polemical questioning of gender oppression came to be posed by individual women, both from the upper castes (notably Pandita Ramabai) as well as lower castes (e.g. Tarabai Shinde).[5] A number of reform organisations widely supported gender causes and took up issues such as the prohibition of child marriage, the promotion of widow remarriage, the education of women, while a large number of these organisations set up schools for girls and homes for widows.[6]

As we have noted, the Bombay presidency (along with Bengal) was at the vanguard of female education and other matters related to gendered social reforms and 'modernisation'. By the nineteenth century enforced female illiteracy had come to be the norm among upper-class/caste women and given this, female education became a priority issue in the mid-century social reform movement. Due to the efforts of missionaries, the colonial government and Indian reformist organisations (notably the Brahmo Samaj in Bengal and, subsequently, the Prarthana Samaj in Bombay), several schools for females were set up in these two presidencies. In addition, western-educated, liberal-minded, reformist husbands also participated in educating their child-wives, taking it upon themselves to teach them at home – generally in the teeth of fierce opposition from disapproving female members in the family who would inflict hardships on the child-wives.[7] Gradually, by the 1880s, some of the colleges in these two presidencies had also started admitting women as students and some women with college degrees even went on to seek careers as doctors or lawyers by the early twentieth century.[8]

What then was the impact of missionaries and their 'civilising mission' in this process? In order to answer that, we need to look at the specific context of Bombay and western India. While, broadly speaking, social reform was visible over the three presidencies, western India differed from the other regions in some crucial ways, and hence gender reform in the Bombay presidency had its own specific features. In contrast to other parts of the country, the purdah system was not rigidly in practice among all the politically dominant castes. Rosalind

O'Hanlon suggests that among the peasant-warrior castes, such as the Marathas, purdah possibly came into existence in this region as late as after the advent of colonialism, as she cites a non-Brahmin, warrior tradition of Maratha women riding 'barefaced on horseback'.[9] Echoing this, Padma Anagol notes that the cultural specificities of the region lent themselves to the early growth of women's assertion of identity.[10] However, we need to remind ourselves that it is difficult to make categorical assertions about caste and caste practices in the nineteenth century, since caste during this period was a fluid category (in this region, as indeed elsewhere), with society being in a state of flux and ferment during the entire era.

European missionaries too played an active role in social reform activities in the Bombay presidency, especially in the sphere of education where they were among the first to set up schools for girls.[11] As in the case of Bengal (which we examined in the first chapter), female evangelicals simultaneously drew attention to the abject condition of high-caste Hindu women, while advocating the idea of a western-style nuclear family life and companionate marriage. Most importantly perhaps they were instrumental in transmitting the post-Enlightenment ideals of equality, progress and mobility which were antithetical to what they perceived to be the traditional brahminical emphasis on rigid gender and caste hierarchies.[12]

Indeed, Padma Anagol maintains in her study on the rise of 'feminism' in late nineteenth-century Maharashtra that Christianity was among the important factors that played a key role in encouraging the early growth of women's assertion of identity in this region. Several Brahmin as well as non-Brahmin women, she points out, were drawn to what they considered to be the more equitable beliefs of Christianity and chose to be converted. And it is indeed true that the first generation of women writing in English (such as Shevantibai and Krupabai), also happened to be Christian converts, while many of these pioneering English-educated Indian women writers' exposure to 'colonial modernity' was through interactions with missionaries.

However, while it is indeed significant that both writers we are discussing in this chapter were Christian converts, we need to perhaps exercise caution while evaluating the role of Christian missionaries and Christianity on the growth of a 'feminist' consciousness in the region, given the fact that contemporary as well as pre-existing social conditions (such as the non-Brahmin movement, the influence of a warrior tradition, as well as the role of Indian reformers) had, *in any case*, sowed the conditions for female reform locally in the region. At any rate, our focus is on the impact of colonialism in inducting and shaping 'modernity' and 'female emancipation' in western India

– and also the manner in which it was negotiated and sometimes interrogated.

At the same time, it is unarguable that one of the key features of Indian women's insertion into the 'modern world' was the gendered transactions that occurred on multiple levels between them and white women, which were mediated by the factors of class, caste, religion and region. Moreover, as we saw in the previous chapter on Steel's writings, in addition to interacting with female evangelicals, school-going Indian girls would sometimes have brief encounters with wives of civil administrators as well, especially during functions at schools.[13] On many counts, moreover, as we shall see in Krupabai's autobiographical novel, these gendered colonial encounters were complicated by tensions and contradictions pertaining to race and class as well as gender.

Education and the companionate wife paradigm: Ratanbai (1895)

Shevantibai Nikambe, who was closely involved with 'native' female schooling, focused in her reformist novel, *Ratanbai: A Sketch of a Bombay High Caste Hindu Young Wife* (1895) – the only work of fiction she would write – on the importance of female education for elite, upper-caste Hindu women along with a reformist critique of the oppression of high-caste widows.[14] Very little is known about Shevantibai, apart from a few scattered facts such as that she had matriculated from a missionary school in Bombay and later came to be connected with female schooling in that city in various capacities: as inspector of primary girls' schools and headmistress of two girls' schools during the 1880s and 1890s. We also know that she was an admirer and close associate of Pandita Ramabai and had taught at the latter's Sharada Sadan school for widows until it shifted out of Bombay to Poona. Subsequently, in 1890 she herself established the 'Married Women's School' in Bombay, which was meant for high-caste Hindu girls, including child-wives, widows and the wives of professional men, where she served as Principal.[15]

In *Ratanbai* (1895), her reformist novel, Shevantibai's emphasis is on the importance of female education for elite, upper-caste Hindu women as well as on the need for reform in the oppression of high-caste widows.[16] She presents issues pertaining to female schooling and 'modernisation' through the figure of the eponymous, eleven-year-old married Brahmin girl who represents the manner in which an educated Hindu wife can, importantly, retain her traditional Hindu norms and practices while combining it with literacy and some of the basic qualities of a Victorian-style companionate wife. As Ratanbai attends a school for Brahmin child-wives which is run by Hindu female teachers, the daily school-going provides both intellectual satisfaction as well as an avenue for pleasurable socialising with classmates who are all 'young wives', like herself.[17] Behind her schooling is the initiative of her father, Vasudevrav Kashinath Dalvi, a progressive and successful advocate at the Bombay High Court in whose house she resides as a pre-pubertal child-wife. Other than going to school, however, she leads the life of a typical upper-middle-class Maharashtrian Brahmin girl, accompanying other female family members at poojas (ritual prayers), religious festivals, marriages and birth celebrations. Purdah is shown to be absent in this liberal family and on some evenings she goes out for a drive with her mother in the family's open-horse carriage, savouring the sights of the city.

It is important to note that despite herself being a Christian convert, Shevantibai takes care to avoid an openly evangelical posture, maintaining instead a studied silence throughout the novel on the idea of conversion and the advocacy of Christianity – except for a fleeting, but crucial gesture at the very end, something that we shall look at in greater detail subsequently.[18] Thus her strategy is to appeal to a wider readership as she centres her reformist agenda around the ideal of the educated Hindu wife who can successfully interweave school education with the observance of traditional Hindu female domestic rituals, fasts, festivals and poojas.[19] Indeed, in aiming to demonstrate how schooling can coalesce seamlessly with traditional, culturally sanctioned Hindu codes of femininity, dress and customs, she seeks to allay fears about the dangers of an educated wife becoming a dominating 'husband-beater', anxieties about which were often expressed in contemporary vernacular discourse.[20] Thus, far from promoting a 'radical', westernised paradigm of the educated female, she reassuringly projects her heroine as docile and obedient.

Among contemporary debates on female education, the subject of what constituted an 'appropriate' female syllabus was most energetically discussed – clearly betraying underlying fears and insecurities about female emancipation. In this regard, the narrative underlines that Ratanbai's 'modern', 'westernised' school syllabus, which consists of English, grammar, spelling, translation, writing, arithmetic, history and geography, does not by any means pose any threat of destabilising her traditional Hindu identity. Notwithstanding her western-style education, she is praised by her teachers as the 'nicest girl that attends our school', as she remains an epitome of passive dutifulness, believing that her 'duty was to please, and to be most obedient'; when at one point she is forcibly taken out of school by her conservative in-laws, she meekly endures their taunts and cries herself to sleep.[21]

[87]

As in the case of Bengal, in western India too it was male initiative that powered female education, with male family members (for instance, Ratanbai's father) deciding on all such matters. Moreover, as in the case of Bengal, the 'modernising' process in matters pertaining to gender and education often generated familial tensions between western-educated male supporters of 'modernity' and hidebound old female guardians of traditional practices. Indeed, it was generally the aged females in the household who were the bitterest opponents of reform, with old great-aunts and grand-mothers assuming the role of self-appointed custodians of orthodoxy. Thus, the greatest hostility to Ratanbai's schooling comes from women, including from tyrannical senior female in-laws, while in her father's house, her mother and especially an old widowed great-aunt shower opprobrium on her liberal father's westernised ideas: 'What are you going to do by learning?' the old great-aunt shrilly demands to know, 'Where did we go to school? Did we even handle a book?'[22] 'We went to the temples daily and worshipped Maravati', she points out, and grumbles that female literacy will disrupt existing gender hierarchies, 'Are girls going to business now, and will you ask your husbands to mind the home?'[23]

The novel and the social reform issue of high-caste
Hindu widowhood
The novel also forcefully projects the social reform issue of the oppression of high-caste Hindu widows, which had become by the second half of the nineteenth century a widely discussed subject. Reformers, including Pandita Ramabai in her reformist tract *The High-Caste Hindu Woman* (1888), sharply indicted the inhuman treatment meted out to upper-caste widows and espoused widows' education and rehabilitation.[24] The 1829 ban on widow immolation had tragically enough only further exacerbated upper-caste widows' sufferings, subjecting them to a life-long, agonisingly protracted 'cold sati'. Despite the legalisation of widow remarriage by an Act in 1856, remarriage rarely took place and Brahmin widows, including child-widows, were subjected to life-long abuse, privations and ostracism, ranging from starvation and torture, to sexual exploitation by male relatives. Besides being forced to wear the hated 'widow's garb' (consisting in western India of a dull maroon coloured sari), they were subjected to the humiliating disfigurement and trauma of fortnightly head-shaving carried out roughly by male barbers who would callously inflict cuts and injuries.[25] Elaborating on the sexual dangers and exploitation which widows were vulnerable to – sometimes resulting in unwanted pregnancies, prostitution and suicides – Mrs Marcus Fuller, a Bombay-based missionary, noted in 1900 that the Hindu widow's life had become 'hopeless and

intolerable', and often ended in 'a life of shame' or 'in a neighbouring tank or well'.[26]

The agonies of the Brahmin widow are presented in the novel through Tarabai, a young aunt of fourteen who suddenly loses her husband to cholera just a year after marriage. When she is brought back as a widow in a semi-prostrated state to her in-laws' house, the pretty young bride of a year ago has undergone a horrific visual transformation, barely recognisable as the cringing, disfigured, tonsured, de-sexualised creature:

> [H]er head, which was shaved but covered with her *padar*, she knocked it against a huge stone, and became desperate with grief ... The young widow again knocked her forehead against a stone in desperate grief. She would have indeed preferred to have followed her husband on the funeral pile. Her life was a blank now. The light – the god of her life – was no more.[27]

Predictably, it is the orthodox old widowed grand-aunt who hurls the loudest curses, accusing the young widow of having 'killed' her husband: 'The wretch has swallowed our Dinu! Why did she marry him? To eat him up in this way! ... She will surely swallow someone here.'[28]

One of the passionately debated issues of the day in western India, as elsewhere in the country, was the remarriage of upper-caste widows, for which there were associations established by reformers.[29] Instead of advocating widow remarriage as the solution, however, Shevantibai's novel underlines the need for the widow's financial independence through education and employment – echoing Pandita Ramabai's stand on this issue. The aim of Ramabai, who had set up her Sharada Sadan home for high-caste widows in 1889, was to make widowed women in this home 'economically self-reliant and also to provide a viable alternative to an oppressive family environment' and Shevantibai similarly promotes widow employment rather than remarriage.[30] Thus, Tarabai, the young widow who is rescued while trying to commit suicide, is sent to a Widows' Home where she is 'trained as a teacher' and reappears towards the novel's end as a transformed figure: her 'hair ... grown again', clad not in a widow's garb, but in a simple 'reformed dress', looking 'very sweet' and exuding quiet confidence as a teacher in a girls' school.[31]

Gendered encounters across race

We earlier noted how, in the 'modernising' process, interactions with white women (usually missionaries or teachers) served as important mediating points in the dissemination of modernity. While inter-racial gendered transactions – and indeed white missionary women's 'civilising mission' – was premised on the notion of western cultural superiority, this paradigm could sometimes be complicated by the contradictions of inverse racism and caste arrogance. Orthodox Indians considered Europeans ritually impure and their touch defiling – a letter in *The Friend of India and Statesman* in 1883 from a 'native' Bengali gentleman disclosed how even in urban Calcutta zenanas, there were 'thousands upon thousands' of orthodox 'native' women 'who would consider themselves defiled by shaking hands with a European' and that English ladies visiting zenanas were 'most strongly' conscious of a sense of 'loathing' from the 'elderly Hindoo ladies' regarding 'shaking hands ... or even of touching their garments'.[32] This particular instance, even though drawn from Bengal, reflects the widely prevalent Hindu viewpoint about the coloniser's inferior, outcaste position. In Shevantibai's novel too the old great-aunt subjects the British colonisers to the orthodox Hindu gaze as she shrilly screeches her race/caste aversion: 'Who are these English?' she demands to know, 'Are not they incarnations of monkeys? Only the tail is not allowed them.'[33] She loudly laments that under the rule of these outcaste foreigners, all upper-caste Hindus are in imminent danger of losing their caste: 'We are Arya, but our Aryanism is getting all defiled.'[34]

Although inter-racial gendered encounters usually occurred through interactions with European missionaries, with this school not being a missionary institution, the only such encounter occurs briefly when Ratanbai's entire class is invited home to tea by a memsahib, a kindly administrator's wife – an encounter that underlines the paradoxes and contradictions that could complicate these transactions. 'Mrs B', the 'kind and beautiful' memsahib (and the sole white woman in this novel), is warmly hospitable, and the excited Brahmin schoolgirls are enthralled by her beautiful bungalow in the posh neighbourhood of Malabar Hill, with its rich furnishings, mirrors, pictures, silk drapes and satin sofas. Moreover, she is not figured as an arrogant 'burra mem' (senior officer's wife) or a patronising purveyor of imperialist 'civilisation', but as kindly and benevolent.[35] As in the case of the administrator's wife (seen in the previous chapter) in Steel's short story, who had distributed prizes at a girls' school in Punjab, here too, the encounter feeds into the trope of benevolent maternalist imperialism.

At first sight this brief inter-racial encounter does appear to project a transaction imbricated in the hierarchies of race, class and social status, seemingly reifying the memsahib's superior positionality. However, these hierarchies stand complicated by the hierarchy of caste (rooted in the 'native' Brahmin girls' superior caste position), when the Brahmin girls refuse to touch anything from Mrs B's beautifully laden table – except for some ritually permitted fruit, and that too served by a Brahmin servant. As these high-caste girl students eat only fruit and wash their hands *outside* the magnificent house at an 'un-polluting' tap to prevent defilement, the incident sharply throws up the contradictions within the race/class/caste hierarchies which complicated such colonial power relationships.

Historically speaking, female education continued to meet with stiff social resistance in western India (as indeed elsewhere in the country) throughout the late nineteenth century. Hence, Ratanbai's schooling is fiercely opposed by her husband's parents, who are wealthy but uneducated and tradition-minded merchants; they even insinuate at one point that literacy has made her sexually immoral, and accuse her of 'looking at the gardener with evil eye'.[36] However, the nineteenth century also witnessed shifting attitudes, and a generational gap between older, traditional males who frowned upon women's schooling, and younger, western-educated men who encouraged their wives and daughters to study, in order to fit them into the Victorian model of the 'companionate wife'. Indeed, one of the prominent features often noted in this 'modernising' process was exactly this. Such a generation gap can be seen here as well. During a short-lived crisis, Ratanbai is removed from school under pressure from her conservative in-laws and forcibly made to sit idly at home. At that time, the situation is saved by the intervention of her young husband, Pratprao. Like many western-educated men at the turn of the century who wanted to have educated wives, this young husband, studying for his BA at Bombay's Wilson College, strongly opposes his family's stand and insists on her resuming her schooling.

Conversion, 'colonial modernity' and the bhadramahila paradigm
One pertinent issue that needs to be addressed here is the nature of the female paradigm. It is striking how the narrative reveals an *absence* of female agency in Ratanbai – her education being espoused initially by her father and later by her young husband, while she passively accepts their decisions. From the very start, therefore, her insertion into 'colonial modernity' feeds into the image of the female social reform programme as a *male* project, propelled by reformist males such as fathers and husbands. It is historically true, of course, that female education during this period often consisted of husbands schooling their child-wives at home – one of the most enduring images of such tutelage from the Bombay presidency being that of Justice M. R. Ranadive teaching his child-wife, Ramabai, at home in the evenings. However, in the process, Shevantibai's novel suppresses an alternative, historical strand that was also visible in western India, namely, the active female

engagement with reform, as seen in the case of pioneering women like Pandita Ramabai or Rukhmabai.[37]

Instead, Ratanbai's gradual transformation into a 'modern' Indian woman is based upon the Victorian model of femininity – the model of the Bengali *bhadramahila*, which had emerged in the 1860s in Bengal and had spread, as Rosalind O'Hanlon notes, in a diluted form to other regions of urban, middle-class India by the next three decades.[38] As we noted in Chapter 1, the concept of the Bengali *bhadramahila* (genteel woman) combined the Victorian lady's moral goodness and basic education with her role as her husband's companion and helpmeet.[39] Indeed, this new feminine model fused 'older brahminical values of *pativrata*, feminine self-sacrifice, and wifely devotion with a Victorian emphasis upon women as enlightened mothers and companions to men in their own "separate sphere" of the home'.[40] The emerging middle classes found this female paradigm especially appealing and unthreatening since it reinforced the ideology of home and the domestic as the 'sacrosanct domains of tradition and religion'.[41] Female subjectivity or agency was not envisaged and the aim was a limited and moderate concept of 'female education' which would help create helpmates for western-educated husbands in a companionate marriage.

In keeping with this, we find at the novel's close that Ratanbai and her husband are clearly located within the domestic paradigm of a companionate marriage; and as she proceeds to leave her father's house for her marital home, she is projected as her husband's ideal helpmate. At the very end, however, when she finally joins her husband who has now returned with a bar-at-law degree from England, there is a sudden, subtle hint that the young husband has since then secretly converted to Christianity. On Prataprao's writing desk there lies a 'beautifully bound, gilt-edged Book', which attracts the young wife's admiration, and on seeing her reaction, the husband declares, 'I must have this Book on my table every day; there are a great many nice things in it which you must know.' At this, the young wife confesses: 'I have this Book too.'[42] The suggestion seems to be that henceforth, the Bible – which is never named but is only cautiously referred to as the 'Book' – will be their guide in acquiring this domestic companionate ideal.

Thus, the novel concludes rather in the manner of some of the missionary novels we discussed in the first chapter, where husband and wife mutually confess their secret conversion. The text, then, gestures at conversion as a furtherance of the domestic companionate ideal and the young couple are linked together by a secret pact that unites them in Christianity. In the end, this unexpected, sudden, surreptitious shift to an evangelising mode opens up the idea of the importance of conversion to Christianity and echoes the typical conclusion of the missionary novel.

This text was published in London (and not in India) by the Marshall Brothers, who were publishers of books on imperial subjects, and dedicated to Queen Victoria 'with profound gratitude and loyalty', besides carrying a Preface written by the wife of the Governor of Bombay. When the heroine, Ratanbai, tries to incorporate 'progressive' ideas within a largely conventional model of passive femininity she is also shaped by the Victorian ideal of the companionate wife. In other words, the text, revealing the virtual seamless interface between the gender ideologies of Victorian patriarchy and that of westernised Indian patriarchies, exchanges 'native' patriarchy for a western style patriarchal model of femininity. 'Colonial modernity', in Shevantibai's text, is thus scripted very much along a Victorian paradigm, reconstituting patriarchies rather than rejecting them – presenting the feminine ideal of the *bhadramahila*, a sweet and docile acceptor of male decisions within the family.

Conversion as emancipation: Saguna (1895)

If Ratanbai projected the *bhadramahila*, then Krupabai Satthianadhan's novel, *Saguna* (1895), may be said to further the idea of the 'New Indian Woman'. Far more questioning of feminine role models than *Ratanbai*, this complex work of fiction takes a radical stand in its critique of patriarchal practices prevalent in Hindu society, and suggests that Christianity provides a 'modernising' and liberating solution to gender oppression, while at the same time raising questions about the Indian Christian's identity.[43]

Before proceeding further, it would be useful to frame this novel within the turn-of-the-century paradigm of the 'modern', 'New Indian Woman' which had gradually started to emerge by the late nineteenth century, based on a generation of modern Indian women who were highly educated, with some even possessing college degrees.[44] In fact, with the Universities of Bombay and Calcutta opening up to women in the 1880s – soon after London University – this generation of women were in advance of many Englishwomen who had no university education. Not surprisingly, many of these 'advanced' women (as they were sometimes termed), came from Calcutta or Bombay, and especially from the Parsee community in western India, since the Bengal and Bombay presidencies were at the vanguard of education as well as in the matter of gendered social reforms. The hallmark of the 'New Indian Woman' (whose numbers were still small in Indian society) was that she was educated and sometimes held a college degree. She was not necessarily satisfied at being confined to the home like a housewife (as the *bhadramahila* was), but sought fulfilment in a career, most popularly as a physician. It is also striking that this category of 'advanced' Indian women had made an impact on the colonising community's consciousness and projected in a laudatory manner in the writings of a number of contemporary memsahibs, such as Mrs E. F. Chapman and Maud Diver.[45]

Krupabai's novel, hailed in its time as a 'New Woman' text, draws attention to the dilemmas and contradictions of 'colonial modernity' that were faced by the intelligent, western-educated, 'New Indian Woman' protagonist.[46] For the most part, the autobiographical novel echoes the life of its author whose parents, Haripunt and Radhabai Khisty, were among the earliest Brahmins converted to Christianity in the Bombay presidency. Much like her protagonist, Krupabai had her early education at the American Mission in Ahmednagar and like many of her educated female contemporaries from Maharashtra – such as Pandita Ramabai, Rukhmabai and Anandibai Joshi – she too sought to become a doctor to help purdah women. However, she failed to achieve her dreams because of ill-health and although she won a scholarship to study medicine in England, her poor health prevented her from taking it up. Even though she enrolled (as the only female student) in Madras Medical College and topped the list of successful students in the examination, here too she was forced to drop out after a year for reasons of health.[47] Nevertheless, Krupabai always remained passionately interested in social issues pertaining to women and published several articles on the subject (which were later collected together and brought out as *Miscellaneous Writings*).[48] Like so many of her contemporaries, she too attributed gender oppression to the brahminical traditions of high-caste Hindu society and suggested that reprieve lay in what she saw as the more democratic principles of Christianity.[49]

Indeed, conversion to Christianity was one of several strands in the idea of 'colonial modernity', as it took shape in late nineteenth-century Maharashtra. Scholars like Rosalind O'Hanlon and Uma Chakravarti have argued in their study of gender in colonial western India that the convergence of brahminism and patriarchy resulted in particularly oppressive social practices against high-caste women, especially widows.[50] Therefore, conversion to Christianity often held an appeal for high-caste Hindu women who suffered the most from harsh brahminical practices and strictures against women, such as child marriage and the prohibition of widow remarriage. In this regard, Padma Anagol notes how 'Christianity in colonial India was perceived by many women to embody customs that favoured women in contrast to what they saw as the harsh reality of Hinduism.'[51] She argues that in nineteenth- and early twentieth-century western India, many pioneering Brahmin and non-Brahmin women converted to Christianity, the most notable of them being Pandita Ramabai in 1883.[52] This trend continued to be seen in the early twentieth century as well, as in the case of the pioneering female barrister Cornelia Sorabji, whose parents were Christian converts.

Critique of high-caste Hindu practices

Christianity is projected in the narrative as a means of liberation for women from the rampant gender discrimination of traditional high-caste Hindu society. Although, strictly speaking, not an evangelical text, it nevertheless shares certain striking similarities with the missionary novel discussed in Chapter 1. These include a sharp critique of women's abject position in Hindu society, the protagonist's (often secret) embracing of Christianity, followed by a glowing account of gendered existence after conversion. The abject condition of the orthodox Brahmin woman Radha (based on her own Brahmin convert mother's experience) is shown in her traditionally low status within the family, the agony suffered by the child-bride as she is transplanted, weeping, to a marital home ruled by a stern mother-in-law, the coldly distant young husband. Nervous, self-effacing, anxious to please, she represents the abject high-caste Indian woman in a patriarchal brahminical society.

However, Radha's life changes dramatically one night when her young husband, rather in the manner of Mrs Mullens' Brahmin hero in *Faith and Victory*, suddenly discloses that he has secretly embraced Christianity. But as the young couple, expelled from home by furious family elders, depart to start a new phase of life in the Christian section of the town, life for a high-caste convert is shown to be fraught with difficulties and struggles, including ostracism by the Hindu community – bearing out what Eliza Kent has described as the complicated process of conversion that Christian converts had to face.[53] The complex gendered implications of conversion are spelled out especially in the case of Radha, who is actually given no choice in this matter. For her, conversion is a highly traumatic experience: weeping and appalled at the thought of the religion of 'untouchables' and *pariahs* and their filthy food (which she shrinks from accepting), Radha has no option but to eventually accept her husband's decision. Paradoxically therefore, she thus remains very much within the paradigm of the obedient and passive Hindu wife who, bound by patriarchy, has to follow her husband's wishes. Till the very end, therefore, although formally a Christian, she retains several Hindu practices pertaining to food, diet and living habits, including the orthodox Maharashtrian Brahmin mode of wearing a nine yard sari.

In congruence with Bernard Cohn's argument about the symbolic significance of clothing in the colonial context (that we also took note of in the previous chapter), it is significant how clothing is shown to symbolically separate European Christians (i.e. missionaries) from Indian Christian converts on grounds of both race and class. In her study of conversions in colonial south India, Eliza Kent has observed how dress was often considered an important marker of 'civilisation' and westernisation among converts: 'One of the most striking ways in which Indian Christians asserted their new identities and claims to respectability was through dress. In nineteenth-century and early twentieth-century south India, visual presentations of the self were key components in the assertion of status.'[54] Consequently, Radha's obstinate (and effectively defiant) retaining of her 'heathen', Hindu way of dressing places her in an inferior position in the eyes of the missionaries. At the same time, dress is also a marker of class, and not only of race – hence, when 'native' Christians wear poor quality western clothing, they too are looked down upon by European missionaries. For instance, when, as a young girl, Saguna, who is dressed in badly cut western clothes and clumsy shoes, encounters an arrogant young white girl, the latter immediately makes her painfully feel 'all the deficiencies in my dress'.[55]

Notwithstanding all these contradictions in her experience of Christianity, however, gendered life after conversion is shown to bring about a significant degree of enfranchisement. Indeed, Krupabai reiterated in a number of her other writings as well that Christianity brought about a liberation from the oppressive Hindu traditions that devalued women.[56] Eliza Kent has argued that companionate marriage was an important aspect of elite Indian Christian life.[57] Indeed, one of the declared cultural objectives behind the agenda of conversion was to encourage companionship between husbands and wives. Radha's relationship with her husband is shown to undergo a change from the cold and formal Hindu style of marital interaction, to a more informal, western-style domesticity.

Undoubtedly, it is the second generation of female converts who are shown to benefit from the greater opportunities that conversion offers. For them Christianity is, to a very large degree, an emancipatory, liberating vehicle of 'colonial modernity', offering western education as well as an entry into the public sphere. Saguna, as one of the brightest of Radha's several children, epitomises this 'modern', educated 'New Indian Woman' of the second generation. Displaying far greater female subjectivity than her mother did, she aspires to be a doctor and even rejects the idea of marriage as a female goal, pointing out in a radical fashion that 'Marriage is not the goal of every girl's ambition.'[58]

Encounters with missionaries, memsahibs and colonial racism
Nevertheless, Saguna's experience of conversion and 'colonial modernity' is rent by ambivalences, especially because of the fact that she and her family are 'native' Christians living under white colonial rule. Krupabai's narrative displays the anguish of the 'native' Christian as it uncovers the problem of missionary racism in a colonial context, thereby overturning the simple optimism of the missionary novel. Although by virtue of being Christians, her family associates closely with British missions and missionaries, most of these encounters, as she increasingly finds, are underlined by colonial racism. An early eye-opener for her is a childhood visit to an 'Indian Christian village' where she notices that at Church, the chief European missionary benignly accepts greetings of 'Salaam! Papa' from the 'native' congregation (suggestive of a paternalistic relationship) – but at all other times he demands that they address him deferentially as 'Sahib' (that is, 'master'). Again, during a courtesy call made to that same missionary's house, she and her mother are humiliated: both of them are deliberately kept standing in order to underline their inferiority – while the missionary's wife arrogantly seats herself on a chair. Moreover, when Saguna, eager to display her sharp intellect to the missionary's daughter, seeks to borrow some books, the latter disdainfully eyes her up and down, with a superior smile: 'She raised her eyebrows … "You read? You can't read what I read. You won't understand."'[59]

Historically, white women missionaries played a pivotal role in these colonial transactions through evangelical as well as reform activities – as Padma Anagol notes: 'When Indian Christian women forged links with the West, an important mediator was the white female missionary.'[60] The bulk of these gendered encounters across race were with European women missionaries – although sometimes there were occasional interactions with memsahibs (administrators' wives), on occasions such as during the latter's visits to school for the distribution of prizes. Wives of colonial bureaucrats, as we saw in the short fiction of Steel in the previous chapter, who were usually ignorant of the local language and insulated from 'native' life and culture, tended to be demonised in colonial discourse as racist, and as repositories of class prejudice. In contrast, missionary women who spoke the vernacular fluently and worked closely with 'native' women in their homes, were projected in colonial discourse as free from racism.

In this regard, it is striking to note that in both the novels under discussion there is, in fact, an *inversion* in the representation of gendered inter-racial relationships. In *both* instances, it is the encounters with memsahibs or administrators' wives which turn out to be free of both overt and covert racism – in contrast to their troubled interactions with the supposedly kind missionaries. As in the case of Ratanbai, the heroine in this novel too discovers in an encounter with a European Collector's wife a surprising absence of the racial arrogance and humiliation that she had suffered at the hands of missionaries. The memsahib is all kindness; she takes Saguna and her sister inside her home, makes them sit beside her and speaks 'so sweetly and gently' to them: 'She asked what I learnt, gave me cake and tea, and I felt as if I were talking to my sister.'[61] One may speculate that the memsahibs shown interacting with 'native' schoolgirls in these works of fiction may have been playing the role of the benevolent maternalist imperialist. But the fact remains that they neither humiliate the young Indian girls they meet nor do they make insinuations about their own race, class, cultural or social superiority.

In other words, the novel throws into sharp focus the contradictions in these inter-racial gendered encounters with different categories of white women, testifying thereby to what Padma Anagol has called, 'tensions between Indian Christian women and their Western sisters'. Such tensions, Anagol has argued, 'increased towards the end of the nineteenth century', with the result that 'Indian Christian women were themselves active in criticising Western missionary attitudes towards Indian culture and Indians'.[62] Moreover, it has sometimes been noted that overt colonial racism was reportedly higher among whites of the lower classes in colonial India and hence these experiences perhaps also gesture at complex, intricate links between class and racism.[63]

Indeed, it is striking how missionaries in this novel are shown up as racist – in sharp divergence from the constructions of the female evangelical that we saw in the previous two chapters. They are neither the kindly, much-loved figures of missionary accounts, nor the servile, eager-to-please mission women of Steel's short fiction. Instead, right through the novel, Saguna's interactions with white missionary teachers – and hence with western culture – is shown to be frictional and conflict-ridden. Moreover, time and again, she finds the much-vaunted promise of female educational opportunities being systematically subverted.

What is more, her reaction is a spirited resistance of this everyday racism and humiliation from evangelicals. When, on the occasion mentioned earlier, she and her mother are kept standing at the local missionary's house, Saguna defiantly pulls up a chair and seats her mother on it (unlike her mother's meek acquiescence: 'they are white and we are black; we ought to be thankful for the little notice that they take of us').[64] Later on, when a white female evangelical humiliates a Bible-woman (who happens to be of Brahmin origin and is a friend of her family), by contemptuously describing her as 'no better than a servant', Saguna retaliates furiously.[65] Stung by this display of European race/class arrogance, she counters it with her own brand of what may be called 'caste arrogance'. She bursts out angrily, reminding the missionary lady that the despised Bible-woman, being a high-caste Brahmin convert, is actually the missionary's superior: 'You are middle-class people ... you are not Brahmins. You are *Sudras*. We are the real aristocrats of this place.'[66]

By hitting out thus, Saguna touches a raw nerve regarding British sensitivities on the issue of caste/class hierarchies. As we saw earlier, and shall be encountering in subsequent chapters as well, the British were considered as outcastes from the perspective of the caste system. What is more, evidently sensitive about this 'untouchable' status, they often employed terms such as 'white Brahmins' and 'ruling caste' to denote themselves – in an apparent attempt to re-inscribe themselves into the power dynamics of the caste system in the colonial imaginary.

Female education and contradictions in colonial Christianity
Even more seriously, the novel raises questions about the brand of Christianity being practised in the colonies by missionaries, as well as its ability to further the intellectual aspirations of women. It reveals the much-vaunted promise of Christianity offering intellectual educational opportunities to women, to be completely hollow. For instance, the same 'racist' female European missionary mentioned earlier (with whom Saguna boards), who initially appears very warm and friendly turns out to be hierarchical and prone to violent fits of temper and mood-swings. Worse still, she actively discourages Saguna's intellectual aspirations; when the young girl eagerly tries to display her quick intellect, she only finds herself being snubbed: 'you know a little too much', she is reprimanded, 'When a horse goes too fast, what does his master do?'[67]

Indeed, throughout, the novel maps the contours of Saguna's increasing disillusionment with the missionary version of 'colonial modernity'. Time and again, her efforts at intellectual growth are stifled. Besides, the colonial version of Christianity turns out to be a narrow 'sin and devil' brand of Christianity. When she later joins a missionary-run school for young 'native' Christian girls in Bombay, she finds the white female teachers intolerant and practising a narrow form of religion that stunts any intellectual growth. The sharpness of her mind is, in fact, frowned upon: 'You may think your intellectual attainments are great', she is admonished, 'but the devil, too, is clever.'[68]

The only teacher to appreciate her intellectual aspirations is a brilliant, eccentric, unpopular American 'lady doctor', who is 'the radical element' in the school, who keeps aloof from her colleagues and disregards all the Mission's ordinances.[69] This white woman encourages her to become a doctor, and at the time of leaving the country, arranges for Saguna's study in England, making arrangements for the expenses to be shared equally by a wealthy philanthropic lady, as well as the Mission. However, Saguna's dreams about becoming a doctor are soon dashed to the ground. Opposition comes, once again, from a missionary – this time, from a pleasant, soft-spoken, white male missionary whom she formerly hero-worshipped. It is this 'Mr A–', who is in charge at the Mission for arranging her visit to England, who suddenly terminates the plan on health grounds, 'I would not recommend you to go ... you would not stand the climate and the hard strain.'[70] Using the very same patriarchal arguments that were being deployed in contemporary Britain to debar women from the universities and medical colleges, he warns that, 'The feeling even in England is very strong against a girl learning medicine, and here it is stronger still.'[71]

Indeed, contemporary Victorian England was witnessing a raging controversy over the subject of women's higher education and one of the central arguments used to oppose it was exactly that of women's allegedly 'weak' health ('The health of women cannot stand much evening reading').[72] Conservative sections in Britain fiercely resisted women's entry into universities and medical colleges, citing 'scientific' studies which, they claimed, had clearly indicated the harmful effects of excessive study on female menstrual cycles, and especially on a woman's ability to conceive.

In colonial India too, this stand was echoed and university education for women was strongly opposed (although some universities did open up to women around the same time as in England). For instance, Mrs Wheeler, a 'native' Christian, who was Inspectress of Schools in Bengal in the 1890s, claimed that university-educated Indian women 'become arrogant, are seldom successful as teachers, and frequently develop hysteria and nervous complaints. It is too great a brain effort with no hereditary preparation.'[73] Higher education was opposed primarily on grounds of health, the argument being that 'the premature development of mind and body rest upon no solid foundation of physical strength'.[74] Indeed, many of the early deaths of several gifted, educated Indian women, such as Toru Dutt in Bengal, or Anandibai Joshi in Bombay who died of tuberculosis a year after obtaining her medical degree from Philadelphia in 1886, were attributed to their being highly educated. In other words, Saguna's 'feminist individual-ism' comes into collision with both traditional 'native' (Hindu) as well as western (Christian) patriarchies and gender norms.[75]

Saguna, bitterly disillusioned by the only white missionary whom she had admired – 'He had been to me the ideal of goodness and nobility ... now he appeared calm, cold, and calculating' – now enrols in a medical college at Madras, as permitted by him, 'You can stay in India and learn', although in the very same breath, he warns her about the 'consequences' of studying medicine even in India:[76]

> Are you ready to brave opposition, loneliness and life in a strange place and among strangers? ... You will have to bear a great deal.[77]

Left with no other option but to enrol at the medical college at Madras, Saguna once again finds herself facing patriarchal discrimination from male fellow-students. Her traditional appearance (head covered with a shawl) elicits loud, curious remarks: 'I heard the students whisper: I say, "a live Zenana", "Orthodox Brahminee", "Gosha woman."'[78] Bent on proving herself, Saguna puts herself through a punishing schedule of study, but so dented is her confidence that she is 'surprised' when she finds she has 'stood highest in my class' in the examination.[79] This, however, results in a severe health breakdown which leaves her permanently weakened – putting an end to her short stint at the medical college and cutting short her intellectual aspirations. Whether one is to read her illness and eventual dropping out of medical college, as feeding into that very same patriarchal myth (i.e. of female unfitness for higher education on health grounds) that the author is trying to demolish is of course a moot point. Perhaps one must bear in mind that, since the narrative is autobiographical, its boundaries of emplotment are by self-definition, thereby limited.

Be that as it may, the novel ends with Saguna's retreat from the larger theatre of public life and finding happiness through the conventional outlet of marriage – something she had always spurned. However, this marriage is not arranged by her relatives in the 'native' manner, but is based on free choice, equality and mutual respect – as she meets, falls in love with and marries the son of a high-caste, highly regarded Indian Christian, who has recently returned from his studies in England. The happy companionate relationship that results from this union seemingly echoes the ending of *Ratanbai*. But this union is rooted in far greater equality than is Ratanbai's companionate marriage. It also needs to be underlined that the ideal gendered goal presented in this novel is not marriage but a medical career and participation in a wider public sphere – aspirations which are explored and reluctantly set aside because of circumstances (her poor health), and only then is she fitted into the role of the clergyman's companionate wife. Nevertheless, the fact remains that larger aspirations and possibilities are explored before being discarded.

Indian Christians and the problem of identity

Finally, one important problem that this text addresses and needs to be emphasised is the problem of Indian Christian identity, which further problematised the notion of the 'civilising mission'. Conversion was of course a product of the missionary 'civilising mission'. But being an Indian Christian was quite distinct from being a European Christian in colonial India. Given the colonial context, an Indian Christian identity was inevitably loaded with dilemmas and contradictions for the community as a whole and, increasingly, there were debates on 'indigenism' as the century progressed. Perhaps, most importantly, the aspect of caste refused to leave the consciousness of high-caste converts, who ended up keeping themselves distinct from low-caste Christian masses.[80]

After her marriage to Samuel Satthianadhan, Krupabai was closely linked with her in-laws, the Satthianadhans, who were a prominent, highly respected Indian Christian family based in Madras. Eliza Kent and Eunice de Souza, among others, have highlighted her marital family's origins and their missionary activism.[81]

For Krupabai (as for many other Indian Christians), the rejection of Hindu social and religious identities by 'native' Christians created the problem of acculturation and posed the danger of creating mimic men and women who would blindly ape western colonial culture – and their colonial masters. She stresses upon the need for Indian Christians to retain their own cultural habits and identity; at one point in the novel, Saguna sharply reprimands an England-returned youth, who calls England 'home' and sneers at everything 'native', by reminding him, 'Surely that is not your home? Your home is here … It is really disgusting to see how many of you imitate the English in manners, dress and other superficial things without imbibing their liberal spirit – that spirit which gives to a woman equal privileges with man, and credits her with noble and disinterested actions'.[82]

Conclusion

We can perhaps make some tentative speculations about the impact of the 'civilising mission' on western-educated Indian women around the turn of the century, through our examination of the two texts. No doubt these writings were a product of a complex process of cross-cultural interactions, missionary efforts at conversion, female education and emancipatory ideas about gender and female subjectivities.

As texts that were written in English by educated Indian Christian women of Brahmin origin, they marked the intersection of several strands pertaining to race, gender, culture, religious and national identities. They were the product of the convergence of several factors in the last decade of the century, such as western education, exposure to Christian ideas, the beginnings of women's entry into the public sphere, a radical 'native' gender movement born out of a rejection of Brahmin orthodoxy, and an interest in the nineteenth-century 'Woman Question'. How did these educated Indian woman respond, react to and negotiate western culture, 'colonial modernity' as well as gendered encounters across race in the nineteenth century? While the most striking factor linking together both texts was their use of English as a vehicle of communication, these contemporaneous writings by two women who were personally engaged in female education, negotiated the questions of conversion, female emancipation, critical appraisal of 'native' and western patriarchies in divergent ways. They pursued distinct trajectories, widely divergent views on reform, conversion and gender paradigms. Shevantibai's focus on the need for female education was seamlessly intertwined with an effort at re-casting the high-caste Hindu wife as a companionate helpmeet, that is to say, to project a Maharashtrian version of the Bengali *bhadramahila* – without disturbing existing gender equations or cultural traditions. In her moderate, reformist perspective, the exemplary feminine model of Indian womanhood was that of the docile Hindu female, eager to please, lacking in agency or female subjectivity – a passive recipient of male, familial educational initiatives and male restrictions. It was a demonstration on how an educated wife/daughter-in-law could fit into the traditional Sati-Savitri role. In fact, even when at the very end, the novel covertly gestured at conversion to Christianity, the gender paradigm remained the same.

In contrast, Krupabai's far more radical perspective sharply interrogated issues connected with the 'civilising mission', such as conversion, colonialism, female subjectivities and 'colonial modernity'. In place of the mild and obedient *bhadramahila*, she valorised the turn-of-the-century paradigm of the 'New Indian Woman': that of the educated, independent-minded woman who raises her voice against patriarchy, and seeks a place for herself beyond the narrow confines of domesticity, rejecting the traditional Victorian notion of marriage as the sole female goal.[83] While valorising the positive aspects of conversion to Christianity, she interrogates at the same time its promise of greater emancipatory potential for females. Dismantling the paradigm of the middle-class European woman that was enjoined by missionary writings, she critically interrogates the prospects of female emancipation by exposing the existing western patriarchal prejudices against women's entry into universities in Britain.

Equally importantly, perhaps, Krupabai contested some important tropes which were part and parcel of missionary discourse. The first trope, as we saw in this book's opening chapter, was the construct of a loving sisterhood (or perhaps, more accurately, a mother–child relationship) between female evangelicals and middle-class 'native' women. Time and again, as Chapter 1 showed us, missionary writings underlined the close and loving bond they shared with Indian zenana women who would call out from their rooftops, begging them to come and visit them. Krupabai dismantles this trope of loving sisterhood by 'returning the gaze', and revealing the overt and covert racism among European missionaries who practice a form of 'colonial Christianity'. She thus subjects to critical scrutiny the rabid racism and class contradictions that sometimes underlay inter-racial encounters with missionaries.

Moreover, her novel debates the important issue of identity, especially Indian Christian identity, which was a particularly vexed question at the turn of the century, carrying with it the negative resonance of the 'colonial colluder', against the background of the Indian national movement. This problem of identity was indeed a question that troubled Indian Christians and emphasis was laid upon the need to reject a highly westernised or Anglicised identity and inculcate a distinct 'Indian' identity (as does Krupabai), rather than blindly ape the colonising culture. Thus, she 'returns the colonial gaze', radically interrogating issues such as conversion, colonial modernities and demonstrating how Christianity's female emancipatory possibilities are undercut by ambivalences.

Notes

An earlier version of this chapter first appeared in the Centre for Women's Development Studies' *Indian Journal of Gender Studies*, 21:1, February (2014), pp. 1–26, published by Sage Publications.

1 Both novels are briefly discussed in Eunice de Souza, 'Recovering a Tradition: Forgotten Women's Voices', *Economic and Political Weekly*, April 29 (2006), pp. 1642–1645.

2 As discussed in earlier chapters, while initially a wide range of social practices were targeted (such as widow immolation, polygamy, infant marriage, female infanticide, enforced female illiteracy, the prohibition of widow remarriage and the practice of female seclusion), the focus increasingly shifted to addressing the problem of female illiteracy through the promotion of education.

3 Other reform organisations included: the Marathi Dnyan Prasarak Sabha ('Marathi Society for the Spread of Knowledge') founded in 1848 by a group of reformers and students of the Elphinstone College; the Paramhansa Mandali ('Society of the Supreme Being') founded in the 1840s by Dadoba Pandurang; and the Vidhava

Vivahottejak Mandal (Society for the Promotion of Widow Remarriage) founded by Vishnu Shastri Pandit in 1865. All of them promoted widow remarriage and female education. For further details, see Rosalind O'Hanlon, *Caste, Conflict and Ideology: Mahatma Jotirao Phule and Low-caste Protest in Nineteenth Century Western India* (Cambridge, Cambridge University Press, 2002), pp. 95–102. See also Parimala Rao, *Foundations of Tilak's Nationalism: Discrimination, Education and Hindutva* (New Delhi, Orient Blackswan, 2010), pp. 96–137.

4 For details about the non-Brahmin movement led by Jotirao Phule (1827–1890) and supported by his wife, Savitribai (1831–1897), which posed a powerful challenge to Brahmin power, see O'Hanlon, *Caste, Conflict and Ideology.*

5 While Pandita Ramabai (1858–1922), who spear-headed the struggle against the oppression of widows and set up homes for widows, was a Brahmin (and later, a Christian convert), Tarabai Shinde's (1850–1910) is a fine example of the questioning of gendered and caste inequities by a lower-caste woman, seen in her *Stripurush-tulana* (A Comparison between Men and Women) (Pune, Sri Shivaji Press, 1882), originally published in Marathi in 1882. Tarabai was also an associate of Jotirao and Savitribai Phule. See Rosalind O'Hanlon (ed.), *A Comparison Between Women and Men: Tarabai Shinde and the Critique of Gender Relations in Colonial India* (Delhi, Oxford University Press, 1994). See also Meera Kosambi, 'Indian Response to Christianity, Church and Colonialism: The Case of Pandita Ramabai', *Economic and Political Weekly*, 27:43–44, 24–31 October (1992), pp. WS61–WS63, and Uma Chakravarti, *Rewriting History: The Life and Times of Pandita Ramabai* (New Delhi, Kali for Women, 1998).

6 These included the Prarthana Samaj ('Prayer Society') formed in 1867 by Atmaram Pandurang and subsequently supported by a few liberal Bombay Brahmins, the Satyashodhak Samaj ('Truth-seeking Society') founded in 1873 by Jotirao Phule, the leader of the non-Brahmin movement, which set up schools for low-caste women and homes for widows, and the Arya Mahila Samaj ('Noble-minded Women's Association') founded in 1882 by Pandita Ramabai. All of them promoted widow remarriage and female education. For details see O'Hanlon, *Caste, Conflict and Ideology*, pp. 95–102, and Rao, *Foundations of Tilak's Nationalism*, Chapter 3, pp. 96–137. However, it needs to be pointed out that later in the period, conservative nationalist leaders and Hindu revivalists opposed many of these issues, including gender reform. Consequently, by the 1890s, social reform for women gradually receded from the forefront of nationalist politics and debate (See O'Hanlon, *A Comparison Between Women and Men*, pp. 15–17; Rao, *Foundations of Tilak's Nationalism*). On this latter point, see also Partha Chatterjee, 'The Nationalist Resolution to the Women's Question', in Kumkum Sangari and Sudesh Vaid (eds), *Recasting Women: Essays in Colonial History* (New Delhi, Kali for Women, 1989), pp. 233–253.

7 This can be seen in the memoir of Ramabai Ranade (1863–1924), the wife of the reformer Justice M. G. Ranade, who was to a large extent taught at home by her husband when she was a child-wife. For details, see Ramabai Ranade, *Ranade: His Wife's Reminiscences*, trans. Kusumavati Deshpande ([1910], New Delhi, Publications Division, Ministry of Information and Broadcasting, Government of India, 1963). See also Chakravarti, *Rewriting History*.

8 In Bengal Chandramukhi Basu (1860–1944) and Kadambini Ganguly (1861–1923) became the first graduates from the University of Calcutta in 1883. The University of Bombay opened admission to women in 1883 and Cornelia Sorabji (1866–1954) became the first BA in 1888. Kadambini Ganguly became a doctor, graduating from the Calcutta Medical College in 1886. In Bombay the medical profession attracted women such as Anandibai Joshi (1865–1887) and Rukhmabai (1864–1955), while Cornelia Sorabji (1866–1954) was one of the earliest women to become a lawyer. For details see Geraldine Forbes, *Women in Modern India*, The New Cambridge History of India, Vol. IV.2 (Cambridge, Cambridge University Press, 2000), pp. 32–53.

9 According to O'Hanlon, as late as the early nineteenth century, colonial accounts

mention how in the Maratha camps, 'women ride on horseback, without taking any pains to conceal their faces; they gallop about and make their way through the throng with as much boldness ... as the men', T. D. Broughton, *Letters from a Mahratta Camp During the Year 1809*, London, 1892, cited in O'Hanlon, *A Comparison Between Women and Men*, p. 22.

10 Padma Anagol, *The Emergence of Feminism in India, 1850–1920* (Hampshire and Burlington, Ashgate, 2005), pp. 32–35.

11 The first school for girls in Bombay was opened by the American Missionary Society in 1824.

12 Gauri Vishwanathan notes that conversion is at the 'nexus of spiritual and material interests'. It is not just the acceptance of a personal religious belief but is also linked to struggles against worldly oppressions like sexism, racism and colonialism, and is thus connected with the 'politics of identity', see Gauri Vishwanathan, *Outside the Fold: Conversion, Modernity and Belief* (New Delhi, Oxford University Press, 2001), pp. xxvi–xxviii. For the impact of European missionaries and Christian ideas on reform in western India see O'Hanlon, *Caste, Conflict and Ideology*, pp. 50–87.

13 For details see Introduction, Indrani Sen (ed.), *Memsahibs' Writings: Colonial Narratives on Indian Women* (New Delhi, Orient BlackSwan, 2008), pp. ix–xxix.

14 Shevantibai Nikambe, *Ratanbai: A Sketch of a Bombay High Caste Hindu Young Wife* (London, Marshall Brothers, 1895). All citations are from the modern re-issue of the text, Chandani Lokuge (ed.), Shevantibai Nikambe, *Ratanbai: A High-caste Child-wife* (New Delhi, Oxford University Press, 2004).

15 According to Chandani Lokuge, the editor of the modern re-issue of the text of *Ratanbai*, Shevantibai was born in Poona in 1865, matriculated from St Peter's High School, Bombay in 1884 and was connected with female schooling in Bombay in various capacities during the 1880s and 1890s – as headmistress of two girls' schools and as inspector of primary girls' schools. She served in Ramabai's Sharada Sadan High School in 1889 but after it shifted to Poona a year later, she established her own school, 'The Married Women's School', in 1890 in Bombay and remained its headmistress till 1934. She also twice visited Europe and America to study Christian work and educational methods. In 1928 she was a delegate at the Second All India Women's Conference on Educational Reform held in Delhi. See Introduction, Lokuge (ed.), Nikambe, *Ratanbai*, pp. xi–xii.

16 Shevantibai Nikambe, *Ratanbai: A Sketch of a Bombay High Caste Hindu Young Wife* (London, Marshall Brothers, 1895). All citations are from the modern re-issue of the text, Chandani Lokuge (ed.), Shevantibai Nikambe, *Ratanbai: A High-caste Child-wife*.

17 Lokuge (ed.), Nikambe, *Ratanbai*, p. 14.

18 Besides, the novel is more or less silent on the related reform issue of child marriage, offering only a mild, indirect critique through the brief periods of petty tyrannies she suffers during her visits to her in-laws.

19 This is rather rare. Most novels and other writings authored by Indian Christians generally promoted conversion as a means of liberation from brahminical patriarchy. See Padma Anagol, 'Indian Christian Women and Indigenous Feminism, c.1850– c.1920' in Clare Midgley (ed.), *Gender and Imperialism* (Manchester, Manchester University Press, 1998), pp. 95–96.

20 For details related to satirical Bengali vernacular tracts and sketches, see Partha Chatterjee, 'The Nationalist Resolution of the Women's Question', in Kumkum Sangari and Sudesh Vaid (eds), *Recasting Women: Essays in Colonial History* (New Delhi, Kali for Women, 1989), pp. 233–253.

21 Lokuge (ed.), Nikambe, *Ratanbai*, pp. 18, 15.

22 *Ibid.*, p. 35.

23 *Ibid.*, pp. 35, 24.

24 Pandita Ramabai, *The High-Caste Hindu Woman* (Philadelphia, n.p, 1888).

25 For details about the agonising head-shaving, see Parvatibai Athavale, *Hindu Widow: An Autobiography*, trans. Rev. Justin E. Abbott ([1930], New Delhi, Reliance Publishing House, 1986), pp. 46–54.

26 Mrs Marcus Fuller, *The Wrongs of Indian Womanhood*, with an Introduction by Pandita Ramabai (Edinburgh and London, Oliphant Anderson and Ferrier, 1900), pp. 52–53. The suicide by a pregnant Brahmin widow led Tarabai Shinde to write her *Stri-purush-tulana* in 1885.

27 Lokuge (ed.), Nikambe, *Ratanbai*, p. 26.

28 *Ibid.*

29 The Society for the Promotion of Widow Remarriage, formed in 1865, did valuable work for more than two decades. For details see Meera Kosambi, 'Life after Widowhood: Two Radical Reformist Options in Maharashtra', in Meera Kosambi (ed.), *Intersections: Socio-Cultural Trends in Maharashtra* (New Delhi, Orient Longman, 2000), pp. 100–101. See also Rosalind O'Hanlon, 'Issues of Widowhood: Gender and Resistance in Colonial Western India', in Douglas Haynes and Gyan Prakash (eds), *Contesting Power: Resistance and Everyday Social Relations in South Asia* (Delhi, Oxford University Press, 1991), pp. 62–108.

30 Kosambi, 'Life after Widowhood, p. 102.

31 Lokuge (ed.), Nikambe, *Ratanbai*, p. 56.

32 *The Friend of India and Statesman* (21 July 1883), p. 1049.

33 Lokuge (ed.), Nikambe, *Ratanbai.*, p. 35.

34 *Ibid.*

35 *Ibid.*, p. 34. The memsahib is not held out as an ideal model of womanhood to be emulated by the Indian girls, quite unlike the white missionary's genteel wife in Hannah Mullens' missionary novel *Faith and Victory*, which we examined in Chapter 1.

36 Lokuge (ed.), Nikambe, *Ratanbai*, p. 54.

37 Rukhmabai (1864–1955), the educated wife whose refusal to live with her unlettered husband resulted in a court case for the 'restitution of conjugal rights', later became a doctor. See Sudhir Chandra, *Enslaved Daughters: Colonialism, Law and Women's Rights* ([1998], New Delhi, Oxford University Press, 2008).

38 Introduction, O'Hanlon, *A Comparison Between Women and Men*, p. 14.

39 Meredith Borthwick, *The Changing Role of Women in Bengal, 1849–1905* (Princeton, Princeton University Press, 1984), pp. 54–59.

40 Introduction, O'Hanlon, *A Comparison Between Women and Men*, p. 14.

41 *Ibid.*, p. 15.

42 Lokuge (ed.), Nikambe, *Ratanbai*, p. 59.

43 Krupabai Satthianadhan, *Saguna: A Story of Native Christian Life*, with a Preface by Mrs R. S. Benson (Madras, Srinivasa Varadachari, 1895). All citations are from the modern re-issue of the text: Chandani Lokuge (ed.), Krupabai Satthianadhan, *Saguna: The First Autobiographical Novel in English by an Indian Woman* (Delhi, Oxford University Press, 1998).

44 This dimension is touched upon in Chapter 4 of Narin Hassan, *Diagnosing Empire: Women, Medical Knowledge, and Colonial Mobility* (London, Ashgate, 2011), pp. 89–105.

45 Mrs E. F. (Georgina) Chapman's *Sketches of Some Distinguished Indian Women* (London and Calcutta, W. H. Allen & Co. Ltd, 1891), paid tribute to pioneering Indian women from Bengal and Bombay, including Toru Dutt (the poet), Chandramukhi Bose (the first female MA from Calcutta University in 1884), Kadambini Ganguly (the first medical graduate), Pandita Ramabai Saraswati, Anandibai Joshi (the first foreign-trained doctor), and Cornelia Sorabji (pioneering barrister). Other contemporary writings on this topic include: Mary Frances Billington, *Woman in India* (London, Chapman & Hall, 1895), and the second section of Maud Diver, *The Englishwoman in India* (Edinburgh and London, William Blackwood & Sons, 1909).

46 Among contemporary reviewers, *The Queen* noted that 'Saguna shows the "new" India woman beside the old'; while Mary Frances Billington remarked in *The Daily Telegraph*, that it was 'a study of the "New Woman" as she is in Indian surroundings'; cited in Kristine Swenson, *Medical Women and Victorian Fiction* (Missouri, University of Missouri Press, 2005), p. 194.

47 In 1881, Krupabai married Samuel Satthianadhan, son of a prominent Indian

convert and missionary from Madras, Rev. W. T. Satthianadhan. She published numerous articles in journals like the *South Indian Observer* and the *National Indian Journal*. Her novel *Saguna* first appeared in serialised form in the *Madras Christian College Magazine* during 1887–1888, and was published as a book post-humously by a Madras-based publishing house, Srinivasa Varadachari & Co. After her early death from tuberculosis, a scholarship for women was set up at the Madras Medical College and a memorial medal for the best female Matriculation candidate at the University of Madras.

48   Krupabai Satthianadhan, *Miscellaneous Writings of Krupabai Satthianadhan* (Madras, Srinivasa Varadachari & Co., 1896).

49   See Krupabai's essays, where she takes up themes such as the critique of women's oppression in Hinduism, the construction of women as promiscuous, sinful crea-tures, the problem of social tyranny, the need for women's education and marriage not being women's only goal in life: 'Woman's Influence at Home'; 'Home Training of Children'; 'Female Education'; and 'Hindu Social Customs' in Satthianadhan, *Miscellaneous Writings*, pp. 1–33, cited in the discussion on Krupabai in Anagol, *Emergence of Feminism in India*, pp. 31–34.

50   See Chakravarti, *Rewriting History*. Pandita Ramabai's delineation of the inhuman treatment of women, especially widows, in her *The High-Caste Hindu Woman* generated a wide interest in the tyranny of brahminical patriarchy.

51   Anagol, 'Indian Christian Women and Indigenous Feminism', p. 93.

52   Notable converts included Soonderbai Powar (1856–1921), daughter of first-genera-tion Christians (Ganderbai and Ramachandra), and an associate of Pandita Ramabai. She wrote *Hinduism and Womanhood* (London, Christian Workers' Depot, n.d.); an earlier version of which was titled, *The Bitter Truths of Hinduism*, published in the 1890s. For details see Anagol, 'Indian Christian Women and Indigenous Feminism'; for a discussion on conversion see also Eliza F. Kent, *Converting Women: Gender and Protestant Christianity in Colonial South India* (New York, Oxford University Press, 2004), pp. 187–190.

53   See Kent, *Converting Women*, p. 187. Krupabai vividly describes her father-in-law's mixed emotions during conversion in her essay, 'The Story of a Conversion' (1893). For details see Eunice de Souza (ed.), *The Satthianadhan Family Album: Miscellaneous Writings of the Members of the Satthianadhan Family* (New Delhi, Sahitya Akademi, 2005), pp. 1–24.

54   Kent, *Converting Women*, p. 199.

55   Lokuge (ed.), Satthianadhan, *Saguna*, p. 99.

56   See Satthianadhan, *Miscellaneous Writings*.

57   Kent, *Converting Women*, pp. 180–187.

58   Lokuge (ed.), Satthianadhan, *Saguna*, p. 149.

59   *Ibid.*, p. 99.

60   Anagol, 'Indian Christian Women and Indigenous Feminism', p. 94.

61   Lokuge (ed.), Satthianadhan, *Saguna*, p. 99.

62   Anagol, 'Indian Christian Women and Indigenous Feminism', p. 96.

63   G. O. Trevelyan noted that racism was higher among the lower classes of whites in colonial India, in *The Competitionwallah* (London, Macmillan & Co., 1864).

64   Lokuge (ed.), Satthinadhan, *Saguna*, p. 99.

65   *Ibid.*, p. 115.

66   *Ibid.*

67   *Ibid.*, p. 114.

68   *Ibid.*, p. 132.

69   *Ibid.*, p. 140.

70   *Ibid.*, p. 150.

71   *Ibid.*, p. 151.

72   Elizabeth Sewell, *Principles of Education* (1865), in Patricia Hollis (ed.), *Women in Public, 1850–1900: Documents of the Victorian Women's Movement* (London, George Allen & Unwin, 1979), p. 143.

73   Billington, *Woman in India*, p. 34.

74 Diver, *Englishwoman in India*, p. 193.
75 Swenson, *Medical Women and Victorian Fiction*, p. 194.
76 Lokuge (ed.), Satthinadhan, *Saguna*, p. 150.
77 *Ibid.*, pp. 150–151.
78 *Ibid.*, p. 153.
79 *Ibid.*, p. 155.
80 As we noted in Chapter 1, Brahmin converts were much cherished by the mission-ary community. For details regarding the persistent regard for caste among mission-aries, see Kent, *Converting Women*. See also Vishwanathan, *Outside the Fold*, and Kevin Ward, *A History of Global Anglicanism* (Cambridge, Cambridge University Press, 2006).
81 Krupabai's father-in-law, Rev. W. T. Satthianadhan, was a highly regarded first-generation Indian Christian missionary of Brahmin origin, while his wife, Anna Satthianadhan, a fourth-generation Christian, belonged to an old Christian family, and was well known as a missionary wife and as the author of a book on child-rearing. This is discussed in great detail in Kent, *Converting Women*, pp. 181–187. See also de Souza, *Satthianadhan Family Album*, and E. M. Jackson, 'Glimpses of a Prominent Indian Christian Family of Tirunelveli and Madras, 1863–1906: Perspectives on Caste, Culture and Conversion', in Robert E. Frykenberg and Alaine Low (eds), *Christians and Missionaries in India: Cross-cultural Communication since 1500* (London, Routledge Curzon, 2003), pp. 315–335.
82 Lokuge (ed.), Satthiadhan, *Saguna*, pp. 147–149.
83 Although Krupabai's views on women as seen in her other, non-fictional essays are said to support a far more conventional feminine ideal (Lokuge (ed.), Satthianadhan, *Saguna*), the fact remains that as far as *Saguna* is concerned, her views are far more militant.

PART II

Colonial domesticity, white women's health and gender disadvantage

The ambivalences of power inside the colonial home: memsahibs, ayahs and wet-nurses

Most memsahibs' preoccupations were quite cut off from any concern with issues such as gendered social reform. Indeed, the average memsahib stayed aloof from the 'native' population, especially from the second half of the nineteenth century onwards after the takeover by the Crown. And their closest, cross-racial gendered contact during this period was confined to the ayah or female domestic servant who worked in their home – and also, occasionally, the wet-nurse who was employed for European infants. Throughout the colonial period, white women maintained diaries, wrote letters home, recorded their memoirs, wrote romantic novels and occasionally published housekeeping manuals in which they wrote copiously about their experiences in running a home in the colony as well as their interactions with their female domestic servants.

Anne McClintock has argued that 'the cultural history of imperialism cannot be understood without a theory of domestic space and gender power'.[1] In recent years, the issue of colonial domesticity as a discourse of power has indeed attracted scholarly attention. Nupur Chaudhuri, Alison Blunt, Elizabeth Buettner and, most importantly, Anne Laura Stoler (in the context of the Dutch East Indies) have written on the interactions between colonial white mistress/female servant/white children.[2] I would like to explore in this chapter the dynamics of these relationships, taking forward some of the explorations, made in particular by Blunt (the study of housekeeping journals) and Buettner (the study of both mistress–ayah and ayah–white child relation). While Alison Blunt has focused on household guides which were 'written for the second generation middle class British women to live in India' and were published between the late 1880s and the mid-1920s, I would like to widen the period under scrutiny, as well as tap a wider range of source materials.[3] Thus, I shall be examining discursive writings from the 1820s to the 1920s; moreover, in the course of exploring this subject, I would like to make the 'native' servant women more foregrounded than they have hitherto been in previous research.

On the face of it, the dynamics of the memsahib–ayah relationship were rooted in race/class hierarchies, domestic power structures and predicated on the superiority of the colonising memsahib. However, in reality these colonial transactions inside the colonial nursery were not so neatly polarised. Rather, these interactions were complicated by tensions and ambivalences which provided oppositional spaces that threatened to destabilise the colonial hierarchies based on race and class and to render the colonial home, and especially the nursery, a contentious space. In fact, in this chapter what I hope to demonstrate is that the colonial household was a site of tension, and to demonstrate Kate Teltscher's point that 'the anxieties of colonial rule manifest themselves most clearly in the home'.[4]

While the subject of the relationship between middle-class memsahib and low-class/caste 'native' female domestic servant inside the colonial home has been written about by scholars, the focus has largely been on the memsahibs' imperial authority and power, while the ambivalences embedded in their interactions have not received much attention. The fact, however, is that while the colonial home was projected in colonial discourse as a site of gendered, imperial power – it was simultaneously a site of imperial anxieties and insecurities. My contention in this chapter is that the complex dynamics of domestic relationships rendered the colonial nursery a troubled, ambivalent and even contested space, and that these insecurities were further exacerbated by the presence of 'marginal' domestics such as the wet-nurse. These memsahibs lived in towns and districts spread across the country, in regions as diverse, geographically, climatically and culturally, as Bengal, Punjab or Madras. We will also be taking note, in passing, of how far the local culture affected their lifestyle or attitudes and perceptions. In order to probe these colonial transactions, I will be drawing mostly upon diaries, memoirs, journals, periodical articles, newspaper reports, medical handbook and housekeeping manuals written by middle-class white women (mostly administrators' wives), living in different parts of colonial India over the nineteenth century as well as the early years of the twentieth century.

I seek to examine in this chapter how female domestic servants were represented in this discourse. What was the nature of the colonial gaze that was directed at low-class/caste ayahs? Did these perceptions reveal shifts and changes over the period? Were there regional diversities, nuances and complexities in their perceptions, or was there a curious sameness in their perceptions and in their discourse?

Domestic empire: an English(wo)man's home is [her] castle

An important aspect of memsahibs' experience of colonial India was the setting up of an English-style home in India. The middle-class memsahib was positioned at the head of a large household consisting of large retinues of servants. Architecturally too, the sprawling colonial bungalows with their spacious compounds and their outhouses for servants contributed to a sense of imperial power and authority.[5] However, embedded within this grand façade were tensions and problems that threatened to undermine the power of the European mistress's 'domestic administration'. To begin with, when faced with the rigidity of the caste system, the memsahib experienced helplessness in reducing the number of servants in her household, since they would refuse to perform tasks and duties not traditionally associated with their caste.[6] Hence, forced to accept Indian customs, she had no option but to employ large numbers of servants throughout the colonial period – resulting in enormous domestic expenditure about which many younger officers' wives habitually grumbled. While in the 1870s one memsahib helplessly complained that the 'number of servants required for only two people' was 'absurd', because in India, 'caste asserts its power'; twenty years later, another exasperated white woman echoed these words almost verbatim, remarking, 'In India one has to keep an absurd number [of servants], three or four at least to do the work of one, because of caste, which interferes with work sadly'.[7]

Nevertheless, the discourse of imperial power dominated the late colonial imaginary, especially in the late nineteenth century, and parallels often came to be drawn between running a home and administering an empire. Around the 1880s and 1890s the memsahib's domestic role was seen as, what an article in the periodical *The Calcutta Review* termed, 'domestic administration'.[8] Scholars such as Alison Blunt have demonstrated how empire and home were virtually interchangeable terms. Not only did the domestic role 'reproduce imperial power relations on a household scale', but the management of empire, in its turn, was perceived as what Rosemary Marangoly George has termed, 'essentially "home management" on a larger scale'.[9] Clearly, the objective of the Englishwoman was to 'replicate the empire on a domestic scale – a benevolent, much supervised terrain where discipline and punishment is meted out with an unwavering hand'.[10]

In this regard, it was of course Flora Annie Steel and Grace Gardiner's influential housekeeping manual *The Complete Indian Housekeeper and Cook* (1888), a text much discussed by scholars of late, which helped in giving firmer shape to the concept of the white woman as domestic administrator. This late nineteenth-century 'bible' of young memsahibs conferred upon housewifery all the practical skills and responsibility of administering a colony. While other household guide-books had appeared prior to it and continued to be published more pro-lifically in later years, it was *The Complete Indian Housekeeper* which always remained the authoritative guidebook for colonial housekeep-ing.[11] Defining domesticity as 'the formation of a home – that unit of civilisation', it compared colonial memsahibs to 'public servants in India', advised them to go on 'regular inspections round the com-pound', maintain monthly audits and keep 'written accounts showing their total yearly receipts and expenditure'.[12] It also urged the learning of 'Hindustanee' since it was 'the first duty of a mistress … to be able to give intelligible orders to her servants'; a command of language that was also underscored by *The Calcutta Review* which argued that 'no lady can be a good mistress, even in the ordinary sense of the word, without a knowledge of the vernacular'.[13]

Anne Laura Stoler has observed how the 'racialised Others invari-ably have been compared and equated with chidren' because such a representation has 'conveniently provided a moral jusification for imperial policies of tutelage, discipline and specific paternalistic and maternalistic strategies of custodial control'.[14] And indeed, servants, according to Steel and Gardiner, were to be managed with a 'balance of rewards and punishments'. Voicing the *mai-baap* (benevolent; literally 'mother and father') paternalism of British colonial administration, they infantalised the 'native' subject, pointing out that the 'Indian servant is a child in everything save age, and should be treated as a child, that is to say, kindly, but with the greatest firmness'. Indeed, the crux of their argument was the by now oft-quoted phrase, that 'an Indian household can no more be governed peacefully, without dignity and prestige than an Indian Empire'.[15]

Architecturally, colonial bungalows constituted the white mis-tress's empire, with her domain spread over the compound in which were located both the sahibs' bungalows and the servants' quarters. The latter were deliberately located at what the Delhi-based colo-nial physician, Kate Platt, termed 'a safe distance', from the sahibs' colonial bungalows.[16] This 'safe distance' racialised the compound and reinforced the hierarchies of race and class in what Alison Blunt defines as the 'imperial geographies of home' and 'reproduced on a household scale the racial distancing of British cantonments and civil lines from the "native" city'.[17]

The Calcutta Review, in that same article, highlighted the mem-sahib's power and imperial responsibilities, by remarking that the 'Englishwoman in her own Bungalow is the centre of an influence …

to which her English life offers no parallel'. It further pointed out that the mistress exercised great sway 'within her own compound', since it was a 'conglomerate not of individuals as in England, but of families'.[18] Indeed, the article encouraged memsahibs to adopt the 'white woman's burden' of uplifting downtrodden 'native' women and to carry out this 'civilising mission' within the ambit of their compounds.[19] Popular colonial novelist, Maud Diver (whose comments on this subject we earlier noted in the second chapter), echoed this idea of imperial responsibility in *The Englishwoman in India* (1909):

> Every mistress of a house has, within her compound, some scope for work in this direction ... every man in her service is certain to possess a wife and family ... any Englishwoman can find material ready to her hand ... to take an active interest in the joys and sorrows of those sister-women whom chance has brought together within her gates.[20]

Ayahs: intricacies of caste, region and religion

Most scholarly explorations of the subject of the colonial home, points out Alison Blunt, suffer from a lacuna, in that they 'render Indian servants largely invisible'.[21] This is something that I shall attempt to rectify in this section, by probing the caste and religious affiliations and their implications of the female domestic servants. In the colonial household where the majority of domestic servants were male, the ayah, according to Steel and Gardiner, was the only female servant in the household. Regarding the number of ayahs employed, however, some of the writings suggest greater variations. For instance, the anonymous housekeeping manual, *The Englishwoman in India* (1864), written by a Madras presidency-based 'Lady Resident', mentioned that there were sometimes two ayahs: the chief ayah and an 'Under Ayah' whose job was to wash and dress the children 'in conjunction with the head ayah'.[22] Edmund C. P. Hull's *The European in India* (1871), on the other hand, which provided a detailed list of colonial domestics in the three presidential towns, suggests further local variations. Hull noted that while in Bombay and Madras only one ayah was employed, in Calcutta households, an ayah as well as a *mehteranee* (sweeper) ayah were kept.[23]

In the early twentieth century, Kate Platt, the Delhi-based physician, who served as the Principal of a hospital for women in that city, mentioned in *Home and Health in India and the Tropical Colonies* (1923) that most homes employed two female servants, 'the ayah and mehtrani [sweeper]'. In this manual, which was part-medical guide-book and part-housekeeping handbook, Platt observed that after a few years, the '[m]ehtrani or sweeper' would sometimes 'rise in station' and be elevated to the position of an ayah, after years of 'doing the menial work of the nursery' and acquiring a 'familiarity with the duties of an ayah'. In fact, Platt even warned against the danger of 'an enterprising' sweeper woman trying to 'pass herself off as an ayah to some unsuspicious [sic] employer' – feeding, thereby, into the old colonial myth of the habitually dishonest 'native' servant.[24]

It was the factor of caste that created one of the main problematic hurdles for colonial domesticity. Memsahibs discovered that since white people were considered 'outcastes', only women from the lowest sweeper caste were usually willing to work for them as ayahs (some of these women happening also to be the wife of the sweeper employed in the household). A large number of households did employ low-caste women in this manner – for instance, in the early nineteenth century, Mary Martha Sherwood, who gave birth to six children during her stay in India as the wife of an army officer, fondly recollected in her diary her son's favourite ayah, who was a 'matranee' (sweeper) by caste.[25] Sometimes, however, memsahibs felt mortified at the idea of low-class 'native' servants harbouring caste prejudices against their European masters and mistresses. Thus, in the 1830s, the unmarried, intellectually inclined Emma Roberts, who made astute observations on colonial society in her numerous books and articles, voiced her indignation at the fact that 'none but a low Hindoo would take the office' of an ayah due to the polluting status of white people.[26]

Other than sweeper-caste women, 'Moossulman' women also worked as ayahs in colonial homes. In fact, most colonial households preferred to employ Muslim women – perhaps to sidestep the ignominy of being rejected by caste servants. However, given the deeply entrenched nature of the caste system, the problem was that Muslim ayahs also refused to do cleaning duties. Indeed, Steel and Gardiner, who preferred low-caste ayahs, admonished the white mistresses for their preference for Muslim ayahs, calling it 'foolish'. Ridiculing the memsahibs' 'dislike to a sweeper or low-caste women', they pointed out that low-caste sweeper women were in fact 'very often cleaner' than Muslim ayahs, who in any case, 'would not 'condescend' to sweeping the house, since like all Indians, they too regarded the 'act of cleansing' to be 'inferior and degrading'.[27]

Occasionally, in order to circumvent this problem of caste, some colonial households even adopted the system of employing two ayahs; one belonging to the relatively higher *mali* (gardener) caste, who would perform all the duties, except that of cleaning the baby's potty or nappies – for which another ayah belonging to the *mehter* (sweeper) caste was employed. Indeed, caste prejudices among the servants were so deeply entrenched that Steel and Gardner, apprehensive about the other domestic servants' contemptuous treatment of a low-caste ayah, even cautioned the mistress to be careful about ensuring that 'whether she be a sweeper or not, it should be generally understood that you hold her to be the equal of any other servant in the house'.[28]

What emerges as most striking in all this is that the white mistresses' own reluctance to employ sweeper-caste ayahs does indeed seem to gesture at the internalisation of caste prejudices by colonial memsahibs. Clearly, these white women had themselves absorbed – even if unconsciously – 'native' social and cultural mores and prejudices. By attaching so much importance to the ayah's caste, they inadvertently participated in reinforcing caste hierarchies and perceptions and, in effect, marginalised themselves as 'outcastes'.

In addition to Muslim and low-caste Hindus, 'native' Christian converts were also occasionally recruited as ayahs. Nupur Chaudhuri and Elizabeth Buettner have argued that there was often a preference for Christian convert ayahs possibly because these women were considered to be 'more distanced from most of Indian society or better acquainted with Western culture'.[29] Echoing this viewpoint, Kate Platt noted in the 1920s that Christian ayahs were generally the most popular among Europeans, and hence most ayahs in colonial homes were either 'Indian Christian' or the 'wife of one of the Mahommedan servants', and very rarely a Hindu.[30]

However, the opposite view was also voiced, earlier on; for instance, the Trichinopoly-based 'Lady Resident', writing in the 1860s, voiced her strong reservations about 'native' Christians. She revealed that she and her husband had been 'robbed and cheated' so often by Christian servants, that it had made her 'resolve[d] never to engage another' again, preferring 'unmitigated heathens' as servants – even 'at the risk of scandalizing a large number' of readers.[31] More importantly, she feared that since Christian domestics belonged to the 'master's-caste', they would give themselves superior airs over the other servants.[32]

We may speculate from these diverse reactions that perhaps Christian convert servants, belonging to the 'master's caste' were sometimes perceived with a certain degree of ambivalence or unease by European masters/mistresses as potentially insubordinate. The fear seems to have been that 'native' servants sharing the same religion with their white masters would undermine the white master's race/ class authority. Indeed, a common religion linking together colonial master and 'native' Christian servant was possibly located as dangerous in the colonial imaginary, threatening to bridge the imperial distance between them.

Dynamics of the memsahib–ayah relationship: the ayah as lady's maid

The dynamics of the memsahib–ayah relationship was indeed a complicated one. Rooted in race/class hierarchies and domestic power structures, it was a part of the everyday colonial 'transactions' of the colonial household. By the latter half of the nineteenth century especially, due to the greater racial segregation, the ayah was the average white woman's closest contact with 'native' India. Besides, as the only female servant inside most households, she was the principal mediator between her mistress and 'native' culture. Although in terms of the domestic hierarchy of servants the *khidmutgar* (butler) was the most senior among servants, the ayah had a special status by virtue of her gendered closeness to the mistress.

In households without children, the ayah–mistress relationship was generally cordial; she played here the role of a lady's maid – a further index of the luxurious lives led by colonial memsahibs who later found it difficult to adjust to their spartan existence after returning 'home' to Britain – a problem examined by Elizabeth Buettner and Georgina Gowans, among others.[33] Regarding the ayah's role as lady's maid, the majority opinion was positive and it was common to find memsahibs showering praises on their ayah as a responsible and faithful assistant.[34] The Madras presidency-based 'Lady Resident' appreciated the number of duties that a good 'head ayah' willingly performed for her mistress in a household without children, such as taking 'care of her mistress's wardrobe and her jewellery', dressing her hair, washing lace and other fine things, and helping in the care of poultry, pets and 'frequently aid unasked in delicate cookery'.[35] As late as 1908, the newly married 'Chota Mem' confessed in her housekeeping manual written for very young memsahibs, that:

> [Y]ou must own it is nice to have one woman in the house. It is such a comfort when you come in hot and tired to have her to take your shoes and clothes off, and put out what you want to wear, to brush, and fold up your things, and generally look after them.[36]

Some male authors too, such as Edmund Hull, valued the ayah as 'a very faithful and affectionate attendant' who was ever-willing to 'perform many little offices about the house when required'. He especially lauded her loyalty and the manner in which she:

> quite identifies herself with her mistress's interests, looks after her property with a jealous anxiety, and is always ready to report any improper proceedings which may be going on among the other servants – against whom, if necessary, she will unhesitatingly range herself on her mistress's side.[37]

Newspapers too had high praise for the ayah; in 1880 the Anglo-Indian newspaper *The Pioneer* hailed her as 'a Confidential Secretary in the Home Dept', employing rather pompous administrative 'officialese' – which further fed into the trope of the 'domestic empire':

> The Ayah smooths down the rough surfaces of life in India ... The servants see their mistress through the Ayah ... and the mistress sees the servants humanised through the intelligible womanly instincts of the Ayah.[38]

Most importantly, Steel and Gardner too gave credence to her value as the memsahib's useful assistant.[39] They spelled out her duties, which included *salaaming* (greeting) the mistress every day, bringing in the early morning tea, attending to all her needs, tidying up the room, attending upon lady guests and so on. The ayah, they pointed out, was especially skilled in brushing the mistress's hair 'very gently and well' and pronounced that a good ayah, with her ability to perform innumerable odd jobs about the house, was 'an immense help' to the mistress and she was hence to be 'treated with consideration and respect' as 'the only woman-servant in the house'.[40]

The stereotype of the lascivious 'native': 'dubious' morality of ayahs

At the same time, however, ayahs were also subjected to a critical colonial gaze in memsahibs' writings and negatively projected as dishonest and lascivious. Commenting on such ambivalent representations of 'native' servants as 'both devotional and devious, trustworthy and lascivious', Ann Laura Stoler has argued that this ambiguity served to further heighten a sense of insecurity, since 'it was their very domestication that placed the intimate workings of the bourgeois home in their knowing insurrectionary hands and in their pernicious control'.[41] Often there appeared the old colonial paradigm of the thieving Indian servant, who was an inveterate liar, adept at extracting high salaries; with the ayah cast as lazy, untruthful and dishonest.[42] 'A Lady Resident' cautioned her readers against the dishonesty of 'native' servants, stressing the need to be 'very careful in examining' their references when engaging them because these certificates were often fabricated.[43] Indeed, this construct of the low-class 'native' ayah's dishonesty and duplicity remained a most enduring one, further reinforced by medical opinion, as we shall see later in this chapter.

Most important of all were prevailing constructions about the ayah's dubious *sexual* morality – a perception that was rooted not only in colonial racism but also in British class prejudice, and in keeping with notions about the sensuality of female domestic servants drawn from the low classes in Britain.[44] The construction of the ayahs as sexually promiscuous seems to have been overwhelmingly predominant. While Emma Roberts warned that 'not one respectable woman out of a hundred' could be found among them, almost fifty years later, the Anglo-Indian newspaper, *The Pioneer*, in 1880 hinted at the ayah's uncontrolled sensuality and her 'strong and warm pulsations'.[45] Similarly, Flora Annie Steel cast aspersions on the sexual morality of her daughter's strikingly handsome ayah, even while praising her efficiency ('A better servant never existed'), claiming that 'years of experience' had taught her that good-looking ayahs usually had, what she termed, a 'lurid' past.[46]

Returning the colonial gaze: the ayah and the memsahib

One important issue that scholars have not adequately taken note of are colonial anxieties over the ayah *returning* the 'colonial gaze'. Indeed (as we saw in our discussion of Flora Annie's short fiction in Chapter 2), the disparaging 'native gaze' did haunt colonials who were uneasily conscious of 'native' disdain for 'immoral' memsahibs, based on their perceptions of western social practices and attire. These included low-cut evening gowns, ball-room dancing (disparagingly called *pugla nautch* or 'mad dance' by 'native' onlookers) and the practice of drinking and dancing in public with men not related to them. The Anglo-Indian newspaper, *The Englishman's Saturday Evening Journal*, for instance, drily cautioned its readers in 1870 against ball-room dancing in the colony, remarking that, 'Englishmen, of course understand that sort of thing; but not so our Aryan brotherhood ... dancing [is] ... characterized by them as *pugla nautch* – or mad dance.'[47]

An important point to note here is that the 'native' ayah's presence (and therefore, inevitably her gaze) inside the household was a ubiquitous one. This was because colonial bungalows lacked European-style privacy. Architecturally, most bungalows were built at the centre of a large plot, with a design that was antithetical in crucial ways to what William Glover terms, the 'nineteenth century European bourgeois ideal' of 'clear separations between less and more private spaces'.[48] Although servants' quarters or outhouses were built at a distance from the main home, nevertheless colonial homes generally had servants (particularly ayahs) hovering around on various duties. Commenting on the architectural lack of privacy in colonial bungalows, Glover further elaborates that '[o]pening the interior rooms of the house to cooling breezes during the summer was indeed one of the critical design criteria for bungalows', and that 'the porosity between the interior rooms of the house and the house's exterior' made 'the less private rooms of the house [open] directly on to more private ones'. This open, airy structure, combined with the 'co-presence of the servants in the innermost recesses of the home', resulted in a 'porosity' between master's and servants' spaces and precluded privacy.[49]

Given this, the role of the ayah as spectator was crucial, since, as Maud Diver cautioned, she was the sole 'native' who was privy to every aspect of the memsahib's daily domestic life. Diver voiced her apprehensions that the 'chattering' of the ayah did much to harm the white woman's imperial image. Cautioning the memsahib that she was under the constant moral surveillance of her 'native' attendant, she reminded her about her imperial responsibilities and cautioned her to ensure that her behaviour did not 'tarnish the honour of her nationality or her sex'.[50] Diver exhorted that:

> she should never forget that the woman from whom little of her social and domestic life is hid, judges her conduct by Eastern standards and communicates those judgements without reserve to an admiring circle of listeners ... for the ayah is a bone-bred gossip.[51]

The ayah's presence therefore effectively exerted an indirect form of 'moral policing' on the memsahib. The situation thus created was fraught with complexities and contradictions. Most strikingly, perhaps, it displayed a colonial reconstitution of patriarchies, with colonisers seeking, in effect, to impose Indian patriarchal notions of 'acceptable' female 'moral' conduct on the white woman, in the name of 'national honour'.[52]

Ayahs and European children

But perhaps most unsettling of all in the colonial imaginary was the ayahs' role as the children's attendant. For many young, dependant memsahibs, the ayah was the 'most important servant in a house with children', exercising great control on child-rearing.[53] One reason for this dependence was the European child's vulnerability in the colony to a host of tropical diseases, such as cholera, malaria, typhoid, and also to the danger of snake and insect bites. Additionally, young mothers' difficulties were further exacerbated in the colony by the absence of their own mothers, aunts and older women who traditionally provided a female support system in metropolitan Britain. Given this, especially in the first half of the century, an experienced old ayah became invaluable for giving advice on child-rearing. Thus Mary Martha Sherwood, who lived in the Bengal presidency in the early 1800s, gratefully acknowledged how she 'ever afterwards' followed an old ayah's advice of engaging a 'daye' for her infant daughter 'till she has cut every tooth'.[54]

Indeed, tributes to ayahs from grateful memsahibs are to be widely found in letters, diaries and memoirs: 'A Lady Resident', whose husband was stationed in the Madras presidency and who chose to withhold her name from her readers, showered encomiums in her housekeeping journal on the comforting presence of a good ayah in the home of any young, white mother:

> A good ayah is a very pleasant and valuable servant; where there is a young family she superintends the under ayah, and always takes the entire charge and responsibility of the infant, often being far more capable of looking after its health and comfort and proper food than its young and inexperienced mother. She is almost always able to take a baby from the moment of its birth, as well as attend to the mother; and the extreme lightness and delicacy of touch which characterises the native, makes the ayah often a very great comfort on these occasions.[55]

It is indeed striking how almost sixty years later, Kate Platt, the Delhi-based female physician, virtually echoed this view in her medical manual – clearly suggesting how some perceptions essentially continued with hardly any change over the decades:

> [The] Indian ayah has many good points; she surrounds her charges with an atmosphere of love and devotion and has infinite patience ... Taking into consideration her home surroundings, her entire lack of training in European customs ... it is wonderful that she is as satisfactory as she is found to be, but too much should not be expected of her.[56]

Newspapers too widely voiced appreciation for the ayah's devotion to European children: *The Pioneer*, a generally conservative newspaper, paid tribute in 1880 to the ayah for having 'given her life for years to her master's family' and appreciating her consequent sacrifice of her own child, 'her own little Sita, merely catching hurried glimpses of her' in the process of her duties.[57] There is, however, the exception of the Madras-based physician, R. S. Mair, who warned in his *Medical Guide for Anglo-Indians* (1871) against 'mischievous practices resorted to by native female servants' like giving infants opium to make them sleep:

> I have known instances, where the amah or the ayah for obvious reasons, has given narcotics, concealed under one of their finger nails, under the pretence that they were quieting the child by allowing it to suck her finger.[58]

However, the majority of the memsahibs, who were otherwise diverse in their opinion, expressed positive sentiments about the ayah in one voice, ranging from the evangelical-minded Mary Martha Sherwood in the early nineteenth century to the imperialist Flora Annie Steel and Maud Diver in the 1880s and 1900s. Sherwood vividly recalled in her memoirs how, when her small son lay dying, his ayah, who was virtually a surrogate-mother to him, walked up and down 'incessantly', carrying him. Remarking that 'a more affectionate creature I never knew', Sherwood recollected how, 'For hours and hours she used to pace the verandah with my boy.'[59] Despite all the ayah's ministrations, however, the child died; years later, the memory of the 'native' woman 'unfeignedly weeping for her boy' led Sherwood to reflect upon the common grief that bound together European mother and low-class 'native' ayah in a common 'maternal' bereavement:

> There are moments of intense feeling, in which all distinction of nations, colours, and castes disappears, and in their place there only remains between two human beings one abiding sense of a common nature … The scene of that weeping woman has power … to cause my tears to flow afresh.[60]

Indianisation and 'indiscipline' among European children

The proverbial affection between ayah and European child was widely hailed; *The Pioneer* remarked in the 1880s that the children would 'carry in their hearts the ayah's laughter and tears … after all else Indian has passed out of their lives';[61] while echoing this forty years later, Kate Platt, the Delhi-based physician, noted how Indian servants:

> almost always love European children and are extremely indulgent to them. Children are as a rule happy with their ayahs and bearers, who are wonderfully good at amusing and interesting them.[62]

Indeed, as Elizabeth Buettner and several other scholars have demonstrated, European children's attachment to their ayahs continued even long after they had returned to England.[63] In the colonial period, this emotional closeness sometimes became a source of deep colonial anxiety and fears were voiced over parents possibly losing their emotional hold over their offspring. Uneasy about children's excessive attachment to their 'native' servants, R. S. Mair warned parents in the 1870s that there was a real danger of their servants replacing the parents in their children's affections:

> The child becomes strongly attached to these servants … indeed it is no uncommon thing to find children in India, preferring the society of their native servants to that of their parents. *Here lies a danger which must be guarded against by every possible means* [emphasis added].[64]

[125]

Edmund Hull too cautioned that 'it is not unheard of to find [children] preferring the society of their native attendants to that of their own parents'. His explanation was that it was the 'pliant, obliging nature of these servants' which 'naturally attaches the children to them'.[65]

Another colonial fear was that servants in their devoted indulgence would encourage 'indiscipline' among European children, leading to 'Indianisation'. Julia Maitland, who lived in various towns in the Madras presidency in the 1830s, complained that her ayah was so weak-willed that all her small daughter had to do was cry 'long enough and loud enough' and she was 'sure to get her own way'.[66] Steel and Gardiner too mentioned that children in India became 'proverbially captious, disobedient, and easily thrown out of gear' and that it was fairly common to find an English child 'eating his dinner off the floor, with his hands full of toys, while a posse of devoted attendants distract his attention, and the ayah feeds him with spoonfuls of *pish-pash*'. They elaborated, 'where, save in India, do we find sturdy little tots of four and five still taking their bottles and refusing to go to sleep without a lullaby?'[67] Maud Diver too expressed concern in the early twentieth century that the adoring servants' 'propensity to worship at the shrine of the Baba-log' made them unable to impose the requisite discipline on 'the small gods and goddesses they serve'.[68]

Elizabeth Buettner has argued that the presence of adoring 'native' servants inculcated a sense of privilege in European children and served to 'create and reinforce a white, middle-class, British imperial identity in children'.[69] However, this kind of tyrannical 'despotism' was in fact, precisely what was considered to be antithetical to the characteristics of leadership, self-control and 'manliness' believed to be requisite in the next generation of imperial rulers. Fears were voiced throughout the colonial period about indulgent 'native' servants sowing indiscipline in the nursery. Kate Platt, for instance, warned that 'the training in obedience, straightforwardness, and self-control, so essential to a child in the earliest years of life' could not be learned from 'native' servants. She added that 'character-formation' was impossible in children who spent most of their time 'in the companionship of ayah and bearer' because their 'plastic young minds' were constantly receiving negative impressions from their Indian attendants.[70] Given all these fears and anxieties, white children were not kept in India beyond the age of five or six and the common practice throughout the colonial period was to send them away to be brought up in England – oftentimes subjected to emotional deprivation by strangers with whom they boarded on payment.[71]

Ayahs as surrogate mothers:
instabilities inside the colonial nursery

For European infants, on the other hand, 'native' ayahs were considered the best option, and in many colonial households the ayah virtually came to play the role of a surrogate mother. Describing her as a 'foster parent', Mary Martha Sherwood in the early 1800s underlined the deep emotional bonds connecting English infant with 'native' servant woman:

> It is touching to see the European babe hanging on the breast of the black woman, and testifying towards her all the tenderness which is due to its own mother. It is not uncommon to see the delicate, fair hand stroking the swarthy face of the foster-parent, and even to observe *that* foster-mother smiling upon the child, really, I believe, usually feeling for it unfeigned and unextinguishable love.[72]

This situation continued more or less unchanged for most of the colonial period, and more than a hundred years later, the physician, Kate Platt, echoed these sentiments, almost verbatim:

> They make a charming picture – the fair haired English child and the swarthy-faced ayah with her voluminous white draperies, twinkling silver bangles, and gay scarlet coat, as she sits soothing him with magnetic touch, crooning an old-world lullaby.[73]

However, the scenario changed with toddlers and older children. Perhaps the most destabilising and alarming effect of 'native' influence inside the colonial nursery was when toddlers started speaking – and learned to speak the vernacular instead of English. Emma Roberts, sharp observer of social life in colonial India in the 1830s, noted that children were 'certain of acquiring Hindostanee' – whereas they were 'very seldom taught a word of English until they are five or six years old'.[74] This, indeed, was a cause for alarm; with European mothers barely able to speak the local language, the result was a serious communication gap between parents and children inside the colonial nursery:

> In British India, children and parents are placed in a very singular position with regard to each other; the former do not speak their mother-tongue ... In numerous instances, they cannot make themselves intelligible to their parents, it being no uncommon case to find the latter almost totally ignorant of the native dialect, while their children cannot converse in any other.[75]

Elaborating on the uniquely dysfunctional mother–child relationships inside the colonial nursery, Roberts critiqued its 'inversion of the usual order of things', where mothers learned the local language from 'the prattles of their infants', having 'perhaps known nothing of Hindostanee' till that time. She added that even when they did understand English, children were 'shy of speaking it' and did not acquire the 'same fluency which distinguishes their utterance of the native language'.[76]

Right through the colonial period this remained the state of affairs. Thus, much later, Rudyard Kipling famously recalled in his autobiography, how, during their childhood in India, he and his sister, having spent the whole day with their much-loved ayah and bearer, would be sent in to meet their parents with the caution, 'Speak English now to Papa and Mamma'. Both the children would then speak 'haltingly' in English, which they 'translated out of the vernacular idiom' that they both 'thought and dreamt in'.[77] Indeed, how unchanged all this remained can be seen in Kate Platt pointing out – almost fifty years after Kipling – that 'children left much with ayahs ... learn to speak Hindustani earlier and more fluently than their mother tongue' and that it was 'not uncommon on board ship to come across children who literally have to learn English during the voyage, while their tongues wag merrily in Hindustani'.[78]

Language, as Ann Laura Stoler reminds us, is 'seen to provide the idioms and cultural referents in which children's "character formation" and internal disposition would be shaped'.[79] And fear of cultural 'contamination' through language was indeed often voiced in the colonial period. Thus, in connection with this problem of communication, 'A Lady Resident' warned in her housekeeping journal that 'the greatest stress should be laid on [children] not understanding any language which their parents do not'. She advised:

> As far as possible, children should be prevented from acquiring native dialects, as with the language they are almost certain to imbibe ideas and knowledge most prejudicial to them in every way.[80]

The fear of language as a culturally corrupting factor was also voiced in the 1880s manual, *Tropical Trials: A Handbook for Women in the Tropics*, written by S. Leigh Hunt and Alexander A. Kenny. The authors warned that by learning the vernacular, the child's 'little mind will soon become contaminated with ideas and expressions that would utterly horrify a mother did she herself understand the language of the country'.[81] Maud Diver, similarly, urged the colonial mother to be 'zealous in guarding her children from promiscuous intimacy with the native servants', while later still, Kate Platt went on to warn that all this made the responsibility of the mother or the European nurse 'all the greater'.[82]

Indeed, these close links between ayah and child threatened to destabilise the power equations and hierarchies within the colonial nursery. The ayah, communicating with the child in a language not accessible to the white mother, was, in a sense, usurping her place and undermining her hold over the child. Not only did this pose the problem of creating an 'Indianised' English but as Nupur Chaudhuri notes, this closeness to native servants threatened to dismantle the 'barrier between the colonisers and the colonised, consequences of which might be an erosion of the foundations of empire'.[83]

In fact, as Nupur Chaudhuri and Elizabeth Buettner, among others, have noted, it was this closeness that evoked colonial anxieties and was often looked at askance by colonial mothers.[84] In the 1830s Julia Maitland, the Madras presidency-based memsahib, alarmed about her child becoming 'Indianised' under the ayah's influence, declared: 'I intend, as much as possible, to prevent her learning the native languages: though it is rather difficult – most English children do learn them ... and grow like little Hindoos.' She went on to add that 'If my child were to stay long in the country, it would be worthwhile to send for an English nurse; but, as it is, I hope to bring her home before it becomes of any consequence' and noted that 'meanwhile I keep her as much as possible with me'.[85] Several decades later, Maud Diver urged the memsahib to be 'zealous in guarding her children from promiscuous intimacy with the native servants'.[86]

The ayah and the Rebellion of 1857

Both Alison Blunt and Nupur Chaudhuri have argued that the upheavals of the 1857 Rebellion further exacerbated the ayah–memsahib relationship, and that servants turned hostile or deserted their employers during that period.[87] Chaudhuri, defining 1857 as 'a watershed year ... which further strained relationships between British women and Indian domestics', observes that 'Memsahibs became increasingly hostile in the criticism of their servants' and that in the period that followed, 'Memsahibs' mistrust of their domestics increased, and they became more negative in their general opinion of Indian servants'.[88] Alison Blunt, in turn, has argued that 'In British India, the desertion of Indian servants during the uprising represented the severity of the imperial crisis on a domestic scale, and memories of the fate of British women and British homes continued to shape imperial domesticity after 1858.'[89] However, as I argue in this section, this is not borne out by memsahibs' diaries and personal accounts, which reveal a far greater range of responses, some negative and some positive.[90]

The upheavals wrought by the Rebellion temporarily disturbed domestic power relations, causing the British memsahib to suffer a displacement from her domestic empire. British imperialism/domesticity was indeed under attack, with rebels attacking, looting and burning down British houses. However, there was also the phenomenon of loyal ayahs protecting memsahibs during this period. A number of first-person accounts such as memoirs and diaries by memsahibs during that period reveal how they sometimes found themselves depending on their domestic servants' loyalty for their survival. In many cases, European families were hidden by faithful servants, both male and female, inside their homes. Colonial servants' quarters used to be built, as we saw, at a 'safe distance' from the colonial master's bungalows inside the same compounds. Paradoxically, it was these servants' huts which now served as a sanctuary and a hiding-place for the English families.[91] Thus, in cases of white people 'on the run' or in hiding, the memsahib–ayah relations temporarily underwent an inversion of power relationships during these turbulent times. Domestic race and class hierarchies were momentarily disturbed by the Rebellion.

Perceptions about domestic servants varied during the Rebellion. Some accounts, feeding into myths of the 'ungrateful' and 'disloyal' native, complained of the 'impudence' of servants who were 'deserting daily', while the ayah was described as greedily eyeing the mistress's belongings 'as her share of the plunder'.[92] Equally, however, accounts by other memsahibs described loyal servants, both male and female, risking their own lives, hiding their master's families or helping them to escape. For instance, Adelaide Case, one of the ladies in the Lucknow Residency, repeatedly mentions in her diary her gratitude towards various servants, including her 'poor ayah' who remained with them during the siege, as well as her sister's 'faithful ayah' who walked all the way from 'Cawnpore' to Lucknow to see her mistress.[93] On the whole, the Rebellion came to be associated in the colonial imagination with the ayah's loyalty, with the wife of a civil servant gratefully remarking in the 1880s that 'many an ayah in the Mutiny proved her devotion at the cost of her life, and many would do so again'.[94]

In particular, whenever there were white *children*, ayahs were said to be deeply devoted during the Rebellion; diaries and first-person accounts by Harriet Tytler at Delhi or Adelaide Case at Lucknow describe how their Indian servants, especially ayahs, continued to nurture deep affection not only for their young charges but also for kind mistresses for whom they risked their own lives.[95] The ayah's role as surrogate mother – ordinarily feared and looked at askance by colonials – now served to save the child's life. Often children survived, with ayahs disguising them as Indians, painting their faces brown and dressing them in 'native' garments.[96] Because the white children could speak the vernacular fluently it often helped them to evade detection. Thus, the ayah–child emotional ties eventually saved white children in these turbulent times – in a context where their parents did not always manage to escape. Colonial anxieties about the 'Indianisation' of the European child therefore came to be turned upon their head. The Rebellion had a further complex fallout on the memsahib–ayah relationship, bringing them both closer together and, at the same time, creating greater distance and suspicion.

British nannies versus Indian ayahs: discipline versus indulgence

One solution to 'cultural contamination' through language was to employ English-speaking ayahs. British nannies were recommended – especially for older children. While Steel and Gardiner observed that 'for tiny babies ... a really good ayah is excellent' and 'often more satisfactory' than English and Eurasian nurses, in the case of older children it was 'absolutely necessary' to engage an English nanny.[97] However, British nannies were expensive and could be afforded only by higher ranking officers and they also tended to get married soon. Sometimes, impoverished British widows or wives of sergeants and quarter masters were employed as nannies.

British nannies also drew a good deal of criticism; Emma Roberts clearly stated her preference for a 'Mossulman ayah' over a European nanny and complained that the latter not only 'demand[ed] enormous wages' but 'soon learn[ed] to give themselves airs' – to the extent that they demanded to be themselves attended by 'native' servants during the hot weather.[98] Even more importantly, there were frequent reports about the *callousness* of English nurses; Mary Martha Sherwood, the Bengal-based memsahib, for instance, indignantly remarked how they seemed unaffected by the deaths of neglected infants of 'native' wet-nurses.[99] Several decades later, 'A Lady Resident' too protested against the 'rough and ready English nurse-maids', and stated her preference for 'native' ayahs who were 'very fond of babies, and gentle and patient with them'.[100] Besides, as Kate Platt admitted, although theoretically speaking an 'experienced English nanny is perhaps the best solution', the problem was that such a woman was 'often autocratic in her methods and may resent interference'. Her suggestion was that a 'trained child's nurse is perhaps the next best thing'.[101]

Inevitably, the British nanny and the native ayah came to clash in their authority inside the colonial nursery. As one would expect, in such cases, the factor of race prevailed. In cases of any dispute, it was the British nanny's version which was accepted over that of the ayah. In one instance in the 1870s when an ayah complained to the memsahib that the nanny had whipped her fourteen-month-old son, the child's mother, Jane Maria Strachey, chose not to believe her – explaining, instead, in her letter to her husband Richard (later Major General) Strachey, that 'As one prefers taking an English woman's word to a native's, I said no more about it.'[102]

Constructing the Indian wet-nurse: dirt, disease and deception

The greatest sense of colonial insecurity for the memsahib, however, came from 'native' wet-nurses. Many colonial households had little option but to keep a wet-nurse (also referred to variously as the *dai* or *amah*) to feed very young infants. In fact, throughout the nineteenth century, almost all colonial physicians advised memsahibs to engage Indian wet-nurses. One physician pointed out that the 'tropical climate undermines and impairs the energies and power of an European consti-tution', making it difficult for European mothers to feed their infants, and hence 'no infant thrives so well as those fed by these women'.[103] At the same time, colonial physicians were extremely negative about the wet-nurse in terms of her hygiene, moral character and honesty, and obsessively made an inventory of all her dishonest practices – something that we shall be examining in the next chapter.

The European mistress's interactions with the wet-nurse, in con-trast to the ayah–memsahib relationship, were far more impersonal and lasted for a much shorter duration, being spread over only a few months. It is worth pointing out here that the wet-nurse's positionality in colonised cultures offers a stark contrast to that in the colonising home. In wealthy Indian homes, keeping a wet-nurse for infants was a traditional practice but the position of the *dai* or wet-nurse within the family presented a dramatically different picture. As Swapna Banerjee delineates in her study of domestic servants in Indian households, the wet-nurse (known as the *dai-ma* or the 'wet-nurse mother'), was a respected 'foster-mother' to the infant in elite Indian households. She wielded great authority and power in the household, occupied an hon-oured position within the extended family and remained with them for her entire life.[104] In middle-class colonial homes, on the other hand, most of the wet-nurses were not only employed for a short duration, they generally came from the lower castes, occupied a much lower position than the ayah and were looked upon with great apprehension by their white employers.

The majority of wet-nurses in Anglo-Indian homes, reiterates Nupur Chaudhuri, belonged to low-caste Hindu or Muslim communities, largely due to the outcaste status of white people from the perspective of traditional caste hierarchies.[105] Hence, inside the memsahibs' bungalow, the *amah* was, as 'A Lady Resident' noted, 'generally a grass-cutter or coolie, or, at all events, a woman from the poorest and hardest worked classes'.[106] Most writings constructed the wet-nurse as cunning and manipulative. For instance, Emma Roberts pointed out indignantly how Muslim wet-nurses who had 'acquired [caste prejudices] from their Hindoo associates', cited daily 'pollution' from the touch of European infants – and succeeded in extracting extra compensatory money from their European employers for 'purchasing their reinstatement to caste'.[107] In the rare instance where the *amah* happened to belong to a higher caste, domestic management became even more problematic for the white mistress, since, as Julia Maitland discovered in the 1830s, in such cases the *amah*'s demands multiplied manifold:

> The amah is a caste woman, and her whims are the plague of my life: I am obliged to keep a cook on purpose for her, because her food must all be dressed by a person of her own caste; and even then she will some-times starve all day rather than eat it, if she fancies anybody else has been near it: she has a house built of coca-nut leaves in the compound, on purpose to cook her food in.[108]

It is striking how throughout the entire colonial period, memsa-hibs' letters, diaries, memoirs and housekeeping journals projected an unmitigated negative image of the wet-nurse – while, at the same time, revealing white women's *dependence* on these women. With little choice but to hire them, memsahibs felt helpless and tyrannised over by *dais* (wet-nurses) and their numerous demands. However, one great source of relief for memsahibs was that, unlike in the case of ayahs, there was little danger of European children forming alarmingly close emotional ties with the wet-nurse, because of the limited duration of their contact. Hence, white mistresses were far less troubled by fears about the *dai* exerting harmful cultural influences over the children.

The need to engage an *amah* remained high, especially over the course of the nineteenth century. While in the earlier decades Mary Martha Sherwood recommended 'dayes' for all 'delicate children', even in cases where the white mother was 'able to nurse her children', the more standard advice – voiced in this case by Emma Roberts – was that a 'dhye' should be hired only where 'mothers are unable to nurse their own children'.[109] In actual practice, however, as 'A Lady Resident' put it in the 1860s, '[a]lmost all infants in India are brought up by amahs, or native wet nurses'.[110]

While the practice of engaging a wet-nurse was commonly found in Britain until about the 1870s, it is notable that in colonial homes in India it continued until a much later period because of the climate and several other factors.[111] There are mixed indications about the continuation of the practice of engaging wet-nurses in the later colonial period as well. On the one hand, Steel and Gardiner noted that by the turn of the century, following the introduction of 'artificial foods' and bottle-feeding, the practice of hiring a wet-nurse was 'now seldom resorted to'. They advised that the *amah* was to be employed only in certain unavoidable cases – such as the mother being 'unable to nurse her baby', or in the case of any 'serious objection' such as 'transmitting any physical or mental disease'.[112] Notwithstanding Steel and Gardiner's claim, however, it seems to appear that the practice of keeping a wet-nurse did continue well into the early years of the twentieth century, at the least. Hence, as late as the 1920s, Kate Platt, the Delhi-based physician, recommended the hiring of 'native foster-mothers' (as wet-nurses were sometimes called), and observed that 'a wet nurse is the best solution of the difficulty' of child-rearing in India – although she did concede that 'the prejudice which exists against native foster-mothers is not without foundation'.[113] Regarding this 'prejudice' against *amahs*, Steel and Gardiner sharply censured the 'race prejudice' which they had sometimes detected in the hiring of 'native wet-nurses', with the tart remark: '[I]f the Western woman is unable to fulfil her first duty to her child, let her thank Heaven for … any one able to do that duty for her.'[114]

Even more unambiguously than in the case of ayahs, colonial writings constructed the wet-nurses negatively, as women who exercised power over and tyrannised their employers in diverse ways.[115] Memsahibs often expressed feelings of helplessness in the face of these women's numerous demands: their main complaint was that *amahs*, knowing that they were indispensable, would extort exorbitant salaries. In other words, this category of low-class 'native' woman was felt to be manipulative and to covertly exercise power over the colonial home. In addition to salary, her food and clothing too had to be provided for. Calling them 'expensive and troublesome appendages to a family', Emma Roberts fumed that they 'demand[ed] high wages' because they were only 'too well aware of their importance', while 'A Lady Resident', terming them 'very expensive luxuries', explained that the expenditure on wet-nurses was exorbitant because they also had to be 'fed, clothed, and highly paid'.[116]

Moreover, there was also guilt about the welfare of the *amah*'s own infant. Some arrangement had to be made for them, such as paying a regular maintenance amount for them. Mary Martha Sherwood suggested that the memsahib should take 'the trouble of keeping the infant within her compound and seeing it daily'.[117] Julia Maitland, in the Madras presidency, also felt 'obliged to keep a separate nurse for her baby, and see after it regularly myself'. She complained in her letters home that otherwise, the wet-nurses were 'so careless about their own children' that they 'would let the poor little creature die from neglect, and then curse us as the cause of it'.[118] On the other hand, 'A Lady Resident' suggested quite the opposite; constructing the wet-nurse stereotypically as the dishonest 'native', she warned that far from being callous, the *amah* was, in fact, more 'apt to nurse' her own child 'by stealth' and hence cautioned that the 'native' infant be taken away from its mother 'by her friends'.[119]

In general, however, memsahibs projected these 'native' women as callous mothers. Martha Sherwood noted how despite the fact that 'something handsome' was paid for their rearing, these woman's own infants usually died. She remarked that not only did the hard-hearted 'native' mothers remain unaffected, but what was more, they exhibited their own brand of racism by preferring white infants to their own:

> The mothers never fret after them; when they nurse a white baby they cease to care for their own. They say, 'White child is good, black child is slave.'[120]

Many housekeeping journals outlined in great detail the diet prescribed for the wet-nurse, of which the mistress was in charge. Their daily diet was considered important since they performed the important task of suckling European infants. Emma Roberts cautioned that this 'diet' had to be 'strictly attended to'.[121] Regarding their diet, the physician author of *A Domestic Guide* (1848) also gave detailed advice. He recommended an early morning breakfast of bread, butter, tea; with dinner consisting of chicken or mutton curry and rice, mild and simply made; and a meal at 7 p.m. when she was to be given bread and butter along with 'rice conjee with milk'. If the baby had wind the *amah* was to be given 'dillseed' or 'aniseed water, or peppermint'.[122] 'A Lady Resident', in turn, advised that the *amah*'s meals 'should be brought to show her mistress daily' and elaborated:

> [T]here is a regular diet provided for them. This consists of about a pint of weak tea, well sweetened with juggree, early in the morning; the same at breakfast, with either half a dozen rice cakes, called 'appahs', or a small loaf of bread. At dinner one pound (half a seer) of boiled rice, with a meat and vegetable curry, and congee or rice-water to drink; the same quantity of rice at night with a fish curry, varied by mulligatawny, pepper-water, and fried meat or fish. Inland, fish is not always to be had, but when procurable, is particularly wholesome for an amah.[123]

Claiming that she had 'had much experience' with wet-nurses, this Madras presidency-based memsahib warned the mistress to reject the *amah*'s demand 'for more chillies and hot spices' and recommended 'ordinary curries' instead, made with 'proper meat and vegetables' which would 'satisfy the amah as well as the infant'.[124]

> Should her milk slightly diminish after several months' nursing, a basin of sago congee, given between her dinner and supper, will almost always produce a sufficient supply; if left to herself she is certain to devour cloves of garlic, which the natives consider a specific in such cases.[125]

At the same time, she reinforced that old construct of the 'lazy native' by insisting that the woman should be made to 'assist in light work', otherwise 'the easy life and good feeding' would 'be sure to disagree with her' and even 'stop the full flow of milk which the native women nearly always have'.[126]

Race and class prejudices intermingled in the horror of 'dirt' that was often expressed in much of the writing on the wet-nurse. Given the *amah*'s close physical proximity with the European infants, she was feared as a potential health threat, and unlike in the case of the ayah, colonial discourse revealed an obsessive preoccupation with the *amah*'s health and hygiene – serving thereby to reinforce colonial constructions of the 'native' as a source of dirt and disease. Among the memsahib authors of housekeeping handbooks, it was 'A Lady Resident' who laid great stress upon the aspect of hygiene, advising that 'on first arrival', the *amah* needed to be provided with 'three cloths or sarees, six cholees or jackets, a comb, mat and blanket, also a tin to drink out of, and a cup and dish for her curry and rice. The clothes are renewed by the mistress when necessary.'[127] She urged young mothers to have the wet-nurse 'examined and duly approved by the medical man'.[128]

It is indeed striking how in their construction of colonial domesticities, colonial writings projected the wet-nurse as a far more negative presence inside the home than the ayah. After all, as we have seen, the ayah was perceived with a certain degree of mixed feelings by the memsahib writers, whose writings often revealed a mixture of both gratitude and suspicion towards her. In contrast, the wet-nurse was projected far more pejoratively as both physically and morally 'dirty' – thereby betraying deep-rooted colonial race and class prejudices. Moreover, as we shall be seeing in greater detail in the next chapter on colonial medical handbooks, physicians too joined hands with memsahibs in discussing the 'native' wet-nurse in great detail and warning against her. The fact that medical discourse (which was virtually silent on ayahs) should have considered it necessary to single out the wet-nurse alone among 'natives' seems to suggest that she was perceived as a deeply ambivalent presence, posing the greater danger of the two women. Clearly, while the ayah was perceived with mixed feelings in colonial discourse, the wet-nurse, in contrast was inscribed with unambiguous negativity.

Conclusion

Colonial writings in the nineteenth and early twentieth centuries projected the colonial home as a microcosm of the empire, with the memsahib at the head of a large retinue of household servants reproducing the power relations characteristic of imperial administration. However, undergirding these relationships was a web of complexities and ambivalences which undermined and mitigated this 'authority'. In particular, it was the complex location of two female servants inside this household, namely, the ayah and the wet-nurse, which frequently evoked colonial anxieties.

While the ayah as lady's maid found widespread appreciation among memsahibs across the entire period, it was the ayah as nursemaid for the European child who was seen as more problematic. Her surrogate motherhood and closeness to European children often generated a tussle between the memsahib and the ayah for cultural and emotional control over the children who were, significantly, the next generation of imperial rulers. Possibly an even more dark and ambivalent a figure was that of the wet-nurse who was perceived as 'tyrannising' over the colonial memsahib. The latter found herself helplessly dependent on this low-class/caste 'native' woman. All these factors together generated various pressures on the colonial memsahib and served in diverse ways to dilute and undermine her imperial authority inside her 'domestic empire'.

A striking feature of this relationship between memsahib and female domestic servants was that it remained more or less unchanging over the entire period, notwithstanding minor variations in emphases in different memsahibs' writings which were based on individual experiences. In fact, most of the interactions seem to have depended on the personal equations of the individuals concerned. This seems to be a feature across the nineteenth and early twentieth centuries, and also across different geographical regions. Thus, whether the memsahib was based in Madras in the 1830s (such as Julia Maitland) or in north India in the 1880s (Flora Annie Steel), it did not affect her attitude to ayahs beyond a point. In other words, living in insulation from 'native' life as they did, European perceptions revealed a curious sameness throughout the colonial period.

Notes

An earlier version of this chapter first appeared in the Centre for Women's Development Studies' *Indian Journal of Gender Studies*, 16:3, September–December (2009), pp. 299–322, published by Sage Publications.

1   Anne McClintock, *Imperial Leather: Race, Gender and Sexuality in the Colonial Contest* (London and New York, Routledge, 1995), p. 133.
2   Alison Blunt, 'Imperial Geographies of Home': British Domesticity in India, 1886–1925', *Transactions of the Institute of British Geographers*, New Series, 24:4 (1999), pp. 421–440; Elizabeth Buettner, *Empire Families: Britons and Late Imperial India* (Oxford and New York, Oxford University Press, 2004), and Ann Laura Stoler, *Carnal Knowledge and Imperial Power: Race and the Intimate in Colonial Rule* (Berkeley, University of California Press, 2002). Others on this subject include Rosemary Marangoly George, 'Homes in the Empire, Empires in the Home', *Cultural Critique*, 26 (Winter, 1993–94), pp. 95–127; Nupur Chaudhuri, 'Memsahibs and their Servants in Nineteenth-century India', *Women's History Review*, 3:4 (1994), pp. 549–562; Georgina Gowans, 'Imperial Geographies of Home: Memsahibs and Miss-Sahibs in India and Britain, 1915–1947, *Cultural Geographies*, 10 (2003), pp. 424–444.
3   Blunt, 'Imperial Geographies of Home', p. 422.
4   Kate Teltscher, *India Inscribed: European and British Writing on India, 1600–1800* (Oxford, Oxford University Press, 1995), p. 145. Teltscher, however, does not probe these master–servant relationships in very great detail.
5   See Philip Davies, *Splendours of the Raj: British Architecture in India, 1660–1947* (London, J. Murray, 1985), and also William J. Glover, '"A Feeling of Absence from Old England": The Colonial Bungalow', *Home Cultures*, 1:1 (2004), pp. 61–82.
6   For details about servants in colonial households see Edmund C. P. Hull, *The European in India or Anglo-India's Vade-Mecum: A Handbook of Useful and Practical Information for those Proceeding to or Residing in the East Indies Relating to Outfits, Routes, Time for Departure, Indian Climate and Seasons, Housekeeping, Servants, etc. etc.* ([1871], New Delhi, Asian Educational Services, 2004), pp. 104–135. For a discussion Nupur Chaudhuri, 'Memsahibs and their Servants', pp. 549–562.
7   E. J. 'Life in India', *Queen*, 2 February (1878), cited in Chaudhuri, 'Memsahibs and their Servants', p. 561; Agatha James, 'Housekeeping and House Management in India', in Anon. (ed.), *The Lady at Home and Abroad: Her Guide and Friend* (London, Abbott, Jones and Co., 1898), p. 372.
8   J. E. Dawson, 'The Englishwoman in India: Her Influence and Responsibilities' (Part II), *The Calcutta Review*, 83:165 (1886), p. 365.
9   Alison Blunt, 'Imperial Geographies of Home', p. 422; George, 'Homes in the Empire', p. 108.
10 George, 'Homes in the Empire', p. 108.
11 Earlier housekeeping manuals include the anonymous 1864 text: 'A Lady Resident', *The Englishwoman in India: Containing Information for the Use of Ldies Proceeding to, or Residing in, the East Indies, on the Subjects of their Outfit. Furniture, Housekeeping, the Rearing of Children, Duties and Wages of Servants, Management of the Stables, and Arrangements for Travelling to which Are Added Receipts for Indian Cookery* (London, Smith, Elder and Co., 1864). Among housekeeping manuals which appeared in the late nineteenth century and early twentieth centuries are E. Garrett, *Morning Hours in India: Practical Hints on Household Management, the Care and Training of Children Etc.* (London, Trubner and Co., 1887); 'Chota Mem' (C. Lang], *The English Bride in India: Being Hints on Indian Housekeeping*, second edition (Madras, Higginbotham and Co., 1909).
12 Flora Annie Steel and Grace Gardiner, *The Complete Indian Housekeeper and Cook: Giving the Duties of Mistress and Servants, the General Management of*

[138]

the House and Practical Recipes for Cooking in all its Branches ([1888], London: William Heinemann, 1909), pp. 7, 19, 4, 19, 2. This manual went into ten quick editions (seven of them in the nineteenth century itself) and was translated into many Indian languages.

13 Steel and Gardiner, *Complete Indian Housekeeper and Cook*, p. 2; Dawson, 'The Englishwoman in India', p. 363.

14 Anne Laura Stoler, *Race and the Education of Desire: Foucault's 'History of Sexuality' and the Colonial Order of Things* (Durham, Duke University Press, 1995), p. 150.

15 Steel and Gardiner, *Complete Indian Housekeeper and Cook*, pp. 3, 3. 9.

16 Kate Platt, *The Home and Health in India and the Tropical Colonies* (London, Bailliere, Tindall & Cox, 1923), p. 2. Kate Platt, MD, was the first Principal of the Lady Hardinge Hospital and College for Women at Delhi, which was established in 1916.

17 Blunt, 'Imperial Geographies of Home', p. 428.

18 Dawson, 'The Englishwoman in India', pp. 359, 365.

19 See Antoinette Burton, *Burdens of History: British Feminists, Indian Women and Imperial Culture, 1865–1915* (Chapel Hill, University of North Carolina Press, 1994); Indrani Sen, *Woman and Empire: Representations in the Writings of British India, 1858–1900* (New Delhi, Orient Longman, 2002), pp. 33–35.

20 Maud Diver, *The Englishwoman in India* (Edinburgh and London, William Blackwood & Sons, 1909), pp. 77–78. Maud Diver (1867–1945), the daughter of an Indian Army officer, was born in Murree and sent to Britain for her education, returning to India at sixteen. She married Lt. Col. Diver when he was a Subaltern in the Royal Warwickshire Regiment, and after her return to England in 1896 she wrote several highly popular novels as well as a number of non-fictional works.

21 Blunt, 'Imperial Geographies of Home', p. 425.

22 'A Lady Resident', *Englishwoman in India*, p. 153.

23 Hull, *The European in India*, p. 130.

24 Platt, *Home and Health in India*, pp. 36, 36, 36.

25 Mary Martha Sherwood, *The Life and Times of Mrs. Sherwood (1775–1851) from the Diaries of Captain and Mrs. Sherwood*, ed. F. J. Harvey Darton (London, Wells Gardner, Darton & Co. Ltd, 1910), p. 296. Mary Martha Sherwood, whose husband was an officer in the Indian army, lived in India for ten years (1805–1815), at places like Dinapore, Berhampore, Cawnpore (Kanpur) and Meerut. Six children were born to her in India, with two of them dying there in infancy, and Mrs Sherwood's diaries delineate aspects of child-rearing, and include glowing accounts of her ayah and wet-nurse, while her appreciation of her children's 'heathen' servants transcend her cultural prejudices and her religious convictions. As mentioned in Chapter 1, Mrs Sherwood also gained fame in England as a writer of evangelical stories for children.

26 Emma Roberts, *Scenes and Characteristics of Hindostan, with Sketches of Anglo-Indian Society*, vol. 1 (London, W. H. Allen, 1835), p. 92. Emma Roberts (1794–1840), who lived in India for four years (1828–1832), with her older sister and her army officer husband, stayed at Agra, Cawnpore (Kanpur), Etawah and Calcutta, before returning to London after her sister's death. Roberts wrote several learned books and articles, and edited newspapers, journals and periodicals. On a later visit to India, she briefly lived in western India and died of a sudden illness in Poona.

27 Steel and Gardiner, *Complete Indian Housekeeper and Cook*, pp. 86, 85, 86.

28 *Ibid.*, p. 87.

29 Buettner, *Empire Families*, p. 59.

30 Platt, *Home and Health in India*, p. 36.

31 'A Lady Resident', *Englishwoman in India*, pp. 54, 55.

32 *Ibid.*, p. 55.

33 For a skilfully delineated account of the memsahibs' feelings of regrets and nostalgia on returning home to Britain as well as their difficulties in adjusting to being 'nobodies', see Chapter 5, 'From Somebodies to Nobodies: Returning Home to

Britain ...', in Buettner, *Empire Families*, pp. 188–239; see also Gowans, 'Imperial Geographies of Home'.

34 Among the few minor complaints against the ayah as lady's maid, is Emma Roberts' annoyed remark for instance, that the ayah had 'no notion of' western dressing, in Roberts, *Scenes and Characteristics of Hindostan*, vol. 1, pp. 92–93.

35 'A Lady Resident', *Englishwoman in India*, p. 52.

36 'Chota Mem', *The English Bride in India*, pp. 61–62.

37 Hull, *The European in India*, p. 129; p. 130.

38 *The Pioneer*, 22 October (1880), p. 5.

39 It is interesting to note how housekeeping manuals often fed off each other. 'Chota Mem', mentioned admiringly in her book's Preface that her 'humble volume' was only 'meant to contain "Simple Hints." For a fuller and more detailed book, I would advise my readers to get an excellent one entitled "The Complete Indian Housekeeper," by G. G. and F. A. S.', in Preface to First Edition, 'Chota Mem', *The English Bride in India*, n.p.

40 Steel and Gardiner, *Complete Indian Housekeeper and Cook*, p. 87.

41 Stoler, *Race and the Education of Desire*, p. 150.

42 Emma Roberts, who was generally critical of ayahs, was nevertheless, one of the few memsahibs who felt that ayahs were generally honest – although they were otherwise 'idle, slatternly ... dissipated... lazy', in Roberts, *Scenes and Characteristics of Hindostan*, vol. 1, p. 92.

43 'A Lady Resident', *Englishwoman in India*, p. 54.

44 For details on female domestic servants in Britain see McClintock, *Imperial Leather*, pp. 85–88.

45 Roberts, *Scenes and Characteristics of Hindostan*, vol. 1, p. 92; *The Pioneer*, 22 October (1880), p. 5.

46 Flora Annie Steel, *The Garden of Fidelity: Being the Autobiography of Flora Annie Steel, 1847–1929* (London, Macmillan & Co. Ltd, 1929), p. 52.

47 *The Englishman's Saturday Evening Journal*, 8 January (1870), p. 21. For more on the 'native' gaze, see Indrani Sen (ed.), *Memsahibs' Writings: Colonial Narratives on Indian Women* (New Delhi, Orient BlackSwan, 2008), pp. 277–285.

48 Glover, '"A Feeling of Absence from Old England"', p. 75.

49 *Ibid.*

50 Diver, *The Englishwoman in India*, p. 86.

51 *Ibid.*, pp. 86–87.

52 Elsewhere I have discussed the imposition of a kind of 'purdah' on the white woman. See Sen, *Woman and Empire*, pp. 21–24.

53 'A Lady Resident', *Englishwoman in India*, p. 52.

54 Sherwood, *Life and Times of Mrs. Sherwood* (1910), p. 365.

55 'A Lady Resident', *Englishwoman in India*, p. 53.

56 Platt, *Home and Health in India*, p. 138.

57 *The Pioneer*, 22 October (1880), p. 6.

58 R. S. Mair, 'Supplement on the Management of Children in India', in his *Medical Guide for Anglo-Indians* ([1871], New Delhi, Asian Educational Services, 2004), pp. 325 and 330.

59 Sherwood, *Life and Times of Mrs. Sherwood* (1910), p. 296.

60 Mary Martha Sherwood, *The Life of Mrs. Sherwood (chiefly autobiographical) with Extracts from Mr. Sherwood's Journal during his Imprisonment in France and Residence in India, ed. by her Daughter, Sophia Kelly* (London, Darton & Co., 1854), p. 337.

61 *The Pioneer*, 22 October (1880), pp. 5–6.

62 Platt, *Home and Health in India*, p. 142.

63 Buettner, *Empire Families*, pp. 25–62; Gowans, 'Imperial Geographies of Home', pp. 424–441.

64 Mair, 'Supplement on the Management of Children in India', p. 341.

65 Hull, *The European in India*, pp. 140, 140.

66 Julia Maitland, *Letters from Madras, during the Years 1836–39, by a Lady* ([1843], London, John Murray, 1846), p. 114. Julia Maitland (1808–1864), who came to India as a bride, lived for three years (1836–1840) in the Madras presidency with her husband, James Thomas, a senior merchant with the East India Company. They stayed at Madras, 'Rajahmundry' and Bangalore, and like most Europeans of this period, socialised with elite Indians, such as zamindars (landowners). They also took an interest in evangelism, and set up schools for Indian boys. Her letters to her mother, full of lively observations on British life in south India, were later published in the form of a book.
67 Steel and Gardiner, *Complete Indian Housekeeper and Cook*, pp. 87, 87, 87.
68 Diver, *The Englishwoman in India*, p. 87
69 Buettner, *Empire Families*, p. 58.
70 Platt, *Home and Health in India*, pp. 138, 139.
71 See Rudyard Kipling, *Something of Myself: For My Friends, Known and Unknown* (London, Macmillan & Co. Ltd, 1937).
72 Sherwood, *Life of Mrs. Sherwood* (1854), p. 406.
73 Platt, *Home and Health in India*, p. 138.
74 Roberts, *Scenes and Characteristics of Hindostan*, vol. 2., p. 125.
75 *Ibid.*
76 *Ibid.*
77 Kipling, *Something of Myself*, pp. 2, 2.
78 Platt, *Home and Health in India*, pp. 138–139.
79 Ann Laura Stoler, 'A Sentimental Education: Native Servants and the Cultivation of European Children in the Netherlands Indies', in Laurie J. Sears (ed.), *Fantasizing the Feminine in Indonesia* (Durham, Duke University Press, 1996), p. 81.
80 'A Lady Resident', *Englishwoman in India*, pp. 106, 106.
81 S. Leigh Hunt and Alexander A. Kenny, *Tropical Trials: A Handbook for Women in the Tropics* (London, W. H. Allen, 1883), p. 403. It needs to be pointed out that the fear of cultural contamination seems to have cut across class, and been present in missionary parenting as well. As Emily Manktelow mentions in a recent book, 'it was parental anxiety about the moral, spiritual and material prosperity of their children that often elicited the most prejudiced responses from missionary parents, whose concerns increasingly shifted from cultural chauvinism to concerns about racial contamination and contact', in Emily J. Manktelow, *Missionary Families: Race, Gender and Generation on the Spiritual Frontier* (Manchester, Manchester University Press, 2013), p. 163.
82 Diver, *The Englishwoman in India*, p. 36; Platt, *Home and Health in India*, p. 138.
83 Chaudhuri, 'Memsahibs and Motherhood in Nineteenth-century Colonial India', *Victorian Studies*, 31:4 (1988), p. 531.
84 For details see Chaudhuri, 'Memsahibs and Motherhood', pp. 517–535, Buettner, *Empire Families*, pp. 52–57.
85 Maitland, *Letters from Madras*, p. 114.
86 Diver, *The Englishwoman in India*, p. 36.
87 See for instance, Blunt, 'Imperial Geographies of Home', p. 426 and Chaudhuri, 'Memsahibs and their Servants', pp. 556–557. Blunt also points out that 'the severity of the conflict was also symbolized by the destruction of British homes through arson and looting, and written and visual depictions of this destruction served to domesticate the imperial crisis in vivid and immediate ways', p. 426
88 Chaudhuri, 'Memsahibs and their Servants', pp. 557.
89 Blunt, 'Imperial Geographies of Home', p. 430
90 A surprisingly large number of them carry grateful accounts of faithful ayahs risking their lives to protect their masters, mistresses and especially the white children in their charge. For more details, see Indrani Sen, 'Discourses of "Gendered Loyalty": Indian Women in Nineteenth Century "Mutiny" Fiction', in Biswamoy Pati (ed.), *The Great Rebellion of 1857 in India: Exploring Transgressions, Contests and Diversities* (London, Routledge,, 2010), pp. 111–128.
91 A faithful *kitmutgar* hides several memsahibs in his hut at great danger to his life

in Ruth M. Coopland, *A Lady's Escape from Gwalior, and Life in the Fort of Agra during the Mutinies of 1857* (London, Smith, Elder, & C., 1859), pp. 122–125.

92 Servants becoming insolent is mentioned by Katherine Harris, *A Lady's Diary of the Siege of Lucknow, Written for the Perusal of Friends at Home* ([1858], New Delhi, Asian Educational Services, 2006), pp. 46–47; the ayah turning greedy is noted in Coopland, *A Lady's Escape from Gwalior*, p. 109.

93 Adelaide Case, *Day by Day at Lucknow: A Journal of the Siege of Lucknow* (London, Richard Bentley, 1858), pp. 4, 33.

94 Mrs. E. Augusta King, *The Diary of a Civilian's Wife in India, 1877–1882* (London, Richard Bentley, 1884), vol. 1, pp. 130–131.

95 See Anthony Sattin (ed.), *An Englishwoman in India: The Memoirs of Harriet Tytler, 1828–1858* (Oxford, Oxford University Press, 1988), Case, *Day by Day at Lucknow*.

96 In Flora Annie Steel's 'Mutiny' novel, *On the Face of the Waters* ([1896], New Delhi, Arnold-Heinemann, 1985), an old ayah saves a neighbour's little son, Sonny Seymour, by staining his face and blonde hair dark, putting him into Indian clothes and passing him off as an Indian child for several months. In Sara Jeannette Duncan's novel, *The Story of Sonny Sahib* (London and New York, Macmillan, 1894), a loyal old ayah lovingly brings up her dead mistress's infant as her own child.

97 Steel and Gardiner, *Complete Indian Housekeeper and Cook*, p. 167.

98 Roberts, *Scenes and Characteristics of Hindostan*, vol. 2, p. 92.

99 Sherwood, *Life and Times of Mrs. Sherwood* (1910), p. 365.

100 'A Lady Resident', *Englishwoman in India*, p. 95.

101 Platt, *Home and Health in India*, pp. 136, 136, 136.

102 Jane Maria Strachey, letter dated 6 January, 1870, MSS. Eur. F127/126, OIOC, cited in Nupur Chaudhuri, 'Memsahibs and Motherhood', p. 532.

103 Anon., *A Domestic Guide to Mothers in India: Containing Particular Instructions on the Management of Themselves and their Children. By a Medical Practitioner of Several Years' Experience in India* ([1836], Bombay, American Mission Press, 1848), pp. 71, 72. One of the rare instances of a colonial physician rejecting the need for a wet-nurse is an early medical guide, Frederick Corbyn, *Management and Diseases of Infants Under the Influence of the Climate of India Being Instructions to Mothers and Parents in Situations where Medical Aid is not to be Obtained, and a Guide to Medical Men, Inexperienced in the Nursery and the Treatment of Tropical Infantile Diseases, Illustrated by Colour Plates* (Calcutta, Thacker, 1828). Colonial physicians' views on the subject of the wet-nurse are discussed in greater detail in the next chapter.

104 See Swapna Banerjee, *Men, Women, and Domestics: Articulating Middle-class Identity in Colonial Bengal* (New Delhi, Oxford University Press, 2004); see also Swapna Banerjee, 'Child, Mother, and Servant: The Discourse of Motherhood and Domestic Ideology in Colonial Bengal', in Avril Powell and Siobhan Lambert-Hurley (eds), *Rhetoric and Reality: Gender and Colonial Experience in South Asia* (New Delhi, Oxford University Press, 2006), pp. 17–50.

105 See Chaudhuri, 'Memsahibs and Motherhood', p. 529.

106 'A Lady Resident', *Englishwoman in India*, p. 53.

107 Roberts, *Scenes and Characteristics of Hindostan*, vol. 2, pp. 121, 121.

108 Maitland, *Letters from Madras*, p. 52.

109 Sherwood, *Life and Times of Mrs. Sherwood* (1910), p. 365; Roberts, *Scenes and Characteristics of Hindostan*, vol. 2, p. 21.

110 'A Lady Resident', *Englishwoman in India*, p. 96.

111 For details on wet-nursing in Britain, see Ann Roberts, 'Mothers and Babies: The Wet-nurse and Her Employer in Mid-Nineteenth Century England', *Women's Studies*, 3 (1976), p. 281, cited in Chaudhuri, 'Memsahibs and Motherhood', p. 529.

112 Steel and Gardiner, *Complete Indian Housekeeper and Cook*, p. 166.

113 Platt, *Home and Health in India*, p. 84. Platt's discussion on wet-nurses seems to contradict the statement by Steel and Gardiner that by around the early 1900s 'the

employment of a dai ... is now seldom resorted to... only to save life, or in the case of very delicate children', in Steel and Gardiner, *Complete Indian Housekeeper and Cook*, p. 166.

114   Steel and Gardiner, *Complete Indian Housekeeper and Cook*, pp. 166, 166, 176.
115   Kate Platt makes a rare, positive comment: 'Indian foster-mothers are usually devoted to their charges, but they need continual supervision', in Platt, *Home and Health in India*, p. 84.
116   Roberts, *Scenes and Characteristics of Hindostan*, vol. 2, p. 121, 'A Lady Resident', *Englishwoman in India*, p. 96.
117   Sherwood, *Life and Times of Mrs. Sherwood* (1910), p. 365.
118   Maitland, *Letters from Madras*, pp. 51, 52.
119   'A Lady Resident', *Englishwoman in India*, p. 97.
120   Sherwood, *Life and Times of Mrs. Sherwood* (1910), pp. 365, 365.
121   Roberts, *Scenes and Characteristics of Hindostan*, vol. 2, p. 21.
122   Anon., *A Domestic Guide to Mothers in India*, p. 75.
123   'A Lady Resident', *Englishwoman in India*, p. 97.
124   *Ibid.*
125   *Ibid.*
126   *Ibid.*, p. 75.
127   *Ibid.*, p. 97.
128   *Ibid.*

CHAPTER FIVE

Marginalising the memsahib: the white woman's health issues in colonial medical writings

In the last chapter we saw how the colonial home was a site of contestation and ambivalences for the white memsahib. Indeed, the role of the white woman within colonial domesticity came to be subjected to critical scrutiny by yet another category of colonial writing. This was the medical handbook which sought to give guidance on health matters to middle-class colonials. From the second half of the nineteenth century onwards and up till the early years of the twentieth century, there appeared a growing spate of medical handbooks and manuals, authored by India-based colonial physicians. These texts, which had the objective of helping the British in India shape their homes and families along the lines of 'home', enjoyed great popularity and also participated in promoting the idea of the white woman's duty as colonial mother. In this chapter we shall examine the construction of gender in these colonial medical texts, scrutinising how they wielded authoritative power over vulnerable young European women in the colonies through the power/knowledge of their medical directives.

The medical manual as tool of empire and colonial misogyny

The colonial medical manual was thus an important category of writing which provides an insight into the manner in which male-authored discursive writings sought to admonish, discipline and control white women inside colonial households. Given the kind of significance that this genre possesses, however, it has surprisingly not received much scholarly attention. Among the very few studies, Elizabeth Buettner's *Empire Families* (2004) comes closest to discussing these texts in some amount of detail, although she does it with regard to child-rearing in colonial India rather than with regard to women's health.[1] Indeed, even historians of the social history of medicine, such as David Arnold or

Mark Harrison, have largely ignored the issue of white women's health in colonial India, while historians who work on colonial maternal and reproductive health such as Barbara Ramusack, Maneesha Lal, Sarah Hodges and more recently, younger scholars such as Samiksha Sehrawat, have focused exclusively on Indian women.[2]

The objective of medical manuals written for Europeans living in remote, far-flung areas or *mofussil* postings, was to bring these colonials under the purview of western medical control. Unlike housekeeping guides which, as we saw in the previous chapter, were generally written by memsahibs, medical handbooks were almost solely authored by male physicians who belonged to the powerful colonial medical services (such as the Indian Medical Service) and held positions of authority in the government.[3] Indeed, the ideological hold that some physicians continued to wield over their readers may be gauged from the fact that several popular texts attained the stature of 'classics' and continued to be reprinted and circulated among readers for generations – even long after medical science had advanced.[4]

As a part of the westernising and 'modernising' impulse of colonial British culture which was amplified further after the mid-nineteenth-century takeover by the Crown, these texts sought to impose the ideas, scientific knowledge and practices of the metropole upon colonials living in the remotest stations of the vast Indian empire, and 'helped to reproduce the Victorian home abroad and convey civilised, ritualised and proper forms of domestic housekeeping and medical care'.[5] Scholars have observed that western medicine was, in many ways, a 'tool of empire' and that the medical conquest of the tropics sought to assist in furthering the colonial subjugation of these regions and reinforce its ideological structures.[6] Indeed, besides carrying out the dissemination of western medicine and medical information, these guidebooks both reflected colonial ideologies and also served to reinforce them. While certain similarities may be discerned between housekeeping manuals and medical handbooks, between colonial domesticity and colonial medicine, it is important to emphasise their fundamental difference.[7] Unlike housekeeping manuals which catered to a female readership and foregrounded the memsahib as mistress of the household, and discussed domestic topics such as managing domestic servants or listing Anglo-Indian recipes, medical handbooks focused largely on European *male* health – and only very occasionally addressed women and children's health issues.[8] Indeed, they displayed an unabashed gender bias, proffering advice mostly on subjects such as preserving male health and combating the climate in tropical colonies through appropriate male clothing, diet and lifestyle.[9] Moreover, as we shall see, this medical discourse was underwritten by colonial gender prejudices and served to 'scientifically' reinforce them under the garb of medical knowledge.

Medical handbooks and the marginalisation of women's health

One striking feature of this medical discourse was that white women were rendered largely invisible in the bulk of these writings. Not only were female health issues addressed only in a relatively small handful of manuals, it is surprising how even in those handbooks which supposedly specialised in 'family health', issues such as child-care and health in the nursery tended to be foregrounded, while the subject of the mother's health continued to remain marginalised.[10] Only very occasionally did handbooks cater to the need of young colonial brides, particularly in remote locations, for practical guidance on the management of pregnancy and childbirth.

In this medical discourse, European memsahibs were subjected by their male compatriots to a gendered, medical gaze that was often critical and disparaging. As I have argued elsewhere, colonial discourse in general – fiction, memoirs, newspaper articles, journals, periodicals, exhortatory writings – widely contributed in constructing and circulating negative stereotypes of the frivolous, party-loving memsahib who had the proclivity 'to laugh, to dance, to sing, to beguile time and to chase dull cares'.[11] Whenever female issues were addressed, medical texts fed into this preoccupation with the white woman's 'morality', her 'womanly' duty in the colony, her gender relationships, as well as her imperial duty and maternal responsibilities. Hence, as we shall be seeing, these writings followed the generally misogynistic trend of highlighting the memsahib's frivolity and her medical vulnerability to the hot climate – in short, in projecting her as both climatically and culturally unfit for living in the colony.

In the nineteenth and early twentieth centuries the need for medical guidance was often voiced. The vastness of the country, the absence of trained doctors in remote areas as well as the lack of easy access to western medical facilities that continued well into the early decades of the twentieth century, fuelled this need. In the 1870s. for instance, Edmund Hull, author of *The European in India* (1871) some of whose exhortations on motherhood we saw in the previous chapter on the colonial home, urged the need for medical handbooks, since large numbers of Europeans were forced to 'live miles away from the nearest resident medical man' and the knowledge of 'a few simple remedies' for common diseases could turn out to be vital for 'averting dangerous illness, or in actually saving life'.[12] Hull may not have been a medical man himself but contemporary colonial physicians also echoed this need. For instance, R. S. Mair, who was Deputy Coroner at Madras in the 1870s, remarked in his *Medical Guide for Anglo-Indians* (1871), that during his sixteen years of service he had frequently been called upon to give 'written directions' to those of his patients who lived in 'remote or isolated districts in the Mofussil'.[13] Mair further observed:

> Europeans in India who live at such great distances from a doctor ... are compelled to fall back upon their own resources, to treat, not only the members of their own household, but also those employed by them: and the author, while engaged for many years in an extensive practice, was frequently called upon to give such written directions ... to such of his patients as left the presidency town for remote or isolated districts in the Mofussil.[14]

According to Mark Harrison, it was from the nineteenth century onwards that Europeans increasingly felt a 'sense of vulnerability' in the tropical climate; prior to that, the belief during the eighteenth century was that European women, in fact, enjoyed better health in warm climates than in cold.[15] Certainly, the sheer plethora of medical manuals which were published in the second half of the nineteenth century gestures at unspoken anxieties about European vulnerability in the tropics and the need for medical guidance. However, what is most striking about these medical handbooks is the veil of silence that they drew over such fears. So that, instead of expressing anxieties about European vulnerability, they sought to project European self-reliance in matters of health, inscribing themselves as courageously coping with disease and medical emergencies in the remotest outposts of empire and proving equal to the task, when 'compelled to fall back upon their own resources'.

As we have already mentioned, a striking feature of this medical discourse was its conspicuous silence on women's health. Indeed, one male gynaecologist writing in the 1870s even complained that female health had been such a neglected area that he had 'only found three lines relating to women' in the classic medical writings of James Johnson and James Ranald Martin, while even contemporary medical writings took 'scant notice' of the health of women.[16] The fact of the matter is that white women's health issues remained peripheral to colonial medical discourse throughout this period – clearly indicating the essentially male-centric nature of the colonial enterprise. So much so, that as late as 1905, a handbook for colonials going out to the tropics, which was written at the specific request of the London School of Tropical Medicine, barely mentioned women.[17] This overall silence on European women's health issues becomes even more striking when we recall that by around the 1860s onwards there was, relatively speaking, a significant presence of English wives in India (even though white men did undoubtedly continue to vastly out-number white women till the very end of the colonial period).[18]

Medical handbooks, pregnancy and childbirth

As Nupur Chaudhuri has pointed out, the circumstances of colonial life in the nineteenth century made the experience of pregnancy and childbirth stressful and difficult for young women.[19] Around much of the century it was the common practice for the bride and groom to proceed to India almost immediately after marriage; alternatively, young women would get married a few months after landing in the country. According to an early medical guidebook, brides were married 'frequently at the age of 16 or 17; indeed, I know several instances of marriage at 14 years of age', and were very young when they became pregnant.[20] Echoing this, another physician pointed out how 'ladies in this country, generally marry very young, and soon afterwards proceed up the country with their husbands, to join their stations'. In many cases, it would be a small station 'with scarcely a lady among it'.[21]

> Thus, she is left to her own resources, timid and inexperienced, and soon brought into the trying period, when she is to bring forth her first-born.[22]

European women in India generally gave birth at home with the help of a European 'midwife' (who was usually a soldier's wife), or more commonly a 'native' *dai*, calling a medical practitioner only if something went amiss.[23] More importantly, the support structures traditionally provided by experienced female relatives as in Britain were absent, while living in remote areas with little access to medical practitioners further aggravated the problem. Sometimes even when physicians were available at military stations, pregnant military wives dreaded consulting misogynistic army doctors who were generally unsympathetic to female ailments.[24] Given such circumstances, the need for medical handbooks and practical advice on childbirth was all the more urgent. And yet, this much-needed guidance on pregnancy, labour or childbirth was rarely forthcoming.

However, two early medical handbooks that did offer practical guidance on handling pregnancy and childbirth at home were Frederick Corbyn's *Management and Diseases of Infants under the Influence of the Climate of India* (1828), and the anonymously written *A Domestic Guide to Mothers in India* (1836). While Corbyn, the Garrison Surgeon of Fort William at Calcutta, was silent on the actual process of giving birth ('the minutiae of delivery is not the intention of this work'), he criticised 'the custom in India for ladies to be solely confined by native women, or the wives of European soldiers' and recommended that 'all ladies ... be near medical aid during confinement, and ... the attendance of a medical gentleman'.[25] Practical guidance on childbirth in a remote area where a doctor may not be available was provided by *A Domestic Guide*, which was authored not by a member of the powerful colonial medical hierarchy but by a more humble, anonymous doctor of 'several years' standing'. Explaining how he had originally written it in sympathetic response to the appeal of a European woman who had lost her only infant in a remote part of India, he noted that '[a] work was required on this side of India' which would offer 'directions to mothers upon the management of themselves and their infants',[26] recalling how:

> A lady remarked to me how ... she herself had felt all the difficulties of ignorance and inexperience ... having had the misfortune to lose her only child, while stationed with her husband at some distance up the country, where she was without any domestic guide to point out to her what to do.[27]

Addressing mothers-to-be directly, he outlined the steps to be taken at various stages of pregnancy and 'accouchement' as well as the precautions to be taken for preventing miscarriages. Noting that a 'delicacy of feeling' often prevented young women from asking anyone, including their husbands, about such matters, he outlined the signs by which the young bride could herself recognise that she might be pregnant (e.g. the stopping of the 'monthly discharge', 'peculiar restlessness and sleeplessness', sickness and retching, irritability, enlargement of neck and breasts, change in colour of areola, and change in nipple, frequent passing of water, swelling and tenderness of the navel, heartburn).[28] Most importantly, he reassured young mothers-to-be that childbirth was a natural phenomenon for which 'very little assistance is required from a medical man' and that 'a good midwife' was 'sufficient', and went on to provide 'a few simple directions how to act when labour occurs'. Like most colonial physicians, he criticised 'native' *dais* whose 'disagreeable and painful' methods only increased 'the already great suffering of the parturient state'.[29] However, texts such as this which provided guidance on the management of childbirth were few and far between; and pregnant white women's needs went largely unaddressed.

The birth of the colonial family medical manual

From around the middle of the nineteenth century onwards, resident wives started to arrive in especially large numbers to set up 'English' style homes in India. Their coming was a part of a government policy initiated after the takeover by the Crown in 1858 and further facilitated by the opening of the Suez Canal in 1869 and subsequent invention of the steamship. It was hoped that this white female presence would help strengthen an imperial identity and consolidate an 'English' lifestyle and values in distant stations. Furthermore, from the mid-nineteenth century onwards, the colonial home and family became important symbols in colonial discourse. Henceforth, the concept of the colonial home as a marker of British cultural identity gradually took shape and its consolidation was sought to be strengthened in diverse ways.[30] Given this, the relative absence of writings on women's health began to be keenly felt. And conscious of this lacuna, the colonial government instituted in 1871 an award of 1,000 rupees for the best medical manual and invited colonial physicians to submit manuscripts for this award. The government gave detailed directives for a handbook which would be useful for its personnel living far removed from medical advice and required that it be 'simple, brief, concise' and suitable for its 'Officers' in remote areas and 'also for the use of their families and establishments'.[31] In 1873 the manuscript on family health submitted by Sir William Moore (who later became surgeon-general with the government of Bombay) was declared to be the winner of this award and in the following year the work was 'published under the authority of the government of India'.[32]

Soon, Moore's *Manual of Family Medicine for India* (1874) came to be regarded as the most authoritative family medical handbook. It was a comprehensive, encyclopaedic work with an alphabetical listing of various diseases and their symptoms, along with advice on their home treatment. This manual was specifically designed to be sold along with a small 'Indian Medicine Chest' which contained the basic medicines and equipment – the medicine chest clearly serving as a symbolic marker of colonial self-sufficiency and control over ailments in the remotest of *mofussil*.[33] The range of subjects that this handbook covered was wide and included diseases affecting men and women as well as children, along with their home remedies. Women's reproductive health was addressed and the discussions centred around diseases of the breast and womb, ovarian dropsy and puerperal fever, along with advice on pregnancy and childbirth.[34] However, in the later chapters which discussed subjects such as climate, clothing and the preservation of health in the tropics, the male bias of the text became glaringly evident and the focus shifted entirely to male health, along with a conspicuous erasure of women's health problems.[35]

Notwithstanding all this, however, Moore's *Manual* did take upon itself to give some degree of advice to memsahibs, focusing upon managing pregnancy and childbirth in remote areas 'in the absence of medical assistance'.[36] Adopting a detached, 'scientific' tone which contrasted with the personalised tone of the earlier handbook, *A Domestic Guide*, Moore gave step-by-step guidance on handling pregnancy and labour as well as childbirth. This included instructions on assisting with childbirth, such as attending to the care of the newborn: clearing its mouth of mucus or any other accumulated discharge; cutting the cord by using a ligature; bandaging the navel and handling any bleeding from the navel; cleaning and washing the newborn; and clothing and even reviving an infant which appeared to be still-born.[37] Besides this, Moore also showed concern for the health and after-care of the newly delivered mother, giving instructions on washing the 'private parts' of the patient, allowing her to sleep for 1½ hours at least, giving her a cup of warm tea, encouraging her to pass urine and clear the bowels, applying an 'abdominal binder' to help contract the womb, and preparing the breasts for suckling the infant.[38] The mandatory 'Medicine Chest' which accompanied Moore's *Manual* with its equipment of medicines, instruments and bandages, was no doubt meant to help in implementing some of the medical advice.

Around this time, possibly inspired by the colonial government's initiative, a number of other physicians also published family medical manuals for European families. Prominent among them was Edward John Tilt's *Health in India for British Women* (1875), a comprehensive study on colonial women's health. In fact, Tilt, a London-based gynaecologist, who had never visited India and based all his observations on years of treating India-returned Europeans, bemoaned in the book's Preface how medical writings generally neglected female health issues, and welcomed the 'increasing interest' being taken in family health. He especially lauded the government's initiative and the imperial considerations that fuelled this thrust, declaring that 'in future we shall hold India at much less cost than hitherto', since such medical books would minimise the 'blood tax' by providing guidance on medical problems.[39]

However, Tilt's handbook carried only very general comments about reproductive health, and this physician who had never practised outside Britain and lacked clinical experience of India, merely mentioned the dangers affecting childbirth in that country, such as puerperal haemorrhage, puerperal tetanus and the risk of miscarriage which, he held, was aggravated by the 'hot season'. His conclusion was that rather than give birth in India, it was better to continue the 'frequent practice for our countrywomen to return to Europe for their confinement'.[40]

The entry of white women as doctors marked the late nineteenth century and by the early twentieth century western medical facilities had greatly improved. So too had European female patients' access to trained physicians and medical care in the larger towns of India where there were enough 'experienced European medical practitioners, both men and women who would undertake the confinement'.[41] By now, important hill stations and some smaller cities too had adequate medical facilities. Nevertheless, in remote postings and *mofussil* towns medical care often continued to remain inaccessible, and practical medical advice continued to be needed in such cases. Kate Platt, whom we took note of in the last chapter, was indeed the sole female physician-author to have written a popular medical handbook in the 1920s. In her *Home and Health in India and the Tropical Colonies* (1923) Platt remarked that in such instances the pregnant European woman could choose to give birth either inside her own home or in a 'hired bungalow', where the 'confinement' could take place 'within reach of an experienced doctor'.[42]

Attempting to set the anxieties of the young mother-to-be at rest, Platt, who had been Principal at the Lady Hardinge Medical College and Hospital for Women at Delhi, reminded her readers (rather like the author of *A Domestic Guide*) that pregnancy and childbirth were but 'natural processes'. If a medical practitioner could not be reached, then a nurse (i.e. a European nurse, preferably someone recommended by the doctor or obtained from a Nursing Association) could be engaged at an early stage for guiding the mother-to-be through the pregnancy. It was important for this nurse to be engaged and kept in the memsahib's residence 'in good time for the event', especially where the doctor was 'not within easy call' or unable to come 'at very short notice'. In case any 'untoward symptoms' appeared at any time, 'the doctor should be sent for at once' – although Platt failed to explain how this could be arranged in remote areas.[43]

Perhaps what emerges most strikingly from Platt's text is that despite all the advances in medical care by the early decades of the twentieth century, white women were even now sometimes left to their own devices for childbirth and child-rearing. The fact that a medical manual carrying practical advice to the 'expectant mother' on pregnancy and childbirth continued to be popular seems to suggest precisely this, further reinforced by Platt's own recommendation of 'an excellent manual of advice' which could be obtained from the Infant Welfare Association at Delhi.[44]

Hot climates and women's reproductive health

White women's physical unfitness to live in the tropical colonies was always a subject of avid debate in medical handbooks, and much of the focus was on the impact of climate on their reproductive health. Physicians divided tropical climates into 'hot and wet' and 'hot and dry' and debates on the ill-effects of tropical climates on European reproductive health prevailed during much of the nineteenth century.[45] The ill-effects mentioned included anaemia, fatigue, sallow colouring and especially reproductive problems. Until the very end of the colonial period, physicians continued to discuss the impact of the climate on female health. The commonly held view was that the hot climate affected European women far more adversely than it did men and that women's reproductive health, in particular, was most vulnerable. Arguably, this all-prevailing construction which appeared in medical discourse about European women's vulnerability to hot climates, also played into the old colonial adage of the tropical colonies being 'no place for a woman'.

As we have seen, a number of texts sought to guide young colonial brides through pregnancy and childbirth as well as menstrual disturbances and uterine diseases. Among the health risks widely discussed was the problem of high diurnal temperatures of a tropical climate and the resultant tendency for miscarriages. In one of the leading medical books of the early nineteenth century, James Ranald Martin, the early nineteenth-century Calcutta-based physician – who according to Mark Harrison, was the 'most-renowned medical practitioner in the city' – observed in the 1840s that 'miscarriages, frequent at all seasons in India, occur yet more frequently in the hot season'.[46] Echoing this, the roughly contemporaneous *Domestic Guide* had agreed that the tropical climate 'impairs the energies and power of an European constitution' and that miscarriages were 'much more common in this country than in a cold climate', because of the 'debilitated state of the constitution'.[47]

However, it needs to be stressed at the same time that doctors sometimes did point out that a warm climate was actually more beneficial than a cold climate in certain ailments, such as 'dyspepsia, languid circulation and cold extremities', and that in this regard European women, in fact, enjoyed *better* health in the tropics.[48] Moreover, in the case of dysmenorrhoea it was felt that women 'benefited by a change to a warm, or even a mild atmosphere'.[49] However, these views were the exceptions to the overwhelming opinion that hot climates affected women's health adversely – an opinion summed by the Madras-based R. S. Mair's observation that in the tropics, 'Females suffer perhaps even more than males' and also 'succumb to the climate sooner'. His conclusion was that a woman's health was 'so affected by the climate of India, after six or eight years unbroken residence, that she [was] compelled to seek that change in her native land which can alone restore her'.[50]

The most detailed exploration of the impact of climate on reproductive health, in fact, was actually made by Edward Tilt, the London-based obstetrician in his *Health in India for British Women*. Speaking with the greatest confidence and authority on the subject, Tilt spoke in imperial tones when he declared climate to be the primary enemy of both health and empire, and remarked that, 'We could conquer India but we succumb to its climate.'[51] Tilt declared that:

> transplantation to India has a marked effect on the reproductive organs of British women. Menstruation is often more abundant.[52]

According to him, not only did white women in India show a proneness to diseases of the reproductive organs, but more seriously, were 'more liable to miscarry' especially 'during the hot season'.[53] Tilt maintained that the hot climate was so inimical to Englishwomen's health that 'eight out of the ten European female residents' suffered greatly from 'deranged menstruation', leucorrhoea, cervical inflammation, inflammation of the womb and 'tropical anaemia' – the latter being aggravated by the intense heat.[54] Tropical climates, he maintained, affected European women so severely that their health broke down sooner than men's – in most cases 'enough … for the patient to return home'.[55] Most importantly, he darkly insinuated, the climate combined with the idleness of colonial life eventually brought about a decline in the 'once hardy Englishwoman' into 'oriental indolence' – and presumably, moral lassitude.[56]

It was around the 1890s that the 'germ theory' of disease came to replace the importance of climate to account for tropical diseases, and the setting up of the London School of Tropical Medicine in 1898 by Patrick Manson marked the advent of modern-day tropical medicine. Diseases now came to be seen as being caused by germs and not by the hot climate – and therefore possible to be overcome and be eradicated. Moreover, the germ theory put paid to the idea that women were especially susceptible to disease and that hence women in the tropical colonies were a liability. However, even after Manson, the 'climate theory' of disease continued to be aired. One of its most vocal proponents in the early twentieth century, Sir Aldo Castellani, the Italian-born tropical medicine specialist at the London School of Tropical Medicine, echoed the view that tropical climates had an important bearing on health.[57] More significantly, like so many had done before him, Castellani also held that the ill-effects of a tropical climate appeared to be more marked on women than on men. According to him, apart from the loss of appetite and indigestion, European women also suffered from reproductive health problems: white girls began to menstruate a little earlier in the tropics and suffered 'more discomfort during their monthly periods', and 'true haemorrhages', with greater 'loss of blood', were not uncommon. Castellani also maintained that pregnancy was 'more trying' in warm climates, with post-partum haemorrhage being far 'more frequent in the tropics'.[58]

The colonial family: motherhood, child-rearing and diseases

We saw in the last chapter how the colonial family and child-rearing were important aspects of the memsahib's life. Indeed, in the late nineteenth century, European women were perceived essentially as child-bearers and, in the colonial context, as progenitors of future generations of imperialists. The colonial family, as a unit of the imperial community, came to be perceived as needing protection and nurture not only culturally, but also medically. And the publication of family medical handbooks became imbricated in an imperial strategy of stabilising colonial domesticities, defining their identities and making medical care available to the colonial family. At the same time, the gendered admonishment and even gender policing which undergirds many of these manuals suggest that the colonial home was, in many ways, an unstable space 'where people can come and go and where belonging and membership are insecure'.[59]

Family manuals focused invariably on reproductive health and on the colonial family. Most tended to prioritise European children's health over that of their mothers. Given the high infant mortality rate, this writing revealed anxieties about European children's health and the imminent danger which they faced from tropical diseases. Young mothers were not only taught to handle a range of issues from giving birth in remote areas to keeping good care of their children's health, but were also advised to take care of their own health, as part of their responsibility as imperial wives and mothers.

To a large extent, colonial medical writings subjected the memsahib's location within the colonial home to a critical gaze. Medical writings sought to emphasise that the memsahib's primary duty and function in the colony was that of being a mother. Indeed, by the late nineteenth century, as Anne Laura Stoler notes, motherhood in Britain was located at 'the centre of empire building' and child-bearing was projected as a woman's 'national, imperial, and racial duty'.[60] Moreover, as Anna Davin has demonstrated, this focus on motherhood and child-rearing was also intrinsically linked to Britain's eugenicist and imperial interests.[61] Colonial women in India were thus perceived primarily as mothers and progenitors of future generations of imperialists. Not surprisingly, most family medical handbooks tended to focus on children and the colonial nursery, since the European family was considered as the key unit of colonisation. Underlying these concerns were considerations of empire and the exigencies of imperial domesticities, since by this time, the health of the white family was closely interlinked with imperial interests.

Colonial medical manuals meant for the white family sought to guide young colonial mothers on child-rearing, health-care and tropical ailments. The need for child-care in the tropics was high, since as we noted in the last chapter, in most colonial households in the nineteenth century children were born and brought up in India during the first few years and then sent to England (to prevent their physical and moral 'decline' in the colony). Further, the colonial perception that the 'colonies were medically hazardous for white women' meant that motherhood in the tropics too was seen as, what Anne Laura Stoler terms, a 'precarious and ambivalent endeavour'.[62] Perhaps what is most striking about most of these early nineteenth-century handbooks is that they discussed child-rearing and the management of tropical diseases in children, but tended to ignore the health of the mother.

The new interest in 'family' health displayed in the 1870s – the period when a spate of family medical handbooks discussing child-rearing appeared – was, as we have noted, closely linked to Britain's imperial interests, which at this time also revolved around the contemporary issue of European colonisation of India. Although the British in India were never a settler community, nevertheless an intensely debated topic that kept surfacing periodically in colonial circles was the possibility of Europeans settling in India. Linked to this issue was the question whether white children could be successfully raised here. Fears about the greater vulnerability of European children (and women) in the tropics that were often voiced were further amplified by the child mortality figures which always remained high.[63] While the chief causes of death for European women in India were puerperal fever, phthisis and enteric fever, European children died of convulsions, diarrhoea and debility.[64]

Although from the 1870s onwards, the new, government-led thrust given to family medicine helped to generate child-rearing manuals, even in the first half of the century there did sporadically appear a few handbooks which discussed child-care. As mentioned earlier in this chapter, these included Corbyn's *Management and Diseases of Infants* (1828), *A Domestic Guide* (1836) as well as H. H. Goodeve's highly popular *Hints for the General Management of Children in India* (1844). While, as we have seen, the earlier two texts paid great attention to both the mother's health as well as to child-rearing, the latter directed detailed attention only towards the care of European children in the colonial home, maintaining a virtual silence on the health of the children's mothers.[65] *A Domestic Guide*, which, as we have seen, voiced a rare sympathy for the European mother, took note of the 'daily sad experience' of child mortality, of 'how few children live to gladden the hearts of their anxious parents', and cautioned that '[i]n a climate like India, it is a matter of great importance that mothers should possess some guide as to the management of their infant offspring'.[66] It advised new mothers on the vaccination, weaning and teething of very young infants, discussed older children's exercise, clothing, diet and diseases and warned that the tropical climate posed the greatest danger to European infants. While in England the European infant was born in a climate 'natural to its temperament and constitution', in a hot climate like India, any weakness in the child's constitution could trigger a 'long train of disease and death'.

> The climate is uncongenial to their tender and exotic constitutions, so that the little ones may be said to maintain, from the very moment of their birth, a struggle for existence.[67]

The spate of family medical manuals which appeared from mid-century onwards focused on the colonial nursery. Anxieties over the health of European children led R. S. Mair to discuss the colonial nursery in his handbook, which was otherwise meant for general and implicitly male health issues. In a lengthy supplementary chapter to this handbook, titled 'On the Management of Children in India', Mair covered the rearing of infants, with detailed instructions on feeding, clothing, exercise, sleep, food, ventilation, suckling and weaning, besides giving advice on the ailments of older children.[68] Unlike most colonial physicians, however, Mair did not consider the climate particularly hostile for European children. Instead, he held that until the age of seven or eight, children actually enjoyed 'as good health on the plains of India as they do in England' and were in fact 'less liable to severe attacks of diseases such as scarlatina, measles, hooping cough'; moreover, these attacks were 'generally much less serious, while the mortality [was] much less also'.[69]

Similarly, Sir William Moore's influential *Manual of Family Medicine for India* which in 1873 had won the prize instituted by the colonial government for the best medical manual, devoted an entire chapter to child-care. Moore observed in the Preface that he had taken it upon himself to add the chapter, 'On the Feeding and Management of Infants', although he had not been required to do so by the government.[70] Focusing on very young infants, he gave detailed instruction on feeding the newborn, including breast-feeding, artificial feeding, the use of condensed milk and other foods, symptoms of over-suckling, as well as methods of weaning.[71] In addition, he discussed older children's diseases, such as 'convulsions of children', mumps, scarlet fever, measles and teething, along with snake and insect bites.[72]

By the early twentieth century, imperialist agendas were more hardened and imperialist vocabulary more pronounced. Strikingly, in Kate Platt's 1920s handbook, *Home and Health in India and the Tropical Colonies*, the white woman's role as the 'imperial mother' was more amplified. By now Delhi was the imperial capital and Platt, who worked in that city, noted that it was the colonial mother's 'responsibility of providing the best possible conditions for the development of the child'.[73] According to her, taking care of her own health was the Englishwoman's wifely and imperial duty, since the 'comfort of the husband and family depend on her good health'.[74] She also pointed out that keeping 'herself in good condition and free from avoidable illness', was a memsahib's way of showing 'good sense as well as true devotion to her family'.[75]

Platt's detailed advice on child-rearing and the management of the nursery included advice on hand-feeding, sterilisation and pasteurisation of milk, as well as the uses of 'dried milk'. Regarding the home treatment of diseases, she touched upon both general 'infantile maladies' and tropical diseases, such as malaria, kala azar, plague, cholera, sleeping sickness, dengue, relapsing fever, sandfly fever, smallpox, dysentery and enteric fever/paratyphoid. In addition she discussed worm infestations, skin troubles, insect bites and stings. Most striking of all, perhaps, was Platt's advice on managing the 'child and its nerves'; among the 'bad habits' of children that she mentioned were 'nail biting', thumb-sucking' and – what was unusual for this genre – the habit of 'masturbation'.[76] In this genre sexuality, especially childhood sexuality, was never mentioned – and this kind of open discussion of such topics reveals the legacy of Freud and modern psycho-analysis.

Clothing, lifestyle and gendered morality

Gender politics was also played out in the sphere of clothing and climate in medical discourse. Combating the hot climate necessitated the use of appropriate clothing – and it is in this sphere that we come across the greatest degree of gender prejudice in colonial medical writings. Right through the nineteenth century, medical manuals focused almost exclusively on European *men's* need for protective tropical clothing; the classic advice being to keep the head shielded from the tropical sun and the loins protected from sudden chills and change in temperature.[77] As late as the 1890s Sir Joseph Fayrer was advising European males to wear:

> a good hat made of solah (pith) or other light material, with a puggrie. The head, temples, back of the neck, and the spine should be protected ...

by a pad of cotton ... It is well, also to have an umbrella, which should be covered with white calico to make it more impervious to the sun's rays ... a light pad inside the hat, wetting the puggrie or even the hair, will add to the protection against the heat.[78]

This protective tropical attire succeeded in constructing the figure in colonial discourse of the hard-worked *male* colonial who sacrificed everything – health, comforts and even sometimes life itself – in the pursuit of duty. Indeed, this enduring colonial trope of the hard-worked white male administrator remained famously mythologised by Rudyard Kipling: 'These die, or kill themselves by overwork or are worried to death, or broken in health ... in order that the land may be protected from death and sickness, famine and war.'[79]

By mid-century the cholera belt and the sola topi (made of 'sola', or 'shola', the term for 'pith' in Hindi and other northern Indian languages) had become the standard British tropical apparel for male colonials in the tropics. Moreover, as Dane Kennedy notes, they gradually became a symbol of imperial power:

[T]he solar [sic] topis and spine pads ... were essential to the protection, privilege and power of the coloniser ... they helped to define and sustain those boundaries, to remind ruler and subject alike of the distance between one another.[80]

Elaborating on this further, Bernard Cohn notes that this 'uniform' of the sahibs – especially the 'sola topi' – became a marker of imperial power and authority in popular perception:

The sahibs had by 1870 generally adopted a 'uniform', the distinctive components of which were sola topi with pugri, spinal pad, and cholera belt or flannel cummerbund. The topi was the most obvious mark of the ruling caste. The British were rarely, from this time until the final demise of the empire, bare-headed. Men, women, and children, each had their versions of the topi.[81]

Colonial medical discourse fed into gender politics by presenting sharply polarised constructions about male and female clothing in the colonies. While the protective 'tropical clothing' that physicians recommended for colonising men signified a hard life in the outdoors, with long hours spent in the sun, the texts carried pejorative descriptions of memsahibs' flimsy and frivolous apparel, which suggested exactly the opposite. Certainly, the idea of a climatically protective 'tropical clothing' was almost never recommended for European women – the implication being that they did not need such apparel, with their leisurely, sheltered and implicitly parasitical life inside their bungalows.[82]

This sartorial inscription fed into the predominant gender tropes governing nineteenth-century colonial discourse, namely that of the idle and flirtatious memsahib. The advice on clothing given to women was generally undergirded by moralistic censure. More than 'protective' attire, the general emphasis was on *responsible* female clothing for women. Indeed, later in the period, European women were frequently admonished for ignoring the practical exigencies of life in the tropics. For instance, in an article in a British medical journal in the 1930s, the physician-author critiqued women's dress in the colonies for being ornamental rather than practical, with the remark that women's lives would be happier if they dressed, not according to London fashion, but according to the needs of the tropical climate.[83]

As a matter of fact – as I have discussed elsewhere – Anglo-Indian culture was underpinned by a profound fear of female sexuality and its destabilising effects on the great brotherhood of male colonisers.[84] Hence, androgyny often became a female paradigm that was deliberately promoted in colonial discourse in order to counter the sexual power of the ultra feminine white woman.[85] For instance, we find a physician in the 1930s urging that changing the excessively feminine nature of 'Englishwomen's dress' was the 'most urgent reform needed in the tropics'. Strongly emphasising that the 'sole aim' in female clothing should be 'health, convenience and utility' rather than adornment, he declared that 'the principle of women's dress should be men's dress modified for women'.[86] At the same time, however, it needs to be underlined that androgyny was only *one* of the numerous female paradigms – and not the overwhelmingly predominant one in the cultural fabric of British India.[87]

Moreover, when it came to the subject of clothing, colonial medical writings identified 'protective tropical attire' as a quintessentially *male* symbol and hardly ever recommended it for white women. Among the few exceptions on this subject of clothing was the physician, Edward Tilt, who advised European women to wear male-type of 'protective clothing' (a hat with 'many folds of a white muslin band twisted around the hat or cap, turban fashion' and a cholera belt, consisting of 'a large cotton or silk band ... worn around the loins'), urged them to protect themselves 'from the direct rays of the sun by a white umbrella', to avoid the use of dark-coloured cloth and certain colours, such as black or red, and to refrain from going outside from ten until three, the hottest part of the day. Hence, interestingly enough, although Tilt was usually one of the sharpest critics of the apocryphal hectic female social life in the colony, in this instance he implicitly figured the white woman as leading an active (and useful) outdoors life in the sun and therefore in need of tropical gear.[88] Another rare instance of a physician recommending the use of 'protective clothing' for women was the equally unlikely W. J. Simpson in his handbook, *The Maintenance of Health in the Tropics*, which, as we saw earlier, otherwise marginalised white women. Simpson advised that a 'spinal pad', a 'good large white umbrella', a 'broad-brimmed topee' and a 'cholera belt' 'should always be worn both by both men and women'.[89]

Indeed, the colonial medical gaze was so deeply masculinist that even the sole female physician-author, Kate Platt, echoed the majority opinion on the subject of female clothing – clearly indicating thereby how deeply ingrained was the patriarchal gender politics of this discourse. Platt's only departure from the general opinion was to concede that women too needed to wear a hat, since 'the direct rays of the tropical sun are always dangerous to those who brave it with unprotected heads'. Indeed, Platt advised protective headgear for white children as well, cautioning that 'they must always be provided with adequate protection from the sun's rays, and they should not be allowed out of doors ... without sun hat or topee and umbrella. The topee should be of material sufficiently substantial to ensure safety and of a shape to protect the nape of the neck.'[90]

Throughout the period, in fact, one recurrent trope to be found in this medical discourse was the censure of women's colonial lifestyles. Female health, lifestyle and morality came to be intertwined, as the white woman's supposedly frivolous lifestyle (and by inference, her morality) was projected as a health risk. This of course also amounted to a dereliction of a woman's imperial duty and responsibility as wife and mother. Many medical handbooks warned about the resultant hazards of a hectic social life to health, especially reproductive health. *A Domestic Guide* ascribed miscarriage to 'extra excitement ... sitting up late at parties' and 'imprudently riding on horseback'. This manual sternly warned that the way to prevent miscarriage was by 'avoiding all fatiguing exertions, all idle visiting, and gay dissipated parties'.[91]

Among the sharpest critiques of this apocryphal gay Anglo-Indian lifestyle was Edward Tilt's *Health in India for British Women*, which advised the new female arrival in India to 'begin by leading a very *quiet life*, so as to learn how to adapt herself to the climate'. Warning against the 'gaieties and fatigues of society, which in such a climate, are far more fatiguing than at home', the manual censured European women who 'give themselves up to the pursuit of pleasure, and set at defiance the laws of hygiene'. Leading a 'fashionable life at one of our Eastern capitals', it warned, would lead to 'abdominal pains, nervousness, depression of spirits, and perhaps hysteria'. In the case of a pregnant woman who was 'bent on pleasure', the consequences were even more serious and 'a miscarriage [was] a likely event'. Moreover, a 'speedy getting up' left the womb permanently enlarged, congested and ulcer-ated, and the results were disastrous:[92]

> Another miscarriage follows, or pregnancy may proceed to its full time. There is a fruitless attempt to nurse, a bad getting up, no power to rally, vaginal discharges, abdominal and back pains, increased by exercise; so the patient is further debilitated by confinement to the house.[93]

This type of linking of the memsahib's health to her lifestyle and morality remained a part of medical discourse well into the later decades as well. In a discussion of the Royal Society of Medicine in 1931 the participating physicians focused as much on the climate as they did on the hazards of the proverbially socially hectic female colo-nial lifestyle. One viewpoint was that the frequency of dysmenorrhoea in tropical climates could be attributed to women's hectic lifestyle in India rather than to the climate.[94]

The 'medical gaze' and the 'native' wet-nurse

We saw in the last chapter how memsahibs expressed in their writings acute anxieties about the 'native' wet-nurse who was generally needed to be employed in Anglo-Indian homes. Colonial medical handbooks too further amplified this negative image and almost all of them gave detailed cautionary advice on the selection of the *amah*. The wet-nurse, who was the only 'native' to be mentioned in colonial medical handbooks (there being a virtual silence on the ayah, for instance), was seen by most colonial physicians as a necessary evil. While they recommended maternal breast-feeding as best for the European infant, the majority of them also admitted that lactation was often a problem in the tropical climate with white mothers unable to feed their infants. Given this, colonial physicians usually conceded that wet-nurses needed to be engaged. As the author of *A Domestic Guide* pointed out, 'ladies are incapacitated from becoming good nurses to their babes, during their residence in this country', a view that persisted throughout the colonial period, and over a hundred years later Sir Aldo Castellani, Professor of Tropical Medicine at the London School of Tropical Medicine remarked that European women found 'secretion from the mammary glands becoming scanty after a short time', with the result that very few could nurse their infants 'for more than a few weeks'.[95]

One of the few exceptions on the subject of engaging wet-nurses was Frederick Corbyn who vehemently opposed in his medical handbook the need to keep 'native' 'dhyes' for white infants. Corbyn argued that not only did these women 'eat opium, and smoke a poisonous narcotic, called *bhang*', they were also ungrateful and exploitative of the young white mothers; most importantly, the European mother's milk (by virtue of her race) was far superior to the 'poor and watery milk of a native woman'.[96] In contrast, the author of *A Domestic Guide* recommended the use of wet-nurses, observing that 'no infant thrives so well in India as those fed by these women [wet-nurses]', although he warned, at the same time, that hiring a wet-nurse meant 'a great deal of trouble and annoyance'.[97]

Colonial physicians universally demonised the wet-nurse. Time and again, they warned European mothers to have the *amahs* medically examined before hiring them.[98] Even physicians like Goodeve or Mair who barely discussed the health issues of the European *mothers* in their medical handbooks, made it a point to give detailed instructions on the method of selecting an *amah*. One of the older medical guide books cautioned that 'natives of this class are generally so dirty', that after being hired, the woman needed to be 'well-cleaned with soap and warm water, and then dressed in clean new clothes' otherwise the baby was in danger of picking up 'some cutaneous disease'.[99] This continued to be the central advice well into the early twentieth century and Kate Platt cautioned that 'no wet-nurse should be employed without a thorough examination by a doctor and a careful enquiry into her antecedents and personal habits'.[100]

The 'correct' method of selecting a wet-nurse thus became an extremely important issue, although the guidance given on this subject varied: some stressed the importance of ensuring that the *amah*'s child was of the same age as the European infant ('because milk undergoes decided changes, and what would be proper for a child of two or three months of age, would disagree with one older'), while others argued, somewhat less logically, that the wet-nurse be, as nearly as possible, of the same age as the mother.[101] Then again, R. S. Mair, combining both viewpoints, recommended that 'the age of the amah should as nearly as possible correspond with that of the mother' and at the same time, that 'the amah's own child should be as nearly as possible the same age as the child for whom she is engaged'.[102]

Most physicians gave minutely detailed instructions on the health and physical appearance to look out for in the prospective wet-nurse. While one physician stressed that the *amah* should look 'young and healthy, and her infant fat and well', another noted that 'a suitable amah' should be 'moderately plump, [with] a fresh clear complexion, clear cheerful eyes, deep red coloured lips'.[103] Goodeve urged that she should be 'temperate in her habits, both as regards food, drink, and smoking' and also advised that she should have:

smooth, sleek skin without eruptions or evidence of previous skin affections ... a well-formed and well-nourished frame; a clear eye; a clean
tongue; good appetite.[104]

Obsessive preoccupations with the *amah*'s health and hygiene
served to reinforce constructions of the 'native' as a source of dirt
and disease. In fact, in much of the medical writing, race and class
prejudices intermingled with notions of hygiene and the horror of 'dirt'
often expressed with regard to these women. As we saw in the last
chapter, most *amahs* who worked in white homes were of low-class/
caste origins and in a conflation of race and class/caste prejudice, the
wet-nurse was fearfully constructed as a potential health hazard in
medical writings. Indeed, as David Arnold notes, 'non-whites continually informed the western understanding of the tropics and of tropical
diseases – as sources of epidemic danger' or 'as sick ... workers'.[105]

This apart, anxieties were sometimes voiced about these women's
sexual morality. However, in this case, sexual morality was perceived
as more of a health problem (rather than a *moral* issue, as it had been
in the case of the ayah), and the *amah*'s promiscuity was considered a
health risk in terms of her contracting venereal disease and posing a
threat to the health of the European infant. Anxieties were thus sometimes voiced about the danger of her having venereal disease. Goodeve
cautioned that she should be 'strictly continent, and moral', while the
Bombay-based William Moore warned that symptoms of venereal disease
as well as epidemic diseases in the woman's locality – such as small-pox,
scarlet fever or measles – needed to be ruled out.[106] It is worth noting how,
virtually without exception, the wet-nurse was constructed as dishonest
and untrustworthy and therefore in need of close monitoring. R. S. Mair,
the Madras-based physician, one of the harshest in his moral estimate
of the wet-nurse, wrote a virtual advisory against these women in his
handbook, accusing them of cheating, deception and lack of hygiene.[107]
He especially warned against the wet-nurse's 'most pernicious of all
habits' of 'administering narcotic drugs' to European infants 'with
the object of inducing sleep' and thus 'relieving' themselves 'of some
part of their duty'.[108] Even the more tolerant Kate Platt admitted that
the general 'prejudice' against 'native foster-mothers' was 'not without
foundation'. 'Indian foster-mothers' noted Platt, were 'usually devoted to
their charges', but they nevertheless 'need[ed] continual supervision'.[109]

Handbooks written by colonial physicians denigrated the wet-nurse
in colonial medical discourse.[110] Doctors warned against the habitual
deception of the prospective wet-nurse – such as passing off a borrowed
baby as her own, or presenting breasts full of milk by not drawing out
the milk for hours before 'inspection'.[111] Goodeve pointed out how

the wet-nurse, 'at the time of examination' presents 'breasts well stored with milk' when in reality she had allowed 'the milk to accumulate over many hours before inspection'.[112] R. S. Mair warned that it was 'no uncommon thing for amahs to borrow children from their friends, in order to deceive the lady engaging them, or even the doctor appointed to examine them'.[113] As a solution he advised that:

> In all cases the amah should be made to draw off half a wineglassful of her milk at her first examination in the presence of the mistress, every attention being at the time paid to the nature of the flow.[114]

Indeed, in a sustained colonial exercise in 'othering', most handbooks turned an intrusive, male, medical gaze on the body of the 'native' woman and recommended that the breasts of a wet-nurse be examined.[115] Male physicians expressed their views on the desired appearance of the wet-nurse's breasts; Goodeve, who was the leading physician in Calcutta in the 1840s, advised that she should possess:

> plump, full, and firm breasts, with nipples of sufficient size and length. The milk should flow freely, on the nipples being gently compressed, whilst it should be of a bluish color, and yielding a generous cream on being collected in quantity and being allowed to cool in the open air.[116]

William Moore, in his turn, pointed out that the wet-nurse's 'breasts should be hard, knotty and round, with prominent nipples', while R. S. Mair recommended 'well formed, moderately firm breasts, with nipples free from soreness or eruption'.[117] Indeed, such detailed anatomical descriptions of the *amah*'s breasts tended to dehumanise her into some kind of a 'milch-cow', displaying a combination of prurience, power as well as race, class and gender prejudices.

Conclusion

As we have seen, the late nineteenth and early twentieth centuries saw a spate of medical manuals and handbooks written for colonials in India, which served to disseminate western medical knowledge, even while reinforcing colonial race, class and gender ideologies. Revealing the inherently masculinist nature of colonial cultures, this discourse largely marginalised women and focused on European men's health – despite a pressing female need for medical advice.[118] It fed into the old adage that the colonies were 'no place for a woman' by underlining European women's enhanced vulnerability to various health problems in tropical climates, which included reproductive problems, miscarriage and also – as we shall be seeing in greater detail in the next chapter – psychological disorders like depression, hysteria and 'tropical neurasthenia'.

Not only did these male-authored medical handbooks marginalise memsahibs, they also constructed them as frivolous, irresponsible and parasitical, indulging in the 'gaieties' of colonial life and risking the danger of miscarriage.[119] While admonishing women against following the latest London fashion in clothing, they projected colonial men, in contrast, as 'hard-worked' sacrificing administrators who required suitable tropical clothing for protection from the sun.

More importantly, perhaps, these medical texts served to buttress race, class and gender ideologies inside the home, as they sought to consolidate and control the domestic space. Racialised pathologies underwrote their 'othering' of the 'native' wet-nurse as dishonest, untrustworthy, unhygienic and a source of disease, while, in a display of arrant sexism and racism, invasive procedures such as 'examining' the body of the 'native' *amah* prior to employing her were recommended.

Finally, as has been noted by modern scholars, Europeans increasingly felt a sense of vulnerability in India's tropical climate during the nineteenth century. Indeed, the presence of numerous medical guides does seem to suggest deep-rooted anxieties and insecurities regarding health in the tropics. In particular, there were fears about European women and children's susceptibilities to the climate. Nevertheless, the readers of these medical handbooks were implicitly constructed as resilient and able to stave off disease and death in the remotest outposts of empire. In other words, even while this medical discourse was haunted by fears of European vulnerability in the tropics, it simultaneously projected the colonialist as scientific, enterprising, self-confident and self-reliant, engaged in conquering and medically subjugating the tropics. In such a masculinist, empire-centric context there was little space for the memsahib in colonial medical discourse, and manifestly even less for the dehumanised 'native' wet-nurse, however crucial her role may have been in lived experience.

Notes

A few points in this chapter are drawn from my article which was originally published in *South Asia Research*, 30:3. Copyright © 2010 SAGE Publications. All rights reserved. Reproduced with the permission of the copyright holders and the publishers Sage Publications India Pvt. Ltd, New Delhi.

1 Elizabeth Buettner, *Empire Families: Britons and Late Imperial India* (Oxford and New York, Oxford University Press, 2004) pp. 25–71, draws upon a range of colonial medical texts in her chapter on child-rearing in colonial India. Other than that, barely passing references are made to medical handbooks in Piya Pal-Lapinski, *The Exotic Woman in Nineteenth-century British Fiction and Culture: A Reconsideration* (New Hampshire, University of New Hampshire Press, 2004) and Narin Hassan, *Diagnosing Empire: Women, Medical Knowledge, and Colonial*

Mobility (London, Ashgate, 2011). The latter rather inaccurately classifies them as 'travel guide books for female travellers', p. 2.

2   See for instance, Barbara Ramusack, 'Embattled Advocates: The Debates Over Birth Control in India, 1920–1940', *Journal of Women's History*, 1:2 (1989), pp. 34–64 and Maneesha Lal, 'The Politics of Gender and Medicine in Colonial India: The Countess of Dufferin's Fund, 1885–1888', *Bulletin of the History of Medicine*, 68:1 (Spring 1994), pp. 29–66. More recent studies include Sarah Hodges (ed.), *Reproductive Health in India: History, Politics, Controversies* (New Delhi, Orient Longman, 2006); Barbara N. Ramusack, 'Women's Hospitals and Midwives in Mysore, 1870–1920: Princely or Colonial Medicine', in Waltraud Ernst and Biswamoy Pati (eds), *India's Princely States: People, Princes and Colonialism* (London, Routledge, 2007), pp. 173–93, and Samiksha Sehrawat, *Colonial Medical Care in North India: Gender, State and Society, c. 1840–1920* (New Delhi, Oxford University Press, 2013).

3   For instance, Henry Hurry Goodeve (1806–1884) was Professor of Medicine at Calcutta Medical College, Sir Joseph Fayrer (1824–1907) was personal surgeon to the viceroy, and later president of the India Office Medical Board and Sir William Moore (1828–1896), was surgeon-general with the Bombay government in the 1870s.

4   Among the most long-lasting 'classic' handbooks were Henry Hurry Goodeve's *Hints for the General Management of Children in India in the Absence of Professional Advice* ([1844], London and Calcutta, Thacker and Thacker, Spink & Co. 1856); and Sir William Moore's *A Manual of Family Medicine for India* (London, Churchill, 1874). Revised and updated editions of both these popular texts kept being brought out periodically by younger colonial doctors over the decades, e.g. Joseph Ewart, *Goodeve's Hints for the General Management of Children in India: In the Absence of Professional Advice*, sixth edition; (Calcutta: Thacker, Spink & Co., 1872); and Cuthbert Allan Sprawson (ed.), *Moore's Manual of Family Medicine and Hygiene for India*, eighth edition (London: J. & A. Churchill, 1916).

5   Hassan, *Diagnosing Empire*, p. 2.

6   Daniel R. Headrick, *Tools of Empire: Technology and European Imperialism in the Nineteenth Century* (Oxford, Oxford University Press, 1981).

7   Narin Hassan argues that medical handbooks were written for and used as a corollary to the colonial housekeeping manual, See Hassan, *Diagnosing Empire*, p. 2.

8   One of the rare medical handbooks to be authored by a female physician was Kate Platt's *The Home and Health in India and the Tropical Colonies* (London, Bailliere, Tindall & Cox, 1923) which we discuss in course of this chapter. Kate Platt was the first Principal of the Lady Hardinge Hospital and College for Women at Delhi, which was established in 1916. Female medical practitioners entered India from the late nineteenth century onwards, first as medical missionaries and later as doctors employed by the colonial administration. For details see Margaret Balfour and Ruth Young, *The Work of Medical Women in India* (London, Oxford University Press, 1929); and for a recent study see Sehrawat, *Colonial Medical Care in North India*.

9   See Indrani Sen, 'Memsahibs and Health in Colonial Medical Writings, c. 1840–1930', in *South Asia Research*, 30:3 (2010), pp. 253–274. The majority of texts maintain a complete silence on white women's health, e.g. James Johnson, *The Influence of Tropical Climates More Especially the Climate of India, on European Constitutions: The Principal Effects and Diseases Thereby Induced, their Prevention or Removal, and the Means of Preserving Health in Hot Climates, Rendered Obvious to Europeans of Every Capacity* ([1813], London, J. Callow, 1815). Later examples include John McCosh, *Medical Advice to the Indian Stranger* (London, William H. Allen & Co., 1841); Sir Joseph Fayrer, *On Preservation of Health in India* (London, Macmillan, 1894), and C. P. Lukis and R. J. Blackham, *Tropical Hygiene for Anglo-Indians and Indians* (Calcutta, Thacker, Spink, 1911).

10 Even today, European women's health issues in colonial India continue to remain a neglected area of research, and are only barely touched upon in leading works, e.g. Mark Harrison, *Public Health in British India: Anglo-Indian Preventive Medicine, 1859–1914* (Cambridge, Cambridge University Press, 1994), pp. 50–51; Mark Harrison, *Climates and Constitutions: Health, Race, Environment and British Imperialism in India, 1600–1850* (New Delhi, Oxford University Press, 1999), p. 90, p. 213; Biswamoy Pati and Mark Harrison (eds), *The Social History of Health and Medicine in Colonial India* (London and New York, Routledge, 2009), p. 8.

11 J. E. Dawson, 'Woman in India: Her Influences and Position', Part I, *The Calcutta Review*, 83:165 (1886), p. 350. For a discussion on this topic see Indrani Sen, 'Between Power and Purdah: The White Woman in British India, 1858–1900', *The Indian Economic and Social History Review*, 34:3 (1997), pp. 363–367.

12 Edmund C. P. Hull, *The European in India or Anglo-India's Vade-Mecum: A Handbook of Useful and Practical Information for those Proceeding to or Residing in the East Indies Relating to Outfits, Routes, Time for Departure, Indian Climate and Seasons, Housekeeping, Servants, etc.* ([1871], New Delhi, Asian Educational Services, 2004), p. x.

13 R. S. Mair, *A Medical Guide for Anglo-Indians*, in Hull, *The European in India*, p. 218. Robert Slater Mair, who practised medicine at Madras for more than sixteen years, was Deputy Coroner at Madras.

14 *Ibid.*

15 For details on the eighteenth century and the nineteenth century, see Harrison, *Climates and Constitutions*, pp. 90, 142.

16 Edward John Tilt, *Health in India for British Women and on the Prevention of Disease in Tropical Climates* (London, J. & A. Churchill, 1875), pp. viii, vii. Edward Tilt (1815–1893), London-based gynaecologist and former president of the Obstetrical Society of London, refers here to James Ranald Martin and James Johnson, *Influence of Tropical Climates on European Constitutions, Including Practical Observations on the Nature and Treatment of the Diseases of Europeans on their Return from Tropical Climates* (London, S. Highley, 1841). Tilt complained that in Ranald Martin and Johnson's classic works, he had 'found only three lines relating to women', and even William Moore's and R. S. Mair's recent family handbooks 'took scant notice' of the health of women, Tilt, *Health in India for British Women*, pp. vii, vii.

17 W. J. Simpson, *The Maintenance of Health in the Tropics* (London, John Bale, Sons and Danielsson Ltd, 1905). Simpson, health officer at the Calcutta Corporation in the 1880s to 1890s, later taught at the London School of Tropical Medicine.

18 In the all-India census conducted in 1881, the total British population was 90,000, of which the number of males was 77,178 and the number of females 12,610 (*Report of the Census of British India 1881*. Vol. IV: Statistics of British Born Subjects, Calcutta, 1883). In the last full-scale census conducted in 1931, out of a total British population of 155,555, the number of males was 110,137 and the number of females was 45,418 (*Census of India, 1931*, Table XIX, Delhi 1933); cited in Mary A. Procida, 'Married to the Empire: British Wives and British Imperialism in India, 1883–1947', PhD thesis, University of Pennsylvania, 1997, p. 4.

19 Nupur Chaudhuri, 'Memsahibs and Motherhood in Nineteenth Century Colonial India', *Victorian Studies*, 31:4 (1988), pp. 520–530.

20 Frederick Corbyn, *Management and Diseases of Infants Under the Influence of the Climate of India, Being Instructions to Mothers and Parents in Situations where Medical Aid is not to be Obtained, and a Guide to Medical Men, Inexperienced in the Nursery and the Treatment of Tropical Infantile Diseases, Illustrated by Colour Plates* (Calcutta, Thacker, 1828), p. 1.

21 Anon., *A Domestic Guide to Mothers in India: Containing Particular Instructions on the Management of Themselves and their Children. By a Medical Practitioner of Several Years' Experience in India* ([1836], Bombay, American Mission Press, 1848), p. vi.

22   *Ibid.*
23   Chaudhuri 'Memsahibs and Motherhood', p. 524.
24   *Ibid.*, p. 523.
25   Corbyn, *Management and Diseases of Infants*, pp. 8, 6, 8.
26   Anon., *A Domestic Guide*, p. iii.
27   *Ibid.*, p. iii.
28   *Ibid.*, pp. 9, 9, 10–13.
29   *Ibid.*, pp. 26, 26, 27, 26.
30   See my discussion on ayahs and wet-nurses in Chapter 4 of this book.
31   Proceedings of the Department of Agriculture, Revenue and Commerce, Government of India, Simla, 31 October, 1871, cited in the Preface of Moore, *Manual of Family Medicine*, p. v.
32   Moore, *Manual of Family Medicine*, Title page.
33   The capacious 'Indian Medicine Chest' meant to be sold with Moore's *Manual of Family Medicine* contained sixty-seven basic medicines, and general medical equipment like mortar and pestle, spatulas, syringes, sponge, bandages, plaster, lint, catheter, scales, weights and measuring glasses.
34   For a discussion of female diseases and complications of pregnancy, see Moore, *Manual of Family Medicine*, pp. 226–267, 404–410.
35   That women's health had become more important by the early twentieth century can be seen in the fact that the eighth edition of Moore's *Manual of Family Medicine*, edited by Sprawson in 1916, carried a new chapter devoted exclusively to women. See Sprawson, *Moore's Manual of Family Medicine and Hygiene*.
36   Moore, *Manual of Family Medicine*, p. 405.
37   *Ibid.*, pp. 496–500
38   *Ibid.*, pp. 405–409.
39   Tilt, *Health in India for British Women*, p. vii.
40   *Ibid.*, p. 60.
41   Platt, *Home and Health in India*, pp. 80–81.
42   *Ibid.*
43   *Ibid.*, pp. 79, 81, 82.
44   *Ibid.*, p. 82.
45   For details see, among others, David Arnold (ed.), *Warm Climates and Western Medicine: The Emergence of Tropical Medicine, 1500–1900* (Amsterdam, Rodopi, 1996); David Arnold, *The Problem of Nature: Environment, Culture and European Expansion* (Oxford, Blackwell, 1996); and Harrison, *Climates and Constitutions*.
46   Harrison, *Climates and Constitutions*, p. 141; Ranald Martin and Johnson, *Influence of Tropical Climates on European Constitutions*, p. 38. Sir James Ranald Martin (1793–1874) was presidency surgeon of Bengal and surgeon at the General Hospital at Calcutta. He later became president of the East India Company's Medical Board at London.
47   Anon., *A Domestic Guide*, pp. 71, 19.
48   Ranald Martin and Johnson, *Influence of Tropical Climates on European Constitutions*, p. 40.
49   *Ibid.*
50   Mair, *Medical Guide for Anglo-Indians*, pp. 222, 222.
51   Tilt, *Health in India for British Women*, p. vii.
52   *Ibid.*, p. 34.
53   *Ibid.*
54   *Ibid.*, pp. 63–64.
55   *Ibid.*, p. 62.
56   *Ibid.*, pp. 64, 62.
57   Sir Aldo Castellani (1877–1971), who welcomed the recent revival of interest in climate, worked at the London School of Tropical Medicine and the University of Rome. His books include *Manual of Tropical Medicine* ([1910], London, Balliere, Tindall, and Cox, 1919), which he co-authored with Albert J. Chalmers; and *Climate and Acclimatization* ([1930], London, John Bale and Sons, 1938).

58   Sir Aldo Castellani in A. R. Neligan, Sir Aldo Castellani, Dr H. S. Stannus, Dr G. W. Bray, Mr A. F. MacCallan, Dr J. B. Christopherson, Dr K. Edmundson and Dr G. W. Theobald, 'Discussion on the Adaptation of European Women and Children to Tropical Climates', *Proceedings of the Royal Society of Medicine*, 24:6 (1931), p. 1320.

59   Esme Cleall, *Missionary Discourses of Difference, Negotiating Otherness in the British Empire* (Basingstoke, Palgrave Macmillan, 2012), p. 27.

60   Ann Laura Stoler, 'Carnal Knowledge and Imperial Power: Gender, Race and Morality in Colonial Asia', in Roger N. Lancaster and Michaela Di Leonardo (eds), *The Gender/Sexuality Reader: Culture, History, Political Economy* (New York, Routledge, 1997), p. 28.

61   Anna Davin, 'Imperialism and Motherhood', *History Workshop Journal*, 5:1 (1978), pp. 9–66.

62   Stoler, 'Carnal Knowledge and Imperial Power', p. 28.

63   Between 1860 and 1869, the death rate of soldiers' children in England below the age of five was 67.58 per thousand, while in the Bengal presidency it was 148.10. See Sir Joseph Fayrer, *European Child-Life in Bengal* (London, J. & A. Churchill, 1873), p. 8. This text studied the health of destitute girl-children and female military orphans with a view to examining the possibility of European colonisation of the country.

64   Harrison, *Public Health*, p. 50.

65   Corbyn, *Management and Diseases of Infants*. Goodeve, *Hints for the General Management of Children* did carry practical instructions on infant-care (e.g. washing the new-born after birth, method of feeding, bathing, clothing, vaccination and so on), and the home-treatment of common 'children's diseases' (e.g. remittent fever, measles, croup, chicken pox, smallpox, scarlet fever, dysentery, cholera, worms and jaundice). For details see Ewart, *Goodeve's Hints For the General Management of Children*. H. H. Goodeve was a Professor of Medicine at Calcutta Medical College.

66   Anon., *A Domestic Guide*, pp. vi, v, v, vi.

67   *Ibid.*, pp. vi, v, v, vi.

68   Mair, *Medical Guide for Anglo-Indians*, pp. 325–351.

69   *Ibid.*, p. 325.

70   Moore, *Manual of Family Medicine*, p. v.

71   *Ibid.*, pp. 484–504.

72   *Ibid.*, pp. 105, 402–404.

73   Platt, *Home and Health in India*, p. 79.

74   *Ibid.*, p. 205.

75   *Ibid.*

76   *Ibid.*, pp. 79–210.

77   James Johnson (1777–1845), surgeon in the Royal Navy, was one of the earliest to conceptualise protective clothing (i.e. the light pith helmet, moistened pad of cotton on the spine and 'cholera belt' or band of flannel worn around the abdomen) which later became a part of nineteenth-century colonial medical commonsense. Johnson based this apparel on a studied adaptation of traditional 'native' garments such as 'the turban and cummerbund'. See Johnson, *Influence of Tropical Climates More Especially the Climate of India, on European Constitutions*, pp. 422–426.

78   Fayrer, *On Preservation of Health in India*, p. 23.

79   Rudyard Kipling, 'On the City Wall', in *Soldiers Three and Other Stories* ([1892], London, Macmillan, 1960), p. 325.

80   Dane Kennedy, 'The Perils of the Mid-day Sun: Climatic Anxieties in the Colonial Tropics', in John M. Mackenzie (ed.), *Imperialism and the Natural World* (Manchester, Manchester University Press, 1990), p. 131.

81   Bernard S. Cohn, *Colonialism and Its Forms of Knowledge: The British in India* (Princeton, Princeton University Press, 1996), p. 159.

82   In this regard, the frivolity of memsahibs' apparel offers a contrast to the sober and practical attire of missionary women. For a discussion see Chapter 2.

83   J. B. Christopherson, 'The Motive in Women's Dress in the Tropics', *The Journal of Tropical Medicine and Hygiene*, 33:14 (1930), p. 205.

84 For a discussion on androgyny in colonial India, see Indrani Sen, *Woman and Empire: Representations in the Writings of British India, 1858–1900* (New Delhi, Orient Longman, 2002), pp. 77–79, 166–168. See also Sen, 'Between Power and "Purdah"', pp. 355–376.

85 For details about white women's psycho-sexual sexual power in the colony, see Sen, *Woman and Empire*, Chapters 1 and 3.

86 Christopherson, 'Motive in Women's Dress in the Tropics', p. 206. Critical of 'too much gaiety' in big stations, he also went on to urge 'useful or healthy pursuits' for women in order to prevent idleness and boredom, p. 205.

87 Mary Procida's argument that the memsahib adopted a masculine persona, 'wearing men's attire, participating in male sports such as polo, or taking up arms in defense of the empire' needs to be treated with caution. This trope of the 'masterful' white woman was not the predominant one in colonial India and may have been relatively prominent in the backdrop of the Indian National movement. See Mary Procida, *Married to the Empire: Gender, Politics and Imperialism in India, 1883–1947* (Manchester, Manchester University Press, 2002), p. 6.

88 Tilt, *Health in India for British Women*, pp. 70, 70, 70.

89 Simpson, *Maintenance of Health in the Tropics*, p. 14.

90 Platt, *Home and Health in India*, pp. 203, 126.

91 Anon., *A Domestic Guide*, pp. 19, 19–20.

92 Tilt, *Health in India for British Women*, pp. 56, 56, 56.

93 *Ibid.*

94 G. W. Theobald, in Neligan et al., 'Discussion on the Adaptation of European Women and Children to Tropical Climates', p. 1331.

95 Anon., *A Domestic Guide*, p. 71; Castellani, 'Discussion on the Adaptation of European Women and Children to Tropical Climates', p. 1320.

96 Corbyn, *Management and Diseases of Infants*, pp. 10, 13.

97 Anon., *A Domestic Guide*, p. 72.

98 Colonial physicians include H. H. Goodeve (Calcutta), William Moore (Bombay), and R. S. Mair (Madras).

99 Anon., *A Domestic Guide*, pp. 73–75.

100 Platt, *Home and Health in India*, p. 84.

101 Anon., *A Domestic Guide*, p. 73. The latter view is expressed by other physicians, such as H. H. Goodeve in the 1840s.

102 Mair, *Medical Guide for Anglo-Indians*, pp. 327–328.

103 Anon., *A Domestic Guide*, p. 74; Mair, *Medical Guide for Anglo-Indians*, p. 328.

104 Ewart, *Goodeve's Hints for the General Management of Children*, p. 9.

105 David Arnold, 'Introduction: Tropical Medicine before Manson', in David Arnold (ed.) *Warm Climates and Western Medicine: The Emergence of Tropical Medicine, 1500–1900* (Amsterdam, Rodopi, 1996), p. 8.

106 Ewart, *Goodeve's Hints for the General Management of Children*, p. 9; Moore, cited in Sprawson, *Moore's Manual of Family Medicine*, p. 492.

107 Mair, *Medical Guide for Anglo-Indians* p. 325.

108 *Ibid.*, p. 329.

109 Platt, *Home and Health in India*, pp. 84, 84.

110 These include H. H. Goodeve and R. S. Mair and William Moore.

111 Sprawson, *Moore's Manual of Family Medicine*, p. 493.

112 Ewart, *Goodeve's Hints for the General Management of Children*, pp. 9–10.

113 Mair, *Medical Guide for Anglo-Indians*, p. 328.

114 *Ibid.*, pp. 328–329.

115 See Goodeve, *Hints for the General Management of Children*, Mair, *Medical Guide for Anglo-Indians*, and Moore, *Manual of Family Medicine*.

116 Ewart, *Goodeve's Hints for the General Management of Children*, p. 9.

117 Sprawson, *Moore's Manual of Family Medicine*, p. 492; Mair, *Medical Guide for Anglo-Indians*, p. 328.

118 For details Sen, *Woman and Empire*, pp. 1–38.

119 *Ibid.*

CHAPTER SIX

The colonial 'female malady': European women's mental health and addiction in the late nineteenth century

We saw in the last chapter how colonial medical discourse tended to either marginalise European women in the colony or to focus on their general unfitness for colonial motherhood. In this chapter we shall turn our attention to the mental health of white women in colonial India, both middle-class memsahibs and lower-class barrack wives.[1] Colonial discourse, including colonial medical writings, sought to project the white woman's vulnerability to specific mental health problems. My aim here is to examine the constructions of female vulnerability in order to probe the significance of their underlying gender politics. In the course of this chapter I concentrate on 'common' mental problems, including 'neurasthenia' among middle-class memsahibs. I also examine the condition called 'delirium tremens' among barrack wives which was related to alcohol addiction and could be life-threatening. It is true that neurasthenia as a mental affliction is no longer recognised today as a valid, scientifically established psychiatric condition. Delirium tremens has of course always been identified as an alcoholism-related condition (and therefore a 'physical' condition), which also happens to have mental, psychological symptoms. However, this chapter seeks to probe the 'social history' of these disorders rather than their 'history of medicine' aspects. The chapter also examines the position of the white woman within the power structures of colonial society, as well as the elements of gendered tensions which existed within these societies. My objective in studying the construction of these mental conditions ultimately seeks to unpack the gendered attitudes and prejudices which undergirded colonial discourse.

White women's mental health in colonial India is an area that has not been much worked upon. Even today Waltraud Ernst's path-breaking work, *Mad Tales from the Raj* (1991) remains the leading study of European (male as well as female) mental health in colonial India. Indeed, Ernst's subsequent essay on white female mental health and numerous other writings on lunatic asylums for Europeans in the various presidential towns defines the scholarship on the subject of mental health.[2] Other than that, little work has been done in the area of white women's mental health in colonial India.[3]

Before we proceed any further, it needs to be pointed out that women's mental disorders have increasingly been understood to be the result of a complex combination of social, economic and cultural factors.[4] Factors like subordinate social status, a heavy burden of house-work, the absence of economic power as well as stress within marriage and the family together contribute to mental illness. In addition, there are links between mental illness and feelings of alienation, powerless-ness and having no control over one's life. Consequently, we have to bear in mind that there are multiple causes of women's distress, and that women's susceptibility to mental illness may be both a myth and also a reality – it may be both socially constructed and also an outcome of the disadvantaged conditions of gendered life which are a feature of all patriarchal societies. Moreover, it has also been argued that this type of 'minor' mental disorder in women could also be an expression of female anger and even protest against their empty and unfulfilled lives.[5]

I begin this chapter by briefly examining some of the medical approaches to female mental health in nineteenth-century Britain, in order to situate the contemporary gendering of madness in the metro-pole as well as examine the prevalent ideas about women's proneness to mental disorders. This is followed by an exploration of middle-class female mental health in colonial India, with a focus on neurasthenia. Here I probe both social realities as well as constructions in colonial discourse about women's greater propensity to suffer from the condi-tion known as neurasthenia especially in the tropical colonies. I then move on to examine mental health problems with regard to white women belonging to the lower social orders (specifically speaking, sol-diers' wives), focusing upon the problem of 'delirium tremens'. I close this chapter with a brief examination of the histories of a few white soldiers' wives, who were admitted to lunatic asylums in Calcutta, Bombay and Madras

The materials that I draw upon include nineteenth- and early twentieth-century medical textbooks, contemporary essays in medical journals, periodicals, literary and non-literary printed books of British India, as well as some case studies drawn from the *Asylum Reports* medical certificates, and certificates of admission. In the case of 'minor' or 'common' mental ailments it is often a challenge to locate pin-pointed or hard-core, incontrovertible evidence, since unlike physical illness, mental ailments are physically not 'visible' to the observer and can often go unnoticed or even unrecognised. One therefore sometimes needs to probe the margins of discursive writings in order to prise out hints and suggestions of female mental illness in the tropics.

Gender and mental illness in the nineteenth century

The Victorian period was particularly significant for its gendering of madness. Leading feminist studies on gender and mental health have pointed out that mental illness came to be perceived specifically as a 'female' disease in the nineteenth century.[6] The Victorians believed that women were more prone to mental illness than men because of their reproductive systems and that madness was caused by female heredity and was carried by women's bodies. Jane Ussher notes that the Victorian era was marked by an important change in the history of women's madness. It was during this period that a close association was established between femininity and pathology in scientific, literary and popular discourse.[7] The Victorian belief in women's greater propensity for mental illness found voice in contemporary theories that linked mental diseases to the 'biological crises of female life-cycles'.[8] Madness was closely associated with the female reproductive organ. The 'wandering womb' was deemed to wander throughout the body, acting as an enormous sponge which would suck the life-energy or intellect from vulnerable women. It was held that a woman's mind was weakened during periods of puberty, pregnancy, childbirth and menopause. Hence madness came to be associated with menarche, menstruation, pregnancy and menopause.[9]

Regarding the nineteenth century, Joan Busfield points out, 'Madness may have been tamed, but men as well as women were part of the new landscape of madness and of nervous complaints: the criminal lunatic, the maniac and the hypochondriac were typically represented as male rather than female, and needed to be counterposed to the female melancholic or hysteric'.[10] Today several western feminist readings of mental illness have pointed out that in many cases female anger and protest at their disadvantaged social circumstances found vent in behaviour that was interpreted as 'hysteria' or 'madness'.

The nineteenth century associated female mental disorders with women's sexual organs and reproductive cycles. Indeed, Victorian culture advocated marriage (and by inference, sexual intercourse) as a cure for numerous female complaints, especially hysteria. Given this, spinsters as a social category were seen to be particularly prone to mental problems, especially hysteria. The Victorians called hysteria the 'daughter's disease' and indeed, hysteria did become the accepted diagnosis of all aspects of female madness.[11] Discussing the occurrence of hysteria in women in his medical handbook, British psychiatrist

J. Michell Clarke observed: 'With regard to sex it is undoubtedly far more common amongst women ... the greatest number of cases occur between fifteen and twenty-five years.'[12] He went on to add that the symptoms which are 'most pronounced in female patients' consists of 'dizziness, noises in the ears ... a feeling of painful pressure, at one spot on the head', 'the sufferer rolls over and over on the floor, or sits up and throws herself back, tears her clothes from off her neck and chest, and tears at her hair'.[13] One extreme treatment for hysteria in women, which was controversial even in its time and rarely used, was the practice of clitorism. Practitioners of clitorism took great pains to defend its usage on both medical and moral grounds; one prominent London gynaecologist argued that the procedure was 'dictated by the loftiest and most moral considerations' and had, for its object, 'the cure of *a* disease that is rapidly tending to lower the moral tone'.[14]

Close inter-connections came to be drawn between madness and female morality, and especially female sexuality. By the Victorian period, the female mind and its maladies had come to be explained in terms of a woman's conformity or departure from attributes considered to be ideally female, such as reproduction, mothering, caring, patience, sympathy and so on.[15] Female madness, melancholia or discontent were somehow associated with 'unnatural desires' and masturbation, illegitimate pregnancy, homosexuality, frigidity, promiscuity and nymphomania came to be included in Victorian psychological nosology.[16] These ideas were further promoted through the influential works of Henry Maudsley, the leading name in British psychiatry in the post-1870s period and much-quoted during the period 1884 to 1904 by contemporary British authors of psychiatric textbooks and other medical writings. Maudsley defined nymphomania in his influential work, *Body and Mind* (1870) as 'a disease by which the most chaste and modest woman is transformed into a raging fury of lust'. He further went on to elaborate that nymphomania especially occurred as a part of 'puerperal mania' and also 'in epileptic mania, and in the mania sometimes met with in old women'.[17]

Neurasthenia

Around the late nineteenth century, there emerged in medical writings the new psychiatric category called 'neurasthenia'. First identified as a distinct nervous disorder by George M. Beard of New York around 1868, this newly developed theory of functional nervous disorder came to be widely discussed in medical discourse from around the 1880s onwards.[18] Beard argued in various lectures and in his notable study, *A Practical Treatise on Nervous Exhaustion (Neurasthenia)* (1880), that this disease was a product of the stresses of a competitive and increasingly industrialised and mechanised modern age, which impacted upon those possessing a refined nervous system, such as intellectuals and professionals. Neurasthenia referred to a cluster of symptoms of excessive mental and physical fatigue, including insomnia, lack of concentration, depression, anxiety and muscle weakness. In 1899, T. D. Savill, the leading London neurologist, observed in his popular study *Clinical Lectures on Neurasthenia* that this condition was marked by 'mental exhaustion and inability to think and study', where the sufferer was 'easily tired, easily startled', and in a 'state of debility and exhaustion'.[19] Savill went on to elaborate:

> I may say that I regard neurasthenia as a generalised irritable weakness of the entire nervous system, characterised (when the brain is chiefly affected) by hyper-sensitiveness of the sensorium, loss of mental and bodily vigour, inaptitude for work, disturbed sleep, and irritability of temper; and (when the spinal cord is chiefly affected) by general muscular weakness, restlessness, nervousness, and vague pains.[20]

Neurasthenia quickly became a popular diagnosis for various symptoms. According to early twentieth-century British physician, Hugh Campbell, it was a nerve disease that was marked by an 'irritability of temper, uncertainty of disposition, defective will', 'melancholia', 'sleeplessness' and 'deficient sleep'; while another contemporary physician described it as 'a persistent state of fatigue', of 'nervous exhaustion or nervous weakness, and irritable weakness', all of which were the result of a weakened nervous system.[21]

There were several different views about neurasthenia. Among the myths that abounded about neurasthenia, the predominant ones pertained to class and gender. For years, it was believed to be a fashionable disease which affected only the 'sensitive' upper classes.[22] The second myth was that neurasthenia was largely a female disorder, affecting women more than men. What was lost sight of in all this was that, as a stress-related condition, neurasthenia was likely, by its very nature, to affect poorer sections of society, subjected as they were to severe pressures of existence, both physical and economic. Regards gender, far from being a female illness, neurasthenia actually recorded a gender ratio of roughly 50:50 in the metropole when the diagnosis first appeared, followed by varying gender trends.[23] Nevertheless, colonial discourse especially highlighted neurasthenia as a female malady, and this is what we shall be probing in the rest of the chapter.

Colonial India and European mental health

Before we proceed, it may be useful to briefly scrutinise the specifics of European gendered life in India. As Alison Bashford has observed in a slightly different context, 'Medical knowledge is always socially constructed and always culture-bound: it is never simply "true"'.[24] Hence, after examining the social context, we shall go on to examine references to and delineations of female mental illness in the colonial discourse of British India.

Waltraud Ernst notes in her classic study, *Mad Tales from the Raj* (1991) that, far more than other European colonising nations, it was the British especially who found the conditions of colonial existence psychologically stressful. When exposed to foreign climes and cultures, the British were inclined to undergo a 'psychological metamorphosis', a tendency that was further exacerbated by their insularity. This predilection expressed itself in the form of eccentricity, 'anxiety, anger or depression' in the colony.[25] Indeed, colonial discursive writings too bear this out, by frequently pointing out the stressful aspect of British colonial existence, irrespective of gender. Contemporary colonial writings often voiced fears that nerve disorders in the colonies were aggravated by the conditions of colonial existence, especially in remote districts and the *mofussil*. As late as the 1930s, civil servant, Dennis Kincaid, for instance, noted how this kind of *lonely*, isolated existence – with its brooding in remote places, and its need to adhere to constant role-playing – often resulted in a 'strange tension' in the minds of district administrators, 'so that even in their most heroic moments is evident a mental condition that seems occasionally unbalanced and almost hysterical'.[26] Echoing this, physicians observed at a contemporary discussion of the Royal Society of Medicine in London, that in the tropical colonies, white men who were compelled by the call of duty to live in 'conditions of isolation and separation from their countrymen', often found themselves 'possessed of an almost unbearable nervous tension'.[27]

Colonial neurosis was, however, not only confined to residing in lonely or isolated areas. Living in crowded places too, surrounded by a teeming 'native' populace, sometimes exacerbated colonial anxieties. The British in India, who were a very small community, always remained vastly outnumbered by the local inhabitants.[28] In this context, the fear of numbers was occasionally voiced, particularly by women in the second half of the nineteenth century, anxieties that may possibly have been exacerbated in the period following the 1857 Rebellion. In a letter to the newspaper, *The Madras Mail*, in the 1860s, a memsahib voiced her fears that 'it does seem very hard to have such numbers against so very few', while several decades later, an administrator's wife expressed feelings of panic on first arriving at Bombay: 'The overwhelming crowds of people frightened me', she wrote. 'What were we in the land, I thought, but a handful of Europeans at the best, and what was there to prevent these myriads from falling upon and obliterating us as if we had never existed?'[29]

Either way, whether affected by isolation or crowds, it was the memsahib, the middle-class European woman, who was projected in discursive colonial writings as being especially vulnerable to anxieties and other 'common' mental disorders. Contemporary writings make repeated references to the frequent occurrence of alienation, monotony, boredom, depression, hysteria and homesickness, all of which were perceived as specifically female problems. In the course of this chapter, I shall examine the issue of gendered mental health problems, exploring their perceived linkages with diverse factors such as hot climates, cultural alienation, loneliness and a hectic social life.

Gender, colonial existence and female mental health

Generally, the isolation of living in remote areas was associated with nerve problems in both sahibs and memsahibs. Women were often required to reside, along with their husbands, in remote *mofussil* towns – generating, as we saw in the previous chapter, a demand for medical advice through handbooks and manuals. Discursive writings too projected the middle-class white woman as a 'tragic exile', cut off from friends, family and 'home', with a life marked by loneliness and boredom.[30] Given the retinue of servants that she was forced to keep (as we saw in Chapter 4), the white woman was often subjected to enforced idleness and absence of meaningful activity. As far back as the 1860s, G. O. Trevelyan, observed that, 'The ladies, poor things come in for all the disagreeables of up-country life. Without plenty of work India is unbearable.'[31] He went on to remark that only 'meaningful activity' for women could:

> stave off languor and a depth of ennui of which a person who has never left Europe can form no conception. In a climate which keeps every one within doors from eight in the morning till five in the evening ... It is very up-hill work for a lady out here to keep up her spirits and pluck, and her interest in general subjects ... none but a very brave or a very stupid woman can endure long without suffering in mind, health, and tournure.[32]

Boredom, homesickness and ennui were thus commonly identified as female colonial complaints; for instance, an anonymous article written by 'an Englishwoman in India' in the journal, *The Calcutta Review* in 1885, described 'homesickness' as a chronic 'disease of the mind' which specifically affected women.[33] The problem of female depression was echoed over the decades; the author of a cookery manual in the 1880s warned that 'if [the mind] be allowed to lie fallow and never exercised, or if the thoughts are unemployed, they act as a depressant'.[34] Around the same time, Flora Annie Steel observed in her memoir that the monotony and boredom plaguing female colonial existence was due to the lack of meaningful occupation or recreation:

> The majority of European women in India have nothing to do. Housekeeping is proverbially easy ... The Anglo-Indian has few companions of her own sex, no shop-windows to look at, no new books to read, no theatres, no cinemas; above all, in many cases, an empty nursery.[35]

As we noted in our discussion on ayahs and child-rearing in Chapter 4, not only were children sent away to England – often to be brought up by strangers in foster homes – the high cost of travel sometimes resulted in parents being unable to meet their children until after several years had elapsed.[36] The negative impact of these separations on family ties and the problem of the loosening of emotional bonds between children and parents were often mentioned as causes of anxiety.[37] Flora Annie Steel confessed that, 'filial affection does not exist at all', and noted the worrisome truth that 'In many Anglo-Indian families it has no chance to grow; so many mothers have bewailed the fact to me.'[38] Indeed, this breaking-up of the precious Victorian institution of the family was frequently lamented by colonial mothers. A letter to the Allahabad-based newspaper, *The Pioneer*, in 1882 from 'A Wife and Mother' pointed out that the 'loosening of the bond between parent and child' was 'the bitterest drop in the cup of our exile in this land'.[39] Echoing this, another memsahib lamented in her letter to *The Pioneer* in 1888:

> [The white woman] too often sees life in its stern aspect and knows too much of its tragedies. Her duty to husband and children often means hardship and self-sacrifice ... Of late years too the Englishwoman's lot in India has become still harder ... and unless some remedy is found, Anglo-India for the Englishwoman will become soon intolerable.[40]

The susceptibility of white women to nerve disorders was further mentioned in Maud Diver's important study on gendered colonial existence, *The Englishwoman in India* (1909), which we have discussed time and again in earlier chapters as well. Diver, drawing attention to the stresses of gendered life in India, ascribed the chronic occurrence of restlessness, irritability, mental and physical fatigue among memsahibs to the 'physical disabilities' of colonial life in India.[41] Her argument was that at the root of these problems there lay nervous exhaustion, aggravated by factors such as the climate, frequent transfers, and long railway journeys:

It is a known fact that the Indian climate, the artificial life its hot season entails, the long railway journeys, and the continuous shifting from place to place ... tends to promote an astonishingly rapid waste of nervous tissue; and it is this fact which renders long residence in India more injurious, as a rule to women than to men.[42]

Although she did not use the term 'neurasthenia', Diver concluded that the 'strain of social pressure' contributed to European woman's mental and physical fatigue in India and affected women more than men.[43]

In the early decades of the twentieth century, many colonial physicians widely agreed that European women in the colonies had a greater propensity for neurasthenia as compared to men. Indeed, it is striking that colonial discursive writings tended to highlight this construction a great deal. However, it was Kate Platt, the Delhi-based physician, who specifically linked the problem of neurasthenia to the memsahib's isolated life in remote districts. She pointed out in *The Home and Health in India and the Tropical Colonies* (1923) that the 'loneliness' caused by the absence of European society and the '[m]onotony of life and surroundings' had a 'most depressing effect on the health and spirits'. In addition, she cautioned that inadequate exercise and lack of activities further aggravated the problem and urged women to take up interesting hobbies or outdoor exercise like walking and especially horse riding. Platt also advocated the beneficial effects of a change of scene and advised that 'when nerves are jarred or over-strained' by the monotony of life in the *mofussil*, 'frequent visits should be paid to neighbouring settlers' or 'an occasional trip ... to one of the large stations or cities'.[44]

This notion that enforced idleness and a lack of meaningful engagement could lead to neurasthenia in women continued to find mention in the 1930s. Sir Aldo Castellani, the well-known expert on tropical medicine, commented in his study, *Climate and Acclimatisation* (1930) that 'neurasthenic conditions are ... more frequently observed in women than in men owing to the somewhat unnatural life many women live in the tropics with lack of serious occupation and very little domestic work'.[45] Indeed, motherhood was sometimes seen as a *palliative* for boredom or neurasthenia and European women were advised to start a family in order to have some meaningful occupation. Kate Platt, for one, prescribed motherhood to childless white women, observing that 'the advent of a child has often been the salvation of a neurasthenic wife'.[46] However, motherhood in the colony was itself undercut by deep-rooted anxieties about the vulnerability of white infants to the tropical climate and disease, and their enhanced risk of death.[47]

Metropolitan specialists on nerve disorders after all did argue that emotionally stressful situations such as illness, nursing a sick family member or bereavement were factors that could trigger off neurasthenia. British physician J. Michell Clarke observed how the 'constant anxiety for the sick person's life', followed by 'grief at loss through death' often laid 'the foundation for severe and long-continued neurasthenia'.[48] One can argue that motherhood in India could itself be an inherently emotionally stressful experience, with anxieties fanned by the infant mortality rate in India, which, during much of the nineteenth century, remained considerably higher than in metropolitan Britain. For instance, Joseph Fayrer noted in *European Child-Life in Bengal* (1873), that from 1860 to 1869, the death rate of soldiers' children in England below the age of five was 67.58 per thousand, while in the Bengal presidency it was as high as148.10.[49] Colonial physicians noted that fears over pregnancy and childbirth often generated stress among pregnant women and young mothers. In a discussion that appeared in the *Indian Medical Gazette*, a Professor at the Calcutta School of Tropical Medicine and Hygiene observed how, 'The dread of the onset of pregnancy is the starting point of neurasthenia in many European women in the tropics'; while a Calcutta-based gynaecologist made the observation that childbirth further exacerbated maternal anxieties, since '[t]he woman's anxiety is now fixed on the dread that perhaps some day a calamity may overtake her child'.[50]

The colonial medical gaze, 'hectic' female social life and neurasthenia

Regarding 'neurasthenia', most physicians also tended to link its occurrence in the colony with the alleged hectic social lifestyle of memsahibs in the larger stations.[51] Dane Kennedy has, in fact, drawn attention to the sharp gender polarisation that often existed in colonial medical discourse: while in the colonies, neurasthenia in males was associated with social isolation, in the case of women, it was largely attributed to a socially hectic lifestyle.[52] Thus, the incipient gender prejudices that underpinned colonial discourse resulted in the heaping of opprobrium on the memsahib's lifestyle for all health evils – ranging from miscarriage to mental health disorders.

To be sure, in the metropole, neurasthenia was held by British and American physicians such as George Beard and Hugh Campbell, among others, to be predominantly a fallout of the pressures of a fast-paced modern life. Contemporary medical theorists widely blamed its occurrence on 'the influence of civilisation' and 'the leading of what is called a "society life"'.[53] As metropolitan physician, J. Michell Clarke, observed:

> Nothing is more exhausting to the nervous system than a constant round of excitement, the continual pursuit of pleasure with enjoyment as the one aim of life, involving, as it does, late hours spent in heated rooms, over-eating, often over-drinking.[54]

Indeed, the phrases, 'constant round of excitement' and 'continual pursuit of pleasure with enjoyment' used by this physician would seem to echo the colonial construct of the hectic social lifestyle of the larger Anglo-Indian stations, with their 'burra khanas' (dinner parties), picnics and amateur theatricals. How exaggerated this construction was, can perhaps be gauged from Flora Annie Steel's acerbic comment that the amusements available to socialite-memsahibs were, in fact, severely limited and largely apocryphal. In a rare *defence* of the white woman, Steel pointed out how, in fact, these forms of entertainments were endlessly *monotonous*:

> Life in a large Indian station is practically the same for all Westerners. Indeed, when you come to an Indian cantonment, *it is almost monotonous in its round of unchangeable amusements* ... badminton parties ... tea parties ... picnics ... theatricals [emphasis added].[55]

Colonial medical discourse too, as we saw in the previous chapter, systematically reinforced this stereotype of the flighty and irresponsible memsahib, subjecting her lifestyle to a critical medical gaze and blaming it for her health disorders. Echoing this, Kate Platt also ascribed the European woman's special susceptibility to neurasthenia in India to her supposedly hectic social lifestyle. Speaking with the knowledgeable authority of having been the Principal of a prominent women's hospital at Delhi, Platt warned European women residing 'in the cities' against excessive socialising since this nerve disorder would be further 'augmented by an excess ... of social distractions'.[56] Indeed, medical opinion linking women's neurasthenia to a hectic social life continued to be voiced over the next decade at least. In the 1930s, a British physician's conclusion at a meeting of the Royal Society of Medicine at London was that, 'The damage caused by residence in the tropics was primarily psychological' and that it was 'aggravated by the evil trinity of late nights, alcohol, and ennui'.[57] These medical writings thereby succeeded in reifying and imprinting on the colonial imaginary an enduring misogynistic stereotype. Thus, as Dane Kennedy puts it, neurasthenia (especially its tropical variant) was 'a socially constructed disease', constructed by colonial medical discourse, which 'stressed the interplay between the physiological and neurological effects of the tropical climate and the cultural and psychological effects of colonial life'.[58]

Hot climates and female mental health

Throughout the colonial period, the question of the effect of climate and the high temperatures of the colonies on mental disorders remained a much-debated issue in colonial psychiatry. Philip Curtin, Dane Kennedy, David Arnold and Mark Harrison, among others, have widely written on the interconnections between climate and colonialism.[59] Nineteenth-century views on this matter were divided; one opinion was that the high temperatures exacerbated mental disorders and Europeans going to the tropics were especially liable to attacks of the nervous system.[60] This popular perception continued to hold currency and was sometimes supported by medical opinion. For instance, in the 1850s, the German physician Friedrich Oesterlen observed in his widely influential work, *Manual of Hygiene* (1851) that:

> The powerful influence of hot climates on the nervous system is manifested by the production of the most varied affections and mental maladies ... even destruction of the memory and mental powers supervenes ... there are superadded to this the at once debilitating and exciting influence of hot climate, sleeplessness, and disappointed hopes, regret at having left home. And nostalgia, the condition of excitable debility proceeds even further and readily ends in incurable madness, or in despair and suicide.[61]

However, this 'hot climate' theory remained a much-debated one and opinions continued to be divided. For instance, the physician, John Macpherson, who was Superintendent of the Bhowanipore Lunatic Asylum for Europeans in Calcutta in the 1850s, strongly contested this point and argued that:

> My own experience, for thirteen years, among Europeans, would not make me suppose cerebral affections to be particularly common – and the records of the General Hospital do not point to any particular prevalence of that class of disease.[62]

In the case of neurasthenia too, there was the theory that a hot climate was injurious to health. The tropical colonies were believed to aggravate nervous disorders due to their high temperatures and the harmful effects of the sun, with the metropolitan British physician, J. Michell Clarke, typically remarking that 'a hot and enervating climate' was 'an important cause in aggravating the disorder'.[63] Female mental health too (rather like their reproductive health) was projected as being susceptible to hot climates. High temperatures were believed to cause nervous exhaustion in women, and were held responsible for female depression, hysteria and neurasthenia. Writing in the 1920s, Kate Platt linked neurasthenia to a hot climate, maintaining that 'nerve strain' in European women was further exacerbated by a hot climate.[64] In order to counter this problem, hill stations were developed by the colonial government in the late nineteenth century as a summer retreat for middle-class white women especially from the heat of the north Indian plains – a yearly flight for which, one might point out, the memsahibs received endless criticism.[65] However, Platt also advised some amount of caution regarding going to the hills, and pointed out that the high altitudes of hill stations too could sometimes trigger neurasthenia, since 'altitude, even with a low temperature', could have a distinctly 'trying effect on the nerves'.[66]

There was also the theory, much debated, that the strong light of the tropics induced depression.[67] However, as was often to be seen in the topic of neurasthenia, the opposite view was also voiced, namely that it was darkness rather than the strong tropical light, which caused neurasthenia. For instance, Flora Annie Steel sharply reprimanded memsahibs for their habit of languishing inside *darkened* interiors of houses to escape the heat, remarking that:

> Half the cases of neurasthenia and anaemia among English ladies arise from the fact that they live virtually in the dark ... The writer believes that the forced inertia caused by living without *light* is responsible for many moral and physical evils among European ladies in the Tropics.[68]

Theories about the impact of climate on female mental health were articulated in other twentieth-century writings as well, the predominant opinion being that in the tropics, women tended to suffer more than men from neurasthenia. Even in the early twentieth century this idea about hot climates aggravating mental disorders continued to prevail. Thus, at a meeting of the Royal Society of Medicine held at London in 1931, most of the physicians agreed that the tropics had been found to exercise a negative effect on the nerves rather than on the individual's physical system, with one of the physicians stating that, 'The more highly strung the individual the less he was suited for the tropics ... The climate affected the mind and through mind, the appetite and the digestion.'[69]

Clearly, this construct continued as late as the 1930s, with physicians such as Sir Aldo Castellani continuing to support the climate theory. Castellani believed that the tropical climate led to 'mild neurasthenic conditions' especially in women, who tended to be more affected by it than men, and noted: 'The average European woman looks much more debilitated and pale and is more "nervy" than the average man and requires more frequent changes to the hills and Europe.'[70] Indeed, the tropical climate continued to play a conspicuous role in medical theories on mental health, and by the early years of the twentieth century, the concept of neurasthenia came to be 'tropicalised' in American and British medical discourse, and the new term, 'tropical neurasthenia' came into existence.[71] 'Tropical neurasthenia' was believed to generally affect white males and most importantly, unlike in western countries (where neurasthenia was believed to be triggered by a fast-paced modern life), the tropical variant was believed to be caused by social isolation combined with climate.[72] An article on 'Neurasthenia Among Europeans in India' in the *British Medical Journal* pointed out how:

> [I]n the tropics normal persons often experienced symptoms which, when strongly marked, were described as neurasthenic ... The symptoms were variously known in different places as 'Punjab head,' 'Bengal head,' 'Burmese head.'[73]

'Tropical neurasthenia' was also believed to affect Europeans but not 'natives'; its symptoms ranged from insomnia to insanity. Medical proponents of this disorder 'stressed the interplay between the physiological and neurological effects of the tropical climate and the cultural and psychological effects of colonial life'.[74] Dane Kennedy points out how, sometimes, the colonists' 'enigmatic ills' were all grouped together under this ailment:

> These included irritability, lack of energy, lack of concentration, loss of memory, loss of appetite, headaches, insomnia, diarrhoea and other digestive disorders, depression, various phobias, heart palpitations, ulcers, alcoholism, irregular menstrual cycles in women, 'weediness' in children, and, in the most serious cases, insanity and suicide.[75]

However, one needs to note that although the term 'tropical neurasthenia' was new, the concept of nerve affliction in the tropics *per se* was not, with theories about the impact of hot climates on mental health long having been a part of colonial lore and common sense. As far back as the early nineteenth century, naval surgeon, James Johnson, had commented in his classic *Influence of Tropical Climates More Especially the Climate of India, on European Constitutions* (1813), that 'ennui reigns triumphant and an unaccountable languor pervades both mind and body of Englishmen in the tropics'.[76] Given this, Dane Kennedy is right when he observes that proponents of 'tropical neurasthenia' merely tried to 'impose the authority and prestige of medical terminology and meaning on a condition long familiar to residents in the tropics'.[77] Even more importantly, physicians writing on the subject of 'tropical neurasthenia' largely held that it affected *men* more than women – especially white men living in isolation from civilisation in the colonial tropics – and that a 'white wife was commonly regarded as the surest safeguard against loneliness, alcoholism and sexual deviancy'.[78] It is important to point out at this juncture that this idea about white men being more susceptible to neurasthenia clearly contradicts the medical theory that we have been seeing all this while, namely that *women* were more prone to the disorder. Indeed, it needs to be underlined that most sources that I came across – medical handbooks, proceedings of the Royal Society, journal articles, household guides, sociological studies, memoirs and letters – constantly reiterated the idea that neurasthenia in the tropical colonies affected white *women* more than men. All this seems to further underline how much of a medical and social construct 'neurasthenia' was all along.

Indeed, its validity did always remain hotly debated among physicians. Thus, at a discussion of the Royal Society of Medicine in the 1930s, the majority rejected 'the existence of a neurasthenia special to the tropics', and urged that 'the use of the phrase "tropical neurasthenia" should be discontinued'.[79] Notwithstanding this, the idea of 'tropical neurasthenia' did continue to predominate in the years following the First World War, with many ailing Europeans being sent back home from colonies in Asia and Africa as invalids suffering from this disorder in the inter-war years. From around the 1930s 'tropical neurasthenia' lost its predominance in medical discourse and broke up and disappeared altogether from medical records after the Second World War. Thus, by the later decades of the twentieth century, neurasthenia as a psychopathological category gradually disappeared and the feelings of fatigue associated with it became incorporated into conditions such as anxiety and the affective disorders.[80]

Social class and health: delirium tremens and the barrack wife

What were the mental health problems among white women belonging to the lower classes, such as soldiers' wives? In what way were their health issues projected differently? To begin with, in contrast to the innumerable references to neurasthenic conditions affecting memsahibs, there is a silence on the mental health of the barrack wife. Indeed, colonial class arrogance and the 'othering' of the barrack wife are glaringly visible here. One military physician openly stated that neurasthenia was 'a matter of class, and it was not surprising that officers should suffer more than the men'.[81] The subject of the mental health of soldiers' wives has largely been ignored, although it is by now well documented how they led harshly brutalised lives that were marked by alcoholism, physical abuse and a high female and child mortality rate.[82] Unlike in the case of officers, there was no clear government policy on soldiers' wives and throughout the nineteenth century, marriage for British 'other ranks' was discouraged, with soldiers tending to form attachments among poor white women or Eurasians.[83] No doubt the combined factors of disadvantaged class, social status and subordinate gender role would have had a bearing on their mental health.

While data on the physical health of soldiers' wives exists in the colonial archives, there is indeed a relative absence of data on the 'common' mental ailments affecting this class of women – an understandable lacuna, given the fact that the recognition of mental health problems has only started taking place in the twentieth century.[84] It is only in cases of major mental health afflictions which required incarceration of the female patient in lunatic asylums (or repatriation to England in the era of the East India Company, as Waltraud Ernst has demonstrated in her *Mad Tales of the Raj*), that we find colonial records.

Regarding the factor of social class and the role that it played in matters of mental health in the colonies, different views prevailed. Dane Kennedy mentions one line of thought in colonial medical discourse – which reveals its own brand of colonial class arrogance – that the less privileged classes of whites, such as missionaries and poor whites, were immune to neurasthenia. Poor whites were believed to lack the 'character and will to put up any serious resistance to local influences' and had 'little will-power ... weak moral and mental character', while missionaries were held to be immune to mental problems because of their 'sturdy and unbending sense of self'.[85] This seems to point towards the insensitivity and class arrogance of the colonial medical gaze. However, there were diverse views on this matter; and numerous physicians held the opposite view, namely that missionaries were in fact *more* susceptible to depression and other mental afflictions because of living in 'such difficult conditions', while their socially marginalised position further 'accentuated their sense of isolation'.[86] Moreover, many of these missionaries were women and, as we have already noted, white females in the tropics were, in any case, considered to be under greater mental stress and at more risk than white males.[87]

Inside the military barracks, alcoholism, wife-beating, desertion by husbands, poverty and squalor were common features. In a rare article in the 1840s on the subject of barrack wives, *The Calcutta Review* voiced the fear that these unfortunate women were devoid of the 'self-respect which even native women may feel'.[88] Deploring 'the condition of mothers and daughters in our barracks – living and growing up without any instruction, principle, or restraint', it described the scene 'in the barracks, on the march, in boats, and in camp' as consisting of 'young girls and married women in the midst of drunken, half-naked men, hearing little but blasphemy and ribaldry, exposed to the extremes of heat and cold, surrounded by influences that render decency nearly impossible'.[89] As a soldier put it in a letter home in the 1840s:

> If I had my mind, no man beneath a commission should be allowed to bring a wife into the army. I have seen simple country girls turn out such low detestable characters under the name of soldiers' wives, that I have often found myself upon the verge of cursing the whole sex. 'It is indeed most awful.'[90]

Indeed, women in the barracks led a brutalised existence. Female drunkenness, marriage and motherhood at a very young age of adolescent girls, giving birth without a minimum degree of privacy, as well as high female and child mortality were regular features. Douglas Peers quotes from an article in a military journal of the 1830s, which vividly described the married quarters in the barracks of one Indian cantonment thus:

> A portion of a verandah eight feet wide, and has two doorways into the centre of the barrack, and two corresponding doors towards the open air, and is divided from the other parts of the verandah by a jaffery, or partition of bamboos and mats; one of which has a door, the other without an aperture. Against the latter jaffery you observe the chupper cot, in front of which is a chintz curtain, let down at night, but drawn up by day, extending from one door to its opposite.[91]

In addition, there was frequent widowhood and numerous subsequent remarriages. That same article in *The Calcutta Review* lamented the practice of 'marriage' among adolescent girls, which was followed by early motherhood, frequent widowhood as well as numerous subsequent remarriages.[92] In fact, in many instances young girls, who were virtually children, were married off by parents to much older men before the Corps marched off – so that the girl-wife could draw a husband's salary or at least a widow's pension. Indeed, this practice of girls marrying very young was a deeply rooted class problem prevalent even among the working classes in the industrial towns of England; the newspaper, *The Friend of India*, pointed out in 1871 how, in the factory towns, 'Poor little lassies, mere children, are commonly enough mothers.'[93]

Given these appalling conditions, a Royal Commission was appointed in 1859 to look into the sanitary state of the Army. It noted in its Report that 'At most places they [married quarters] are reported as "sufficient", at some "insufficient", at others "very bad", and at a few there are none. Where they are insufficient or non-existent, the "married quarters" are men's barrack rooms or huts, divided off by curtains or partitions'. The Commission also pointed out that the cause of the deaths of a large number of wives and children left in the barracks at Dumdum (Calcutta) during the Rebellion of 1857 had been 'intemperance, immorality, filth and foul air'.[94] In her co-authored housekeeping manual, Flora Annie Steel attributed the high mortality in the barracks to 'the result of crowding, errors of diet, intemperance, exposure, immorality' and 'imperfect ventilation and sanitation'.[95]

The culmination of the brutal hardships of colonial barrack existence were the gruelling marches undertaken under the blazing sun in the hot season when a regiment had to move to a new station. Barrack women and children routinely participated in them, with predictably high fatalities.[96] Indeed, barrack life was characterised by mortality rates for women and children which always remained higher than for men. In 1870, after hygienic conditions had been improved, following the recommendations of the Royal Commission, although the adult male mortality rate dropped to 26.55 per 1,000, the rate for women (46 per 1,000) and children (80 per 1,000) remained the same.[97] Similarly, in 1889, while the male mortality rate in India was 16 per 1,000, the figures for females was a little over 20 per 1,000 and for children as high as 48 per 1,000.[98] Indeed, with regard to child mortality in the barracks, one surgeon commented:

> Few children of pure English blood can be reared in the plains of India ... The mortality of barrack-children is appalling, especially in the months of June, September and October. At Cawnpore from twenty to thirty have died in one month.[99]

Besides the social and economic factors affecting women's mental health that we mentioned earlier, there are also strong connections between class, gender and mental illness. The linkages between mental health problems, poverty, alienation and a sense of helplessness found among women in poorer sections of society no doubt played a vital role in the case of colonial barrack wives, given their brutalised existence. One may recall that in the metropole in the late nineteenth century neurasthenia and other mental disorders were also believed to be triggered by the stresses of poverty and powerlessness. This was in addition to the apparently contradictory causative factors already mentioned (e.g. boredom, loneliness *as well as* leading a wild, hectic social life). Voicing a widely held contemporary medical opinion, the metropolitan physician J. Michell Clarke noted in *Hysteria and Neurasthenia* that when this disorder occurred among the poorer sections of society, it appeared far more predominantly among the women ('women predominate').[100] Neurasthenia, he pointed out, was also triggered by the 'stress of disadvantaged circumstances', or what T. D. Savill defined as 'prolonged anxiety ... and worry of making both ends'.[101] Other additional factors were 'frequent child-bearing, the drain of repeated lactation, and the cares of a large family with insufficient means for its support'.[102] This was clearly in contrast to its supposed pattern among the middle and upper classes, where a hectic social life was often felt to be the cause. Thus, neurasthenia was believed to be aggravated by stresses that were generated by poverty as well. All this further indicates that barrack wives in colonial India, who suffered the dual disadvantage of class (poverty) and gender (women), would also have been as likely to suffer from neurasthenia as memsahibs.

Notwithstanding this, a notable silence prevails in colonial medical discourse on neurasthenia among poorer whites, and till the very end it continued to be constructed as a condition affecting the 'sensitive' middle- and upper-class white 'ladies'. Instead, when it comes to women of the lower social orders, such as soldiers' wives, mental health problems are constructed as more befitting their coarser, less sensitive natures, and references to 'cruder' mental health disorders such as 'delirium tremens' are to be found.[103] Delirium tremens or 'shaking delirium' was a fairly widely occurring disorder among soldiers and their wives in India. This condition was linked to alcoholism and was a severe form of alcohol withdrawal that involved sudden and severe mental or nervous system changes.[104]

It also happened to be the only mental disorder that, according to Dr Macpherson of the Bhowanipore Lunatic Asylum at Calcutta, was aggravated by a hot climate. According to him, it was only in the case of delirium tremens that there existed a strong link between the hot climate of the colonies and the occurrence of mental disorder. 'I am hardly prepared to admit', he observed 'that, *with the exception of delirium tremens*, cerebral affections are more common among Europeans in India than at home' [emphasis added].[105] The incidence of delirium tremens was thus medically confirmed to be higher among Europeans in India than in England.

This condition, which could be life-threatening, was characterised by both mental symptoms (e.g. confusion, disorientation, delirium, hallucinations, restlessness, agitation, fear and excitement) as well as physical symptoms (e.g. seizures, palpitations, fever and fatigue). Indeed, the problem of alcoholism was rampant in the barracks among both the soldiers and their women. Intemperance was a long-standing problem among the European soldiery in India, affecting the rank and file rather than the officers.[106] Regarding the women, Harald Fischer-Tine points out that 'the majority of European women who fell on "black days" in colonial India were soldiers' wives'. Contemporary sources described these wives as 'greater drunkards than the men' and responsible for 'scenes of misery and vice in the married barracks'.[107]

In the Victorian imagination inter-connections were often drawn between class, gender and intemperance. Kipling's short fiction famously delineates the hard, brutal realities of female barrack existence, where alcoholism was overwhelmingly prevalent and women perpetually drunk and abusive.[108] While contemporary discourse discerned an 'innate affinity between the lower classes and intemperance', alcoholism was moralistically perceived as the root cause of Victorian 'female downfall', while the impact of alcoholic excess was considered to be much more harmful on women than on men.[109] More recently, Erica Wald notes how the 'wayward' wives of European soldiers, who indulged in 'immoral' activities, including prostitution or illicitly selling liquor in the barracks, were the target of 'extreme anger and censure from both commanding and medical officers'.[110] When soldiers' European wives or widows sold liquor in the bazaar to make ends meet, they were blamed for the 'threats to the men's health'.[111] It was sometimes also alleged that barrack wives prostituted themselves, occasionally 'with the understanding or support of their husbands'.[112] In such cases, these '"dissolute" European women' were 'systematically ring-fenced', declared to be 'both low-class and bad character' and expelled from the cantonment. Care was also taken to underline that such women were 'anomalies' and provided a contrast to the '"respectable" and "quiet" women of the regiment'.[113] In this manner, the barrack wife was the object of a censorious medical and military gaze in the colony.

Colonial discursive writings too mention the prevalence of both moral degradation and 'delirium tremens' among soldiers' wives. In *The Competitionwallah* (1864), his study of mid-century Anglo-Indian society, G. O. Trevelyan described how, during a Sunday morning sermon, an army chaplain exhorted these women to meekly endure ill-treatment (presumably from their husbands) and abjure taking to the common recourse of despair, drink or 'evil courses' (i.e. prostitution).[114] The chaplain then went on to paint for these women a lurid, cautionary tale of 'the horrors of delirium tremens and the other temporal consequences of gross sin'.[115]

In her essay on 'European Madness and Gender in Nineteenth-century British India', Waltraud Ernst refers to the case of one 'Mrs Catherine D', a Madras-based barrack wife in the 1820s. This woman who was an Irish private's wife, 'indulged in intemperate habits' and her derangement was supposed to have been 'produced by intoxication and other Vices incidental to a Barrack'. She remained as she had been before the onset of her mental malady, and her behaviour in the Madras lunatic asylum, too, was 'uniformly Violent and Mischievous'; and was described by the physician who recorded her case as 'uneducated and disposed to be uncleanly in her person and vulgar in her Manners'.[116]

In yet another instance of female alcoholism resulting in the neglect of maternal and wifely duty by an alcoholic barrack wife, Fischer-Tine cites a case in the 1880s of an Irish Gunner's wife who was also the mother of three children. Somewhat like the previous case, this Dublin-born woman's drunk and disorderly behaviour was so extreme that she had to be 'removed from the married establishment of the Battery for misconduct and deported by Government'. After returning at her own expense, she chose to live not with her husband and children, but in Bombay where she worked as a 'bar maid' in a hotel. However, from here too she had to quit, 'being ill from the effects of drink'. After having 'twice suffered from delirium tremens', she was admitted in the J. J. Hospital and was eventually put in Bombay's female workhouse in late 1885.[117]

The incidence of alcoholism and delirium tremens among lower-class white women is mentioned by Flora Annie Steel too in her autobiography *The Garden of Fidelity*. Recalling her experience in one dreary Anglo-Indian station in Punjab, where alcoholism was rife among the lower-class whites, Steel observed:

> We were the only sober people there. I had to nurse a young English woman – a lady by birth and education – through delirium tremens. It was a terrible experience ... I wrote to the woman's parents: the father was an English country clergyman.[118]

While traditionally, intemperance was associated with morality, it came to be increasingly identified as a life-threatening health problem by the second half of the century. As medical, rather than moral, arguments tended to be presented against excessive consumption of alcohol, linkages also came to be drawn between alcoholism and madness, with 'medical experts ... convinced that over-drinking was also often responsible for the growing number of Europeans who had to be sent to the newly created lunatic asylums'.[119]

Barrack wives in lunatic asylums in India

Indeed, in nineteenth-century colonial India, when white women exhibited signs of violence and 'severe' mental disorders, they were incarcerated in lunatic asylums in the country.[120] During this period, metropolitan Britain saw an unprecedented increase in the number of women admitted to asylums, with the 1871 census revealing that for every 1,000 male lunatics, there were 1,182 females and for 1,000 pauper male lunatics, there were 1,242 females.[121] One has to, of course, bear in mind that in colonial India, with the white female population always having been small, comparable gendered figures cannot be expected. Nevertheless, it is illuminating to consider some of the cases that are to be found in the records of the three asylums located in Calcutta (Bhowanipore), Bombay (Colaba) and Madras.[122] 'Domestic distress' was among the leading factors for 'insanity' recorded among female patients at Bhowanipore during the 1850s and 1860s.[123] In addition, 'grief and child-birth', as well as the related complication of 'puerperal fever' were prominent among the aggravating factors in both Bhowanipore and Colaba.[124]

A number of the cases of female asylum patients who were soldier's wives throw light on the disadvantaged social and economic condition as well as the pressures of class and gender which 'barrack widows' especially would be subjected to. In the case of a young barrack widow admitted to the Dinapore asylum in the winter of 1854, one notes several anomalies. Twenty-five-year-old Johanna Sheridan was described in the Medical Certificate as 'very excitable' and suffering from 'violent Cephalagia, the effects of exposure to the sun'.[125] The doctor's certificate also hinted that she was suffering from delusions of being pregnant (she 'labours under the delusion that she is pregnant and near her confinement'). However, she was obviously not hallucinating about being pregnant, because as the physician's certificate noted, she 'Gave birth on the 20th May '55 to her first-born, a healthy male babe' – a seeming contradiction on which it remained silent.

The stresses that the poorer female sections of white society in colonial India could be subjected to is once again visible in the case of another young widow, thirty-three-year-old Maria Augustina Martin, who was confined in the Lunatic Asylum at Madras in 1850. In her medical history, provided by surgeons of the asylum, she was said to be a widow who 'had a child born about 11 years ago'.[126] She was described as 'under excitement, walking about in a restless manner, talking with great volubility … and desiring that she may be permitted to return to Bellary, to meet a Corporal there who she believes to be her husband'. Though the records disclose no more details about her, there is little doubt that a combination of several factors, including her disadvantaged class status as well as personal bereavement in the form of the loss of her child and husband, may have played a triggering role in this case.

An even more striking case of disadvantaged gender and class status is that of Anne Morgan, another barrack wife admitted into the Colaba Lunatic Asylum at Bombay in 1845, a scrutiny of whose medical history discloses an interface of family circumstances, poverty, economic and sexual exploitation – in other words, a classic cycle of class and gender exploitation.[127] According to these records, she had been married 'to a soldier, but who he was, or in what corps he served' was difficult to ascertain. 'Subsequent to his death or her separation from him she led ... a life of prostitution and was for a time, it is said, in the keeping of an officer.' In other words, after having lost her husband and having become economically helpless, she appears to have taken recourse to the only available means of livelihood available to a woman of her economic background – that of becoming a prostitute. It is striking how the only 'assistance' she seems to have received from her connections with the British army in India was being kept as a personalised prostitute by an army officer.

The medical records further admit that from the beginning her treatment had been 'moral rather than medicinal', and attempts were made to 'reclaim her to the path of virtue'. Ann Morgan also 'frequently engaged in soliloquy' and appeared to have 'hallucinations'. The doctors noted that her mind appeared to be in a 'state of constant chaos and excitement – her thoughts are incoherent and her temper violent'. She also seemed to suffer delusions of grandeur: 'From expressions which she occasionally drops, it is inferred that she fancies herself a Lady ... She is constantly demanding that her diet, dress, accommodation and attendance should be in a style corresponding with her imaginary greatness.' It may not be fully off the mark to read in the last point mentioned above (i.e. in the woman's delusions of grandeur), hints and signs suggestive of class aspirations in a woman who had been sexually exploited earlier on by a socially superior male in the army barrack.

Interestingly, the medical records also express concern about the influence of the climate and 'native' culture on her condition: 'Should she remain in this country it seems inevitable that she must go on from bad to worse ... The climate is against her and ... surrounded as she necessarily is with native servants and native Inmates', it was feared that she could not have 'the means and appliances to bear on her mind by which alone it can ever be repaired'. But the hope was expressed that 'under more favourable circumstances' she would show 'improvement, if not of cure' and she was recommended to be 'sent to England with a view to treatment in an asylum there'.

These three cases of female lunacy discussed above, which are taken from the records of lunatic asylums in widely divergent regions and located in the three presidency capitals of Calcutta, Madras and Bombay, though otherwise different in their details, share one strikingly similar pattern of female suffering. All three white women belonged to the lower- classes and all of them were impoverished widows (or abandoned wives) of soldiers. These cases reiterate the same gendered narratives of straitened circumstances, economic hardship, sexual vulnerability, serious susceptibility to mental illness and the need for institutional confinement.

Conclusion

In this chapter we explored some aspects of European female mental disorder in colonial India. Colonial life, it is widely recognised, sub-jected colonisers of both sexes to constant mental stress and tension. We examined how the white woman negotiated mental stress as well as the medical construct of 'tropical neurasthenia' which was used to define her condition, through a scrutiny of articles in medical journals, medical case histories, as well as women's writings. Both objective realities as well as colonial perceptions were examined; in other words, both the perceived as well as actual middle-class female vulnerability to chronic mental health problems were kept in mind.

Without trying to build up a comprehensive picture, this chapter attempted to touch upon some of the various dimensions related to questions pertaining to gender and mental health. A scrutiny of dis-cursive writings in nineteenth-century colonial India did suggest the fairly wide occurrence of mental health problems – although these may not even have been fully recognised or properly identified as such. Psychologists recognise the links between mental illness and feelings of alienation, powerlessness and having no control over one's life. Consequently, the multiple causes of women's distress and women's susceptibility to mental illness are both a myth and also a reality – it is both socially constructed and also an outcome of the disadvantaged conditions of gendered existence which are a feature of all patriarchal societies.

The 'colonial medical gaze' displayed submerged gender prejudices. Although neurasthenia may have been a social construct of medical discourse, perceptions about its occurrence in the colony varied according to class and gender. White men's neurasthenia, it is strik-ing, was attributed to their hard lives in lonely, isolated outposts and exposure to the tropical sun. In other words, their nerve problems were projected as a badge of honour, a symbol of their sacrifice – of health, comfort and even mental balance – in the service of empire, thereby feeding into the myth of the administrator-hero who sacrificed every-thing in the pursuit of duty (a myth that we also took note of in the previous chapter).

In contrast, white women's susceptibility to neurasthenia was widely attributed to their inability to tolerate the high temperatures – but equally to their supposedly idle and frivolous lifestyle. Indeed, their hectic social life came to be blamed for every female health problem – ranging from reproductive problems (as we saw in the previous chapter) to neurasthenia. More seriously, evidence suggests that it was the alienating and stressful conditions of gendered life in colonial India that aggravated problems of mental health among both middle-class memsahib and lower-class barrack wife. Clearly, these colonial women's mental disorders were the result of a complex combination of social, economic and cultural factors, such as loneliness and absence of meaningful activity – in addition to the hard work, poverty and brutalisation among the soldiers' wives. Thus, there were multifarious linkages between the social and cultural specificities of gendered colonial life and the problem of female mental disorder.[128]

In the case of the lower social orders, such as the soldier's wife, we saw how the problem of 'delirium tremens' (which was characterised by psychological disturbances such as delusions), was brought about by chronic alcoholism affecting this class of white woman. We also looked at this class of woman's vulnerability to serious mental breakdown, as well as institutionalisation in colonial lunatic asylums. A scrutiny of the case studies of severe mental disorders requiring institutionalisation, as well as a scrutiny of their records in asylums, revealed that a fair number of those affected and admitted were from the lower classes, including soldiers' wives or widows. The details of the case histories of these barrack wives voice their own unspoken story of female vulnerability, sexual exploitation as well as class and gender oppression in the colony.

In conclusion, feminist scholars such as Phyllis Chesler and Elaine Showalter have argued (in the context of the metropole) that beneath the outbreaks of female hysteria and other nervous disorders, which peaked in the nineteenth century, there lay submerged anger against the limited role that was assigned to women.[129] In the case of colonial India then, was the occurrence of 'minor' problems a symbol of female victimhood? Or was this complicated by elements of resentment and anger on her part against the limited choice allowed her in colonial society? Perhaps we may speculate that in this context too, woman's mental health problems signified *both* victimhood and resentment. Consequently, we need to see the white woman in colonial India as *both* victim *and* rebel. Hence, although the predominant construct may appear to be that of victim, there is a submerged female frustration and even anger that can be discerned.

Notes

1 Mental disorders are categorised as either 'common' or 'severe'. In the case of 'common mental disorders' (e.g. depression, panic disorder, obsessive-compulsive

disorder and anxiety), strong inter-connections are believed to exist between gender and mental health with the occurrence being higher among women, with a male–female ratio of at least 1:2. With perceptions about gender and mental health having undergone changes over the centuries, the roots of 'common' mental disorders among women are increasingly being seen as enmeshed in complex social, cultural and ideological factors.

2   See Waltraud Ernst, *Mad Tales from the Raj: The European Insane in British India, 1800–1858* (London and New York, Routledge, 1991) and Waltraud Ernst, 'European Madness and Gender in Nineteenth-century British India', *The Social History of Medicine*, 9:3 (1996), pp. 357–382, among her numerous essays and chapters on the subject of mental health.

3   Among the few essays on the subject are my article: Indrani Sen, 'The Memsahib's "Madness": The European Woman's Mental Health in Late Nineteenth Century India', *Social Scientist*, 33: 5/6 (May–June, 2005), pp. 26–48; and Dane Kennedy's important essay, 'Diagnosing the Colonial Dilemma: Tropical Neurasthenia and the Alienated Briton', in Durba Ghosh and Dane Kennedy (eds), *Decentring Empire: Britain, India and the Transcolonial World* (New Delhi, Orient Longman, 2006), pp. 157–181.

4   Elaine Carmen, Nancy Felipe Russo and Jean Baker Miller, 'Inequality and Women's Mental Health: An Overview', in Patricia Perri Reiker and Elaine (Hilberman) Carmen (eds), *The Gender Gap in Psychotherapy: Social Realities and Psychological Processes* (New York, Plenum Press, 1984), p. 23.

5   Elaine Showalter, *The Female Malady: Women, Madness and English Culture, 1830–1980* (London, Virago, 1987), Chapter 5, pp. 121–144. For arguments supporting this idea about women's mental breakdown being an expression of female anger and protest, see Phyllis Chesler, *Women and Madness* (Harmondsworth, Penguin Books, 1979). See also Florence Nightingale's essay, 'Cassandra', in *Suggestions for Thought to Searchers after Religious Truth*, 3 vols, privately printed (London, Eyre & Spottiswoode, 1860); and Sandra Gilbert and Susan Gubar, *The Mad Woman in the Attic: The Woman Writer and the Nineteenth Century literary Imagination* (New Haven, Yale University Press, 1978).

6   See Showalter, *Female Malady*.

7   Jane Ussher, *Women's Madness: Misogyny or Mental Illness?* (London, Harvester Wheatsheaf, 1991), p. 64.

8   Showalter, *Female Malady*, p. 55.

9   Ussher, *Women's Madness*, p. 74.

10 Joan Busfield, *Men, Women and Madness: Understanding Gender and Mental Disorder* (Hampshire, Macmillan, 1996), p. 29.

11 Showalter, *Female Malady*, p. 147.

12 J. Michell Clarke, *Hysteria and Neurasthenia* (London, John Lane, the Bodley Head, 1905), p. 6. J. Michell Clarke (1859–1918) was Physician at the General Hospital and Professor of Pathology, University College at Bristol.

13 *Ibid.*, pp. 11, 17, 18.

14 Isaac Baker Brown, *On the Curability of Certain Forms of Insanity, Epilepsy, Catalepsy and Hysteria in Females* (London, Robert Hardwicke, 1866), pp. 12, 17. Isaac Baker Brown (1811–1873), a prominent London gynecologist, attracted enormous controversy in the 1860s for practising clitoridectomy without patient permission. He was eventually expelled from the Obstetrical Society of London in 1873.

15 Showalter, *Female Malady*, pp. 121–163.

16 Ussher, *Women's Madness*, pp. 72–73.

17 Henry Maudsley, MD, *Body and Mind: An Inquiry into their Connection and Mutual Influence, Specially in Reference to Mental Disorders* ([1870], London, Macmillan & Co., 1873), p. 82.

18 George M. Beard first wrote on the subject of neurasthenia in, 'Neurasthenia or Nervous Exhaustion', *Boston Medical and Surgical Journal*, 3 (1869), pp. 217–221. In 1880 Beard published his views on the subject in book form entitled, *A Practical*

Treatise on Nervous Exhaustion (Neurasthenia) (New York, William Wood & Co, 1880).

19 T. D. Savill, *Clinical Lectures on Neurasthenia* ([1899], London, Glaisher, 1906), pp. 48–49. Thomas Dixon Savill was a London neurologist who worked at the Paddington Infirmary.
20 *Ibid.*, p. 35.
21 Hugh Campbell, *The Anatomy of Nervousness and Nervous Exhaustion (Neurasthenia)* (London, Henry Renshaw, n.d.), pp. 10, 17, 19. Michell Clarke, *Hysteria and Neurasthenia*, p. 189.
22 Hospital records and observations by specialist physicians confirm that it was not only an upper-class disease. T. D. Savill found its frequent occurrence among the poor and the inmates of the Paddington workhouse; for details, see Ruth E. Taylor, 'Death of Neurasthenia and its Psychological Reincarnation: A Study of Neurasthenia at the National Hospital for the Relief and Care of the Paralysed and Epileptic, Queen Square, London, 1870–1932', *The British Journal of Psychiatry*, 179 (2001), p. 555.
23 In the case of neurasthenia, the gender ratio showed varying increase and decrease after the initial figure of 50:50 (e.g. slight decrease among males between 1891 and 1905, slight increase among males during the First World War, and slight increase among females between 1916 and 1920). For details, see Taylor, 'Death of Neurasthenia', p. 555.
24 Alison Bashford, *Purity and Pollution: Gender, Embodiment and Victorian Medicine* (London, MacMillan, 1998), p. xvii.
25 Ernst goes on to add that the Briton's '[e]xposure to unfamiliar cultural conditions' had 'psychological consequences ... of which anxiety, anger or depression are the most common', See Ernst, *Mad Tales from the Raj*, p. 4.
26 Dennis Kincaid, *British Social Life in India: 1608–1937* ([1938], London, Routledge & Kegan Paul, 1973), p. 181.
27 Dr H. C. Squires in Dr Millais Culpin, 'An Examination of Tropical Neurasthenia', *Proceedings of the Royal Society of Medicine*, 26:7 (May, 1933), pp. 919–920.
28 As mentioned in the previous chapter (note 18), in the first all-India census conducted in1881, the total British population numbered 90,000.
29 *The Madras Mail* (18 May 1869); Anne Campbell Wilson, *Letters from India* ([1911], London, Century, 1984), pp. 2–5.
30 See Indrani Sen, *Woman and Empire: Representations in the Writings of British India, 1858–1900* (New Delhi, Orient Longman, 2002), pp. 1–38.
31 G. O. Trevelyan, *The Competitionwallah* (London, Macmillan & Co., 1864), pp. 141–142.
32 *Ibid.*
33 An Englishwoman in India, 'Englishwomen in India', *The Calcutta Review*, 8:159 (1885), p. 137.
34 W. H. Dawe, *The Wife's Help to Indian Cookery* (London, Elliot Stock, 1888), p. 21, cited in Mary A. Procida, 'Married to the Empire: British Wives and British Imperialism in India, 1883–1947', PhD thesis, University of Pennsylvania, 1997, p. 69.
35 Flora Annie Steel, *The Garden of Fidelity: Being the Autobiography of Flora Annie Steel, 1847–1929* (London, Macmillan & Co. Ltd, 1929), pp. 122–123.
36 Rudyard Kipling, *Something of Myself: For My Friends, Known and Unknown* (London, Macmillan & Co. Ltd, 1937).
37 This subject of the break-up of families is explored in, among others, Georgina Gowans, 'Imperial Geographies of Home: Memsahibs and Miss-sahibs in India and Britain, 1915–1947, *Cultural Geographies*, 10 (2003), pp. 424–441 and Elizabeth Buettner, *Empire Families: Britons and Late Imperial India* (Oxford and New York, Oxford University Press, 2004). For a literary delineation of the tragic alienation between an Anglo-Indian mother and her grown-up daughter returning to India, see Sara Jeannette Duncan's short story, 'A Mother in India', in Sara Jeannette Duncan, *The Pool in the Desert* (New York, D. Appleton and Company, 1903).

38 Steel, *Garden of Fidelity*, p. 105.
39 Letter to the Editor, *The Pioneer* (20 February, 1882).
40 Letter to the Editor, *The Pioneer* (10 November, 1888).
41 Maud Diver, *The Englishwoman in India* (Edinburgh and London, William Blackwood & Sons, 1909), p. 8.
42 *Ibid.*
43 *Ibid.*, p. 9.
44 Kate Platt, *The Home and Health in India and the Tropical Colonies* (London, Bailliere, Tindall & Cox, 1923), pp. 204, 204, 204.
45 Sir Aldo Castellani, *Climate and Acclimatization* ([1930], London, John Bale and Sons, 1938), p. 54.
46 Platt, *Home and Health in India*, p. 204.
47 For a discussion, see Nupur Chaudhuri, 'Memsahibs and Motherhood in Nineteenth Century Colonial India', *Victorian Studies*, 31:4. (1988), pp. 528–529.
48 Michell Clarke, *Hysteria and Neurasthenia*, p. 181.
49 See Sir Joseph Fayrer, *European Child-Life in Bengal* (London, J. & A. Churchill, 1873), p. 8.
50 Hugh W. Acton, 'Neurasthenia in the Tropics', *The Indian Medical Gazette*, 62:1, January (1927), p. 4; V. B. Green-Armytage, in Acton, 'Neurasthenia in the Tropics', p. 7. Major Hugh W. Acton was Professor of Bacteriology at the Calcutta School of Tropical Medicine and Hygiene, while Major V. B. Green-Armytage was Professor of Midwifery and Gynaecology at Calcutta University.
51 An exceptions here is Kate Platt, one of the few female physicians who wrote a medical handbook. Platt recognised *both* isolation and *also* a hectic social life equally as the cause of nerve disorders.
52 Kennedy, 'Diagnosing the Colonial Dilemma', pp. 157–181. Kennedy also uses the term 'tropical neurasthenia' in the entire essay. See also Dane Kennedy, 'The Perils of the Mid-day Sun: Climatic Anxieties in the Colonial Tropics', in John M. Mackenzie (ed.), *Imperialism and the Natural World* (Manchester, Manchester University Press, 1990), p. 131.
53 Campbell, *Anatomy of Nervousness and Nervous Exhaustion*, p. 2; Michell Clarke, *Hysteria and Neurasthenia*, p. 181.
54 Michell Clarke, *Hysteria and Neurasthenia*, p. 181.
55 Steel, *Garden of Fidelity*, p. 122.
56 It is striking that while metropolitan physicians link neurasthenia to hectic social activity, colonial writings do not make this connection very often, and generally tend to link the condition to social isolation. Platt is one of the few colonial physicians who makes this connection between hectic social activity and neurasthenia in the context of colonial India in her *Home and Health in India*, p. 205.
57 Dr G. W. Theobald's comments in A. R. Neligan, Sir Aldo Castellani, Dr H. S. Stannus, Dr G. W. Bray, Mr A. F. MacCallan, Dr J. B. Christopherson, Dr K. Edmundson and Dr G. W. Theobald, 'Discussion on the Adaptation of European Women and Children to Tropical Climates', *Proceedings of the Royal Society of Medicine*, 24:6 (1931), p. 1332.
58 Kennedy, 'Diagnosing the Colonial Dilemma', p. 157.
59 Philip Curtin, *Death by Migration: Europe's Encounter with the Tropical World in the Nineteenth Century* (Cambridge: Cambridge University Press, 1988); Kennedy, 'The Perils of the Mid-day Sun', pp. 118–140; David Arnold, 'Introduction: Tropical Medicine before Manson', in David Arnold (ed.), *Warm Climates and Western Medicine: The Emergence of Tropical Medicine, 1500–1900* (Amsterdam, Rodopi, 1996), pp. 1–19; Mark Harrison, *Climates and Constitutions: Health, Race, Environment and British Imperialism in India, 1600–1850* (New Delhi, Oxford University Press, 1999).
60 See also James Johnson, *The Influence of Tropical Climates More Especially the Climate of India, on European Constitutions etc.* ([1813], London, J. Callow, 1815); James Ranald Martin and James Johnson. *The Influence of Tropical Climates on European Constitutions*, sixth edition (London, S. Highley, 1841); Sir

Joseph Fayrer, *On the Climate and Fevers of India: Being the Croonian Lectures Delivered at the Royal College of Physicians* (London, J. & A. Churchill. 1882) and Sir Joseph Fayrer, *On Preservation of Health in India* (London, Macmillan, 1894).

61 Friedrich Oesterlen, *Manual of Hygiene* (original German title: *Handbuch der Hygieine für den Einzelnen wie für eine Bevölkerung* (Tubingen, H. Laupp, 1851), quoted in John Macpherson, MD, *Report on Insanity among Europeans in Bengal, founded on the experience of the Calcutta Lunatic Asylum*, quoted in *The Calcutta Review*, 26:52 (1856), p. 602.

62 Macpherson, *Report on Insanity Among Europeans in Bengal*, p. 602. He goes on to cite several instances from doctors from other tropical colonies, such as Senegal, Algeria or other regions in India, such as Bombay.

63 Michell Clarke, *Hysteria and Neurasthenia*, p. 175.

64 Platt, *Home and Health in India*, p. 205.

65 It was not only white women who systematically escaped to the hill stations. From 1864 Simla became the summer capital of the British colonial government as well. So, in a way, the memsahibs were rather unfairly targeted in this matter. Simla became mythologised as a place of female flirtation and frivolity especially by Rudyard Kipling in his many writings, such as 'Nursery Rhymes for Little Anglo-Indians' in *Echoes* (Lahore, Civil and Military Gazette Press, 1884) and his hugely successful collection of short stories, *Plain Tales from the Hills* ([1888], London, Macmillan, 1960). For a discussion of Kipling's projection of Simla, see Indrani Sen, 'Gendering (Anglo) India: Rudyard Kipling and the Construction of Women', *Social Scientist*, 28:9/10 (September– October, 2000), pp. 12–32; for hill station life in general, see Dane Kennedy, *The Magic Mountains: Hill Stations and the British Raj* (Berkeley, University of California Press, 1996).

66 Platt, *Home and Health in India*, p. 203.

67 See Major Charles E. Woodruff, *The Effects of Tropical Light on White Men* (Rebman, New York, 1905).

68 Flora Annie Steel and Grace Gardiner, *The Complete Indian Housekeeper and Cook* ([1888], London, William Heinemann, 1909), p. 178.

69 Dr G. W. Theobald's comments in A. R. Neligan et al. 'Discussion on the Adaptation of European Women and Children to Tropical Climates', p. 1332.

70 Sir Aldo Castellani in A. R. Neligan et al. 'Discussion on the Adaptation of European Women and Children to Tropical Climates', p. 1332.

71 This term 'tropical neurasthenia' seems to have been first used by American doctors, probably around the year, 1905, based on the American experience of colonisation in the Philipines. Among the first to voice white people's vulnerability in the tropics was the American, Major Charles E. Woodruff, in *The Effects of Tropical White Light on White Men*, and 'The Neurasthenic State Caused by Excessive Light', *Medical Record*, 23 December, 1905. One of the earliest to use the term was W. W. King, 'Tropical Neurasthenia', *Journal of the American Medical Association*, 46:20 (May 1906), p. 1519. For details see Warwick Anderson, 'The Trespass Speaks: White Masculinity and Colonial Breakdown', *The American Historical Review*, 102:5 (December, 1997), pp. 1343–1370 and Kennedy, 'Diagnosing the Colonial Dilemma', pp. 160–161.

72 For details, see Kennedy, 'Diagnosing the Colonial Dilemma', pp. 157–181 and also Anna Greenwood, 'Looking Back: The Strange History of Tropical Neurasthenia', in *The Psychologist*, 24:3 (March 2011), pp. 226–227.

73 'Neurasthenia Among Europeans in India', *The British Medical Journal*, 1:2778 (March 28, 1914), p. 72.

74 Kennedy, 'Diagnosing the Colonial Dilemma', p. 157.

75 *Ibid.*, p. 165.

76 Johnson, *Influence of Tropical Climates More Especially the Climate of India, on European Constitutions*, p. 403.

77 Kennedy, 'The Perils of the Mid-day Sun', p. 123.

78 *Ibid.*, p. 169.

79 Millais Culpin, 'An Examination of Tropical Neurasthenia', p. 911. British psy-

chologist, Millais Culpin (1874–1952), was professor in industrial and medical psychology at the London School of Health and Tropical Medicine. Among his publications was a 1935 article for the *Practitioner*, 'Neurasthenia in the Tropics', which argued that white people could inhabit the tropics without ill effects. He became president of the British Psychological Society in 1944.

80   German E. Berrios, *The History of Mental Symptoms: Descriptive Psychopathology since the Nineteenth Century* (Cambridge, Cambridge University Press, 1996), p. 373.

81   Dr M. Cameron Blair, in Col. R. J. S. Simpson et al. 'The Causes of Invaliding in the Tropics', *The British Medical Journal*, 15 November (1913), p. 1296, cited in Kennedy, 'Diagnosing the Colonial Dilemma', p. 171.

82   See Myna Trustram, *Women of the Regiment: Marriage and the Victorian Army* (Cambridge, Cambridge University Press, 1984) and also Joanna Trollope, *Britannia's Daughters: Women of the British Empire* (London, Hutchinson, 1984).

83   Earlier writers and commentators (e.g. Dennis Kincaid) tended to be silent on the barrack wife.

84   See for instance Sumit Guha, 'Nutrition, Sanitation, Hygiene, and the Likelihood of Death: The British Army in India *c.* 1870–1920', *Population Studies: A Journal of Demography*, 47:3 (1993), pp. 385–401.

85   Kennedy, 'Diagnosing the Colonial Dilemma', p. 170.

86   *Ibid.*, p. 171. Indeed, this is supported by a pre-First World War study which reveals that large numbers of missionaries in tropical colonies were, in fact, repatriated to Britain due to a 'nervous condition of a neurasthenic type'. See G. Basil Price, in Col. R. J. S. Simpson et al. 'The Causes of Invaliding in the Tropics', pp. 1290–1293.

87   See Geraldine Forbes, 'In Search of the "Pure Heathen"': Missionary Women in Nineteenth Century India', *Economic and Political Weekly*, 21:17, 28 April (1986), pp. WS2–WS8.

88   'English Women in Hindustan', *The Calcutta Review*, 4:7 (1845), p. 124.

89   *Ibid.*, pp. 121, 126.

90   Letter of Lance-Corporal David Banham of the 94th Regiment of Foot, Moulmein, Burma, to a friend in England, dated 1 August, 1845, National Museum, London, www.nam.ac.uk/exhibitions/online-exhibitions/wives-sweethearts/women-regiment/lives-misery-transcript-1 (accessed 26 August 2016).

91   [Sylvanus Crowquill], 'Barrack Sketches: The Sentry and the Teapot', *East India United Service Journal*, xxxvii (1837), p. 513, quoted in Douglas Peers, 'Privates Off Parade: Regimenting in the Nineteenth-century Indian Empire', *The International History Review*, 20:4 (December 1998), p. 849.

92   'English Women in Hindustan', *The Calcutta Review*, p. 121.

93   *The Friend of India* (29 June 1871), p. 744.

94   *Report of the Commissioners Appointed to Inquire into the Sanitary State of the Army in India, with Abstract of Evidence and of Reports Received from Indian Military Stations* (London, Printed Under the Superintendence of Her Majesty's Stationery Office, 1864), pp. 339, 339.

95   Steel and Gardiner, *Complete Indian Housekeeper and Cook*, pp. 177–178.

96   Rudyard Kipling describes such marches in stories such as 'The Daughter of the Regiment', in *Plain Tales from the Hills*, and 'The Courting of Dinah Shadd' in *Life's Handicap: Being Stories of My Own People* ([1891], Oxford, Oxford University Press, 1987).

97   'Review of the Progress of Sanitation in India', *The Calcutta Review*, 50:99 (1870), p. 103.

98   Mark Harrison, *Public Health in British India: Anglo-Indian Preventive Medicine, 1859–1914* (Cambridge, Cambridge University Press, 1994), p. 50.

99   J. Jeffreys, *The British Army in India: Its Preservation by an Appropriate Clothing, Housing, Locating, Recreative Employment, and Hopeful Encouragement of the Troops* (London, 1858), p. 172, cited in Peers, 'Privates Off Parade', p. 847.

100 Michell Clarke, *Hysteria and Neurasthenia*, p. 174.

101 Michell Clarke, *Hysteria and Neurasthenia*, p. 171; T. D. Savill observed, 'Great grief, emotional strain of any kind, and prolonged anxiety, including the trouble and worry of making both ends, are all potent causes', in Savill, *Clinical Lectures on Neurasthenia*, p. 45.

102 Savill, *Clinical Lectures on Neurasthenia*, p. 181.

103 Berrios, *History of Mental Symptoms*, pp. 238–240. Delirium tremens (or acute confusional state) was associated with alcohol withdrawal and referred to a cluster of mental symptoms and behaviour occurring in the wake of acute brain disease. Debates went on until the end of the nineteenth century whether acute delirium was distinct from insanity. The definition of 'delirium' underwent changes in the course of the nineteenth century. From being a state of excited behaviour accompanied by fever, 'delirium' became associated with a disorder of consciousness, attention, cognition and orientation.

104 For a discussion on alcoholism in the British Indian army see Douglas Peers, 'Imperial Vice: Sex, Drink, and the Health of the British Troops in North Indian Cantonments, 1800–1858', in David Killingray and David Omissi (eds), *Guardians of Empire: The Armed Forces of the Colonial Powers, 1700–1964* (Manchester, Manchester University Press, 1999), pp. 25–52.

105 Macpherson, *Report on Insanity Among Europeans*, p. 602.

106 For a discussion on intemperance among soldiers and lower-class Europeans, see Peers, 'Privates Off Parade', pp. 823–854; Harald Fischer-Tine, '"The Drinking Habits of Our Countrymen": European Alcohol Consumption and Colonial Power in British India', *The Journal of Imperial and Commonwealth History*, 40:3 (September 2012), pp. 383–408; and Erica Wald, *Vice in the Barracks: Medicine, the Military and the Making of Colonial India, 1780–1868* (London, Palgrave Macmillan, 2014). See also Harald Fischer-Tine, *Low and Licentious Europeans: Race, Class and 'White Subalternity' in Colonial India* (New Delhi, Orient BlackSwan, 2009).

107 Frederick John Mouat, *The British Soldier in India* (Calcutta, R. C. Lepage & Co., 1859), p. 72, and Monier Williams, *A Few Remarks on the Use of Spirituous Liquors among the European Soldiers; and on the Punishment of Flogging in the Native Army of the Honourable East India Company* (London, D. S. Maurice, n.d. [1823?], quoted in Harald Fischer Tine, *Low and Licentious Europeans*, p. 137.

108 With such hard lives, this class of women are shown to age fast; a once-beautiful woman becomes unrecognisably bald and grotesque, another winsome girl is transformed after some years of married life into a 'gigantic figure' without the remotest claim to beauty; 'Mother Sheehy', the colour-sergeant's wife, is drunk and abusive. See Rudyard Kipling, 'The Courting of Dinah Shadd', in *Life's Handicap*.

109 Judith Rowbotham, '"Only When Drunk": The Stereotyping of Violence in England, c. 1850–1900', in Shani D'Cruze (ed.), *Everyday Violence in Britain, 1850–1950, Class and Gender* (Harlow, Longman-Pearson Education, 2000), p. 165.

110 Erica Wald, 'Health, Discipline and Appropriate Behaviour: The Body of the Soldier and Space of the Cantonment', *Modern Asian Studies*, 46: 4 (July 2012), p. 855. See also Erica Wald, *Vice in the Barracks*, pp. 140–145.

111 Wald, 'Health, Discipline and Appropriate Behaviour', p. 821.

112 *Ibid.*, p. 839.

113 *Ibid.*, p. 840.

114 Trevelyan, *Competitionwallah*, p. 241.

115 *Ibid.*, p. 241.

116 APAC: Letter from Medical Board to Government of Madras, 8.1.1821, 7; Military Letter from Madras, 3.4.1821 [Case of Mrs Catherine D.] in Waltraud Ernst, 'European Madness and Gender in Nineteenth-century British India', p. 365. pp. 357–382.

117 Maharashtra State Archives, Go Bom, Jud. Dept Proc., vol. 47, 1886, letter no. WF 15, P. Cooper, Governor, Government Female WH Bom, to Go Bom Jud. Dept, 10

March 1886, quoted in Fischer-Tine, '"The Drinking Habits of Our Countrymen"', p. 403.

118 Steel, *Garden of Fidelity*, pp. 141–142.

119 Fischer-Tine, '"The Drinking Habits of Our Countrymen"', p. 387.

120 'Severe' disorders are marked by a high degree of cognitive and social impairment (e.g. schizophrenia, depressive psychoses, mania), and display no particular gender propensity. See D. Goldberg and P. Huxley, *Common Mental Disorders* (London, Routledge & Kegan Paul, 1992), p. 54–56.

121 Showalter, *Female Malady*, p. 52.

122 While the Bombay (Colaba) and Madras asylums were mixed-race institutions, the Bhowanipore asylum at Calcutta was a 'whites-only' institution, housing various classes of patients, and a numerically much higher number of women than the other two asylums. For details about lunatic asylums for whites in the early nineteenth century, see Ernst, *Mad Tales from the Raj*.

123 In 1856, out of forty-five female patients in Bhowanipore the highest number of 'Supposed Causes' was 'Domestic Distress: 5'. See *Reports on the Asylums for European and Native Insane Patients at Bhowanipore and Dullunda, for 1856 and 1857* (Calcutta, John Grey, 'Calcutta Gazette Office', 1858), p. 21. In 1857, out of the twenty-seven female patients at Bhowanipore, there were three Gentlewomen, seven soldiers' wives, and seventeen tradesmen's wives. See *ibid.*, pp. 23–24.

124 In 1868, out of a total of twenty-two female inmates in Bengal, seventeen suffered from 'chronic mania', two from 'dementia' and two from 'puerperal mania' (p. 60) *Annual Report of the Insane Asylums in Bengal for the Year 1868* (Calcutta, Office of the Superintendent of Govt. Printing, 1869), p. 56. In the records of the Colaba asylum in 1873, childbirth and poverty are mentioned as leading causes; in two out of the eight cases, the cause of insanity being recorded as childbirth. See *Annual Administration and Progress Report on the Insane Asylums in the Bombay Presidency for the Year 1873–74* (Bombay, Government Central Press, 1874), p. 7.

125 APAC (PELA), Medical Certificate 1856, [Case of Mrs Johanna Sheridan]. This section draws heavily on Ernst's path-breaking essay on white female mental illness in colonial India, 'European Madness and Gender in Nineteenth-century British India'.

126 APAC (PELA), Medical Certificate, dated 26 February, 1850, [Case of Mrs Maria Augustina Martin].

127 AOAC (PELA), Medical Certificate 1854, [Case of Mrs Anne Morgan]. 'Summary Statement of the case of Mrs Anne Morgan, Admitted into the Lunatic Asylum, 18 December, 1845', and signed by the 'Superintendent Lunatic Asylum, dated Colaba, Bombay, 1st January, 1854'.

128 Carmen, Felipe Russo and Baker Miller, 'Inequality and Women's Mental Health: An Overview', p. 23.

129 Showalter, *Female Malady*; Chesler, *Women and Madness*.

CONCLUSION

This book explored diverse aspects related to the white woman's experience of colonialism in India during the late nineteenth- and early twentieth- centuries. One of its central concerns and areas of inquiry was the sphere of gendered transactions across the race divide. An important concern was to prise out colonial and gender constructs in narratives – both overt as well as submerged beneath the surface. What emerged from our reading of colonial discursive writings was a complex picture replete with tensions and contradictions.

In the colonial imaginary, the 'native' woman tended to be simplified into the monolithic figure of the 'oppressed zenana woman', but our readings of various encounters brought out instead the complexities among 'native' women from various regions (namely, Bengali, Maharashtrian or Punjabi women). Missionary accounts of middle-class/high-caste Bengali zenana women, or Steel's representations of the Jat peasantry or impoverished school girls from small-town Punjab, served to underline these cultural complexities among 'native' women who were linguistically, regionally and geographically distinct from each other. The image of the 'native woman' thus proved to be complicated by variations of class, caste, religion and region.

Moreover, by the turn of the century, inter-racial gendered relationships were further complicated by the emergence of the educated 'New Indian Woman', a new generation of western-educated women who served to present a sharply critical perspective on the 'civilising mission'. Indeed, when these educated women also happened to be upper-caste Christian converts their experiences served to highlight the contradictions within colonial modernities, including 'colonial Christianity', conversion, evangelical racism as well as the inferior status of 'native' Christians within missionary hierarchies.

Besides regional variations, caste hierarchies too played a profound role in inter-racial gendered colonial transactions. Numerous instances gestured at Indian women's disdain for colonisers on the basis of the latter's outcaste status. Moreover, the white community's perspective on caste also appeared to have been riddled with ambivalences – sometimes even gesturing at an *internalisation* of caste hierarchies (suggested by the memsahibs' reluctance to employ low-caste ayahs, or in missionaries valorising and treasuring their Brahmin converts). Further indicating the internalisation of the caste system were certain self-appellations adopted by British colonials such as 'ruling caste' or 'white Brahmins' – suggesting their attempt to re-inscribe themselves into a caste hierarchy which had rejected them as 'untouchable'.

In addition, one of the objectives of this book was to probe class contradictions *within* white colonial society and its hierarchies – a subject not adequately addressed in most studies. The idea was to uncover and disentangle the various strands that constituted the heterogeneous gendered category of the 'white woman' in Anglo-Indian society. In this highly hierarchical society class contradictions separated memsahibs (wives of civil administrators or military officers) from missionaries, and even more so from lower-class soldiers' wives, with whom virtually no contact existed. Besides, female evangelicals too were looked down upon by memsahibs.

Apart from class contradictions, gender relations between memsahibs and sahibs were also undergirded by ambivalences, underlining the gender disadvantage inherent in the middle-class woman's position. In other words, the power relations *within* the colonising community were revealed to be complicated by gender contradictions discernible in diverse ways. Memsahibs were subjected to hostility by male compatriots in colonial discourse, further reinforcing negative constructions about them as flighty and irresponsible. For instance, medical manuals and handbooks authored mostly by male colonial physicians highlighted the misogyny which underpinned colonial medical discourse – evident in its advice on white woman's physical as well as mental health.

The trope of the colonial female gaze as well as the 'return of the gaze' by 'native' women were key features in this entire monograph. While most existing studies on the female colonial gaze, notably Indira Ghose's study, have focused on white women's imperial gaze, this book laid stress upon the dialectical nature of the gaze involving both white as well 'native' spectatorship.[1] While the white woman's gendered imperial gaze across race and class was primarily a patronising, maternalist one (namely, the missionary gaze directed at upper-caste Bengali zenana women, Steel's imperialist spectatorship of Punjabi rural women's sufferings, or the average memsahibs' disparaging and uneasy gaze directed at lower-class 'native' ayahs and wet-nurses), the race and class disdain in memsahibs' diaries, letters and memoirs often betrayed deep insecurities, anxieties and feelings of powerlessness inside the colonial home. In their turn, missionaries were subjected to the memsahib's gaze of class superiority for their perceived servility towards 'natives'. In other words, the 'colonial gaze' was complex, multi-layered, diverse, consisting of gaps, tensions and even self-contradictions between the missionaries' and memsahibs' perceptions. Moreover, gendered transactions, as we have noted, were complicated by the *return* of the 'native' gaze. Time and again, there was an uneasy awareness among the white female spectator of the *return* of the gaze by 'native' females of various classes – be it the purdah women's denigration of white women's 'immorality' or 'shameless' memsahibs dancing in low-cut ball gowns, or the ayahs' penetrative 'native' gaze within the private spaces of the colonial home – a danger against which memsahibs were constantly cautioned. Most importantly, educated Indian women turned a critical gaze upon western patriarchies and prejudices prevalent in contemporary western society, especially in regard to university education for women.

One of this book's most significant features was the richly diverse sources that it drew upon, ranging from colonial memoirs, fiction and housekeeping manuals, to lesser known texts from the colonial and missionary archives, including the category of the missionary novel and the medical manual.[2] Moreover, it revisited certain well-known colonial figures such as Flora Annie Steel and brought a fresh perspective on her by exploring her largely forgotten short stories which addressed issues pertaining to patriarchal practices affecting women in Punjabi society – thereby uncovering important, yet neglected dimensions about colonial discursive narratives.

Most importantly perhaps, this monograph prised open colonial medical discourse, an area that remains virtually untouched in current research. We recuperated a host of nearly forgotten medical handbooks and manuals authored predominantly by highly influential, powerful male colonial physicians, which addressed the subject of the *health* of the white woman in colonial India – an aspect of the colonial medical narrative that remains almost completely invisibilised.[3] The male 'medical gaze' which was directed at white women in this discourse served to reinforce patriarchal constructions about the memsahib as frivolous and irresponsible, while medical journals and textbooks underscored female vulnerability to chronic mental health problems among middle-class memsahibs and lower-class barrack wives – thereby helping to propagate the age-old adage of the colonies being 'no place for a woman'. By thus uncovering the gendered hostility embedded in this medical discourse, this book further demonstrated how the colonial 'medical gaze' served to reinforce colonial patriarchies.

At the same time, we need to remind ourselves that there are dimensions and complexities in the status of the white memsahib which may not have been highlighted in this book. With regard to the sahib–memsahib relationship, for instance, the misogyny of colonial discourse was essentially rooted in a fear of white female sexuality and the power it exercised in a context where, at the highest point, men outnumbered women 3:1. The 'disorderly' white woman always posed a threat to the male order of colonisers.[4]

In conclusion, we saw in this book an exploration of the white woman's race, class and gender interactions in colonial India. The different strands constituting the chapters were woven together into an underlying pattern rooted in her complex positionality. Taking into account the tensions, contradictions as well as fluidities inherent in this situation, this book discussed a range of inter-related issues which emanate from the central locus of the European woman's contradictory position/location in the colony.

Notes

1 Indira Ghose, *Women Travellers in Colonial India: The Power of the Female Gaze* (Delhi, Oxford University Press, 1998).
2 Among missionary novels are Mrs Mullens' *Faith and Victory* (1865) and Mary Leslie's *The Dawn of Light* (1868), both of which are discussed in Chapter 1.
3 The numerous texts examined in Chapter 5 and Chapter 6 included, among many others, the anonymous *A Domestic Guide to Mothers in India* (1836), the rare Frederick Corbyn's *Management and Diseases of Infants under the Influence of the Climate of India* (1828), Sir William Moore's *A Manual of Family Medicine for India* (1874) and Edward Tilt's *Health in India for British Women* (1875).
4 The fear of adultery and divorce as well as the obsession with the 'disorderly woman' and the married flirt in colonial discourse were rooted in 'the numerical sex imbalance and the critical stress it created' in colonial society. For details see Indrani Sen, *Woman and Empire: Representations in the Writings of British India, 1858–1900* (New Delhi, Orient Longman, 2002), p. 19.

SELECT BIBLIOGRAPHY

Primary sources

Unpublished primary sources
Asia, Pacific and Africa Collections, British Library, London
  Records of Pembroke House and Ealing Lunatic Asylum, 1818–92
  (PELA)
  Medical Certificates
  Certificates of Admission

Newspapers and journals
The Calcutta Review
The Englishman's Saturday Evening Journal
The Friend of India (1870–1876)
The Friend of India and Statesman (1877–1883)
The Indian Medical Gazette
The Journal of Tropical Medicine and Hygiene
The Madras Mail
The Pioneer
Proceedings of the Royal Society of Medicine

Reports
Reports on the Asylums for European and Native Insane Patients at Bhowanipore and Dullunda, for 1856 and 1857. Calcutta, John Grey, 'Calcutta Gazette Office', 1858.
Report of the Commissioners Appointed to Inquire into the Sanitary State of the Army in India, with Abstract of Evidence and of Reports Received from Indian Military Stations. London, Printed Under the Superintendence of Her Majesty's Stationery Office, 1864.
Annual Report of the Insane Asylums in Bengal for the Year 1868. Calcutta, Office of the Superintendent of Govt. Printing, 1869.
Annual Administration and Progress Report on the Insane Asylums in the Bombay Presidency for the Year 1873–74. Bombay, Government Central Press, 1874.

Published primary sources
Acton, Hugh W. 'Neurasthenia in the Tropics', *The Indian Medical Gazette*, 62:1, January (1927).
Anon. *A Domestic Guide to Mothers in India: Containing Particular Instructions on the Management of Themselves and their Children. By a Medical Practitioner of Several Years' Experience in India.* [1836], Bombay, American Mission Press, 1848.

[208]

Anon. (ed.), *The Lady at Home and Abroad: Her Guide and Friend.* London, Abbott, Jones and Co., 1898.

Armstrong-Hopkins, Saleni. *Within the Purdah: In the Zenana and Homes of Indian Princes and Heroes and Heroines of Zion.* New York, Eaton & Mains, 1898.

Athavale, Parvatibai. *Hindu Widow: An Autobiography*, trans. Rev. Justin E. Abbott. [1930], New Delhi, Reliance Publishing House, 1986.

Baker Brown, Isaac, *On the Curability of Certain Forms of Insanity, Epilepsy, Catalepsy and Hysteria in Females.* London, Robert Hardwicke, 1866.

Balfour, Margaret and Ruth Young. *The Work of Medical Women in India.* London, Oxford University Press, 1929.

Baptist Zenana Mission. *JUBILEE, 1867–1917: Fifty Years' Work among Women in the Far East.* London, Carey Press, 1917.

Beard, George M. *A Practical Treatise on Nervous Exhaustion (Neurasthenia).* New York, William Wood & Co, 1880.

— 'Neurasthenia or Nervous Exhaustion'. *Boston Medical and Surgical Journal*, 3 (1869), pp. 217–221.

Billington, Mary Frances. *Woman in India.* London, Chapman & Hall, 1895.

Campbell, Hugh. *The Anatomy of Nervousness and Nervous Exhaustion (Neurasthenia).* London, Henry Renshaw, n.d.

Case, Adelaide. *Day by Day at Lucknow: A Journal of the Siege of Lucknow.* London, Richard Bentley, 1858.

Castellani, Sir Aldo. *Climate and Acclimatization.* [1930], London, John Bale and Sons, 1938.

Castellani, Sir Aldo in A. R. Neligan, Sir Aldo Castellani, Dr H. S. Stannus, Dr G. W. Bray, Mr A. F. MacCallan, Dr J. B. Christopherson, Dr K. Edmundson and Dr G. W. Theobald 'Discussion on the Adaptation of European Women and Children to Tropical Climates', *Proceedings of the Royal Society of Medicine*, 24:6 (1931), pp. 1315–1333.

Castellani, Sir Aldo and Albert J. Chambers. *Manual of Tropical Medicine.* London, Balliere, Tindall, and Cox, 1919.

Chapman, Mrs E. F. (Georgina). *Sketches of Some Distinguished Indian Women.* London and Calcutta, W. H. Allen & Co. Ltd, 1891.

Chapman, Priscilla. *Hindoo Female Education.* London, R. B. Seeley and G. Seely, 1839.

Chota Mem (C. Lang). *The English Bride in India: Being Hints on Indian Housekeeping.* Second edition. Madras, Higginbotham and Co., 1909.

Christopherson, J. B. 'The Motive in Women's Dress in the Tropics', *The Journal of Tropical Medicine and Hygiene*, 33:14 (1930), pp. 201–207.

Coopland, Ruth. *A Lady's Escape from Gwalior, and Life in the Fort of Agra during the Mutinies of 1857.* London, Smith, Elder, & Co., 1859.

Corbyn, Frederick. *Management and Diseases of Infants under the Influence of the Climate of India Being Instructions to Mothers and Parents in Situations where Medical Aid is not to be Obtained, and a Guide to Medical Men, Inexperienced in the Nursery and the Treatment of Tropical Infantile Diseases, Illustrated by Colour Plates.* Calcutta, Thacker, 1828.

Culpin, Millais. 'An Examination of Tropical Neurasthenia', *Proceedings of the Royal Society of Medicine*, 26: 7 (May, 1933), pp. 919–920.

Darling, Malcolm Lyall. *The Punjab Peasant in Prosperity and Debt*. [1925], New Delhi, Manohar Book Service, 1978.

Dawson, J. E. 'Woman in India: Her Influence and Position' (Part I), *The Calcutta Review*, 83:165 (1886), pp. 347–357.

— 'The Englishwoman in India: Her Influence and Responsibilities' (Part II). *The Calcutta Review*, 83:165 (1886), pp. 358–370.

Diver, Maud. *The Englishwoman in India*. Edinburgh and London, William Blackwood & Sons, 1909.

Duncan, Sara Jeannette. *The Pool in the Desert*. New York, D. Appleton and Company, 1903.

Englishwoman in India, An. 'Englishwomen in India'. *The Calcutta Review*, 8:159 (1885), pp. 137–152.

'English Women in Hindustan'. *The Calcutta Review*, 4:7 (1845), pp. 96–127.

Ewart, Joseph. *Goodeve's Hints For the General Management of Children in India, in the Absence of Professional Advice*. Sixth edition. Calcutta, Thacker, Spink & Co. 1872.

Fayrer, Joseph Sir. *European Child-Life in Bengal*. London, J. & A. Churchill, 1873.

— *On the Climate and Fevers of India: Being the Croonian Lectures Delivered at the Royal College of Physicians*. London, J. & A. Churchill, 1882.

— *On Preservation of Health in India*. London, Macmillan, 1894.

Fuller, Jenny (Mrs Marcus). *The Wrongs of Indian Womanhood*. Edinburgh and London, Oliphant Anderson and Ferrier, 1900.

Garrett, E. *Morning Hours in India: Practical Hints on Household Management, the Care and Training of Children Etc.* London, Trubner and Co., 1887.

Goodeve, Henry Hurry. *Hints for the General Management of Children in India in the Absence of Professional Advice*. Fourth edition. [1844], London and Calcutta, Thacker and Thacker, Spink & Co. 1856.

Green-Armytage, V.B. 'Neurasthenia in the Tropics'. *The Indian Medical Gazette*, 62:1, January (1927).

Harris, Katherine. *A Lady's Diary of the Siege of Lucknow, Written for the Perusal of Friends at Home*. [1858], New Delhi, Asian Educational Services, 2006.

Hull, Edmund C. P. *The European in India or Anglo-India's Vade-Mecum: A Handbook of Useful and Practical Information for those Proceeding to or Residing in the East Indies Relating to Outfits, Routes, Time for Departure, Indian Climate and Seasons, Housekeeping, Servants, etc. etc.* [1871], New Delhi, Asian Educational Services, 2004.

Hunt, Leigh S. and Alexander A. Kenny. *Tropical Trials: A Handbook for Women in the Tropics*. W. H. Allen & Co., 1883.

Johnson, James *The Influence of Tropical Climates More Especially the Climate of India, on European Constitutions: The Principal Effects and Diseases Thereby Induced, their Prevention or Removal, and the Means of Preserving Health in Hot Climates, Rendered Obvious to Europeans of Every Capacity.* [1813], London, J. Callow, 1815.

King, Mrs E. Augusta. *The Diary of a Civilian's Wife in India, 1877–1882.* Vol. 1. London, Richard Bentley, 1884.

King, W. W. 'Tropical Neurasthenia'. *Journal of the American Medical Association*, 46:20 (May 1906), pp. 518–519.

Kipling, Rudyard. 'Nursery Rhymes for little Anglo-Indians' in *Echoes*. Lahore, Civil and Military Gazette Press, 1884.

— *Plain Tales from the Hills.* [1888], London, Macmillan, 1960.

— *Life's Handicap: Being Stories of My Own people.* [1891], Oxford, Oxford University Press, 1987.

— 'On the City Wall', in *Soldiers Three and Other Stories.* [1892], London, Macmillan, 1960.

— *Something of Myself: For My Friends, Known and Unknown.* London, Macmillan & Co. Ltd, 1937.

Lady Resident, A. *The Englishwoman in India: Containing Information for the Use of ladies Proceeding to, or Residing in, the East Indies, on the Subjects of their Outfit. Furniture, Housekeeping, the Rearing of Children, Duties and Wages of Servants, Management of the Stables, and Arrangements for Travelling to which Are Added Receipts for Indian Cookery.* London, Smith, Elder and Co., 1864.

Leslie, Mary. *The Dawn of Light: A Story of the Zenana Mission.* London, John Snow, 1868.

Lukis, C. P and R. J. Blackham. *Tropical Hygiene for Anglo-Indians and Indians.* Calcutta, Thacker, Spink, 1911.

Macpherson, John, MD. *Report on Insanity Among Europeans in Bengal, Founded on the Experience of the Calcutta Lunatic Asylum. The Calcutta Review*, 26:52 (1856), pp. 592–602.

Mair, R. S. 'Supplement on the Management of Children in India', in his *Medical Guide for Anglo-Indians.* [1871], New Delhi, Asian Educational Services, 2004.

Maitland, Julia. *Letters from Madras, During the Years 1836–39, by a Lady.* [1843], London, John Murray, 1846.

Maudsley, Henry, MD. *Body and Mind: An Inquiry into their Connection and Mutual Influence, Specially in Reference to Mental Disorders.* [1870], London, Macmillan & Co., 1873.

McCosh. John. *Medical Advice to the Indian Stranger.* London, William H. Allen & Co., 1841.

Michell Clarke, J. *Hysteria and Neurasthenia.* London, John Lane, the Bodley Head, 1905.

Moore, Sir William James. *A Manual of Family Medicine for India.* London, Churchill, 1874.

Mullens, Hannah Catherine. *Faith and Victory: A Story of the Progress of Christianity in Bengal.* London, James Nisbet & Co., 1865.

— *Prasanna and Kamini: The History of a Young Hindu.* London, Religious Tract Society, c. 1885.

Neligan, A. R., Sir Aldo Castellani, Dr H. S. Stannus, Dr G. W. Bray, Mr A. F. MacCallan, Dr J. B. Christopherson, Dr K. Edmundson and Dr G. W. Theobald, 'Discussion on the Adaptation of European Women and Children to Tropical Climates'. *Proceedings of the Royal Society of Medicine*, 24:6 (1931), pp. 1315–1333.

Nikambe, Shevantibai. *Ratanbai: A Sketch of a Bombay High Caste Hindu Young Wife*. London, Marshall Brothers, 1895.

— *Ratanbai: A High-caste Child-wife*, ed. Chandani Lokuge ([1895], New Delhi, Oxford University Press, 2004).

Oesterlen, Friedrich. *Manual of Hygiene* (original German title: *Handbuch der Hygieine für den Einzelnen wie für eine Bevölkeru*ng), Tubingen, H. Laupp, 1851.

Pitman, Emma Raymond. *Indian Zenana Missions: Their Needs, Origin, Objects, Agents, Modes of Working and Results*. London, John Snow and Co., 1903.

Platt, Kate. *The Home and Health in India and the Tropical Colonies*. Bailliere, Tindall & Cox, 1923.

Postans, Marianne. *Western India in 1838*. 2 vols. London, Saunders and Otley, 1839.

Ramabai, Pandita. *The High-Caste Hindu Woman*. Philadelphia, n.p. 1888.

Ranade, Ramabai. *Ranade: His Wife's Reminiscences*, trans. Kusumavati Deshpande. [1910], New Delhi, Publications Division, Ministry of Information and Broadcasting, Government of India, 1963.

Ranald Martin, James and James Johnson. *Influence of Tropical Climates on European Constitutions, Including Practical Observations on the Nature and Treatment of the Diseases of Europeans on their Return from Tropical Climates*. London, S. Highley, 1841.

'Review of the Progress of Sanitation in India'. *The Calcutta Review*, 50:99 (1870), pp. 94–158.

Roberts, Emma. *Scenes and Characteristics of Hindostan, with Sketches of Anglo-Indian Society*, vols 1 and 2. London, W. H. Allen, 1835.

Satthianadhan, Krupabai. *Saguna: A Story of Native Christian Life* (with a Preface by Mrs R. S. Benson). Madras, Srinivasa Varadachari & Co. 1895.

— *Saguna: A Story of Native Christian Life*, in Chandani Lokuge (ed.) *Krupabai Satthianadhan, Saguna: The First Autobiographical Novel in English*. [1895], Oxford Classic Reissue; Delhi, Oxford University Press, 1998.

— *Miscellaneous Writings of Krupabai Satthianadhan*. Madras, Srinivasa Varadachari & Co., 1896.

Sattin, Anthony (ed.). *An Englishwoman in India: The Memoirs of Harriet Tytler, 1828–1858*. Oxford, Oxford University Press, 1988.

Savill, T. D. *Clinical Lectures on Neurasthenia*. [1899], London, Glaisher, 1906.

Sherwood, Mary Martha. *The Life of Mrs. Sherwood (chiefly autobiographical) with Extracts from Mr. Sherwood's Journal During His Imprisonment in*

France and Residence in India, ed. by her Daughter, *Sophia Kelly*. London, Darton & Co., 1854.

— *The Life and Times of Mrs. Sherwood (1775–1851) from the Diaries of Captain and Mrs. Sherwood*, ed. F. J. Harvey Darton. London, Wells Gardner, Darton & Co. Ltd, 1910.

Simpson, W. J. *The Maintenance of Health in the Tropics*. London, John Bale, Sons and Danielsson Ltd, 1905.

Sprawson, Cuthbert Allan. *Moore's Manual of Family Medicine and Hygiene for India*. Eighth edition, re-written by the editor. London, J. & A. Churchill, 1916.

Steel, Flora Annie. 'At a Girls' School'. *From the Five Rivers*. [1893], London, William Heinemann, 1897.

— 'Gunesh Chand'. *From the Five Rivers*. [1893], London, William Heinemann, 1897.

— 'Feroza'. *The Flower of Forgiveness and Other Stories*. [1894], London, William Heinemann, 1900.

— 'In the House of a Coppersmith'. *The Flower of Forgiveness and Other Stories*. London, Macmillan & Co., [1894], London, William Heinemann, 1900.

— 'Mussumat Kirpo's Doll'. *The Flower of Forgiveness and Other Stories*. [1894], London, William Heinemann, 1900.

— 'Amor Vincit Omnia'. *In The Permanent Way and Other Stories*. [1897], London, William Heinemann, 1898.

— 'On the Second Storey'. *In The Permanent Way and Other Stories* ([1897], London, William Heinemann, 1898.

— 'The Sorrowful Hour'. *In the Permanent Way and Other Stories*. [1897], London, William Heinemann, 1898.

— 'Uma Himavutee'. *In the Permanent Way and Other Stories*. [1897], London, William Heinemann, 1898.

— *The Garden of Fidelity: Being the Autobiography of Flora Annie Steel, 1847–1929*. London, Macmillan & Co. Ltd., 1929.

Steel, Flora Annie and Grace Gardiner, *The Complete Indian Housekeeper and Cook: Giving the Duties of Mistress and Servants, the General Management of the House and Practical Recipes for Cooking in all its branches*. [1888] London, William Heinemann, 1909.

Tilt, Edward John. *Health in India for British Women and on the Prevention of Disease in Tropical Climates*. London, J. & A. Churchill, 1875.

Trevelyan, G. O. *The Competitionwallah*. London and Cambridge, Macmillan & Co., 1864.

Urquhart, Mrs Margaret. *Women of Bengal: A Study of the Hindu Purdahnashins of Calcutta*. [1925], Calcutta: Association Press, YMCA, 1927.

Ward, William. *A View of the History, Literature, and Mythology of the Hindoos*. Serampore, 1822.

Weitbrecht, Mary. *Women of India and Christian Work in the Zenana*. London, James Nisbet & Co., 1875.

Wilson, Anne Campbell. *Letters from India*. [1911], London, Century, 1984.

Woodruff, Charles E, Major. *The Effects of Tropical Light on White Men*. New York, Rebman, 1905.
— 'The Neurasthenic State Caused by Excessive Light'. *Medical Record*, 23 December, 1905.

Secondary sources

Allender, Tim. 'Anglican Evangelism in North India and the Punjabi Missionary Classroom: The Failure to Educate "the Masses," 1860–77'. *History of Education: Journal of the History of Education Society*, 32:3 (2003), pp. 273–288.
— *Ruling through Education: The Politics of Schooling in the Colonial Punjab*. New Delhi, New Dawn Press, 2006.
— 'Surrendering a Colonial Domain: Educating North India, 1854–1890'. *History of Education: Journal of the History of Education Society*, 36:1 (2007), pp. 45–63.
— *Learning Femininity in Colonial India, 1820–1932*. Manchester, Manchester University Press, 2016.
Anagol, Padma. 'Indian Christian Women and Indigenous Feminism, c.1850–c.1920', in Clare Midgley (ed.), *Gender and Imperialism*. Manchester, Manchester University Press, 1998, pp. 79–103.
— *The Emergence of Feminism in India, 1850–1920*. Hampshire and Burlington, Ashgate, 2005.
Anderson, Warwick. 'The Trespass Speaks: White Masculinity and Colonial Breakdown'. *The American Historical Review*, 102:5 (December 1997), pp. 1343–1370.
Arnold, David. *The Problem of Nature: Environment, Culture and European Expansion*. Oxford, Blackwell, 1996.
— (ed.). *Warm Climates and Western Medicine: The Emergence of Tropical Medicine, 1500–1900*. Amsterdam, Rodopi, 1996.
Ballhatchet, Kenneth. *Race, Sex and Class Under the Raj: Imperial Attitudes and Policies and their Critics, 1793–1905*. New York, St. Martin's Press, 1980.
Banerjee, Swapna M. *Men, Women, and Domestics: Articulating Middle-class Identity in Colonial Bengal*. New Delhi, Oxford University Press, 2004.
— 'Down Memory Lane: Representations of Domestic Workers in Middle Class Personal Narratives of Colonial Bengal'. *Journal of Social History*, 37:3 (Spring 2004), pp. 681–708.
Barr, Pat. *The Memsahibs: The Women of Victorian India*. London, Secker and Warburg, 1976.
Bashford, Alison. *Purity and Pollution: Gender, Embodiment and Victorian Medicine*. London, MacMillan, 1998.
Bellenoit, Hayden J. A. *Missionary Education and Empire in Late Colonial India, 1860–1920*. London, Pickering & Chatto, 2007.
Berrios, German E. *The History of Mental Symptoms: Descriptive*

Psychopathology since the Nineteenth Century. Cambridge, Cambridge University Press, 1996.

Blunt, Alison. 'Imperial Geographies of Home: British Domesticity in India, 1886–1925'. *Transactions of the Institute of British Geographers*, New Series, 24:4 (1999), pp. 421–440.

Borthwick, Meredith. *The Changing Role of Women in Bengal, 1849–1905*. Princeton, Princeton University Press, 1984.

Buettner, Elizabeth. *Empire Families: Britons and Late Imperial India*. Oxford and New York, Oxford University Press, 2004.

— 'Three Weeks' Post Apart: British Children Travel the Empire', in Miles Taylor (ed.), *The Victorian Empire and Britain's Maritime World, 1837–1901*. London and New York, Palgrave Macmillan, 2013, pp. 129–148.

Burton, Antoinette. *Burdens of History: British Feminists, Indian Women and Imperial Culture, 1865–1915*. Chapel Hill, University of North Carolina Press, 1994.

— *At the Heart of the Empire: Indians and the Colonial Encounter in Late Victorian Britain*. Berkeley, University of California Press, 1998.

— *Dwelling in the Archive: Women Writing House, Home and History in late Colonial India.* New Delhi, Oxford University Press, 2003.

Busfield, Joan. *Men, Women and Madness: Understanding Gender and Mental Disorder.* Hampshire, Macmillan, 1996.

Carmen, Elaine, Nancy Felipe Russo and Jean Baker Miller, 'Inequality and Women's Mental Health: An Overview', in Patricia Perri Reiker and Elaine (Hilberman) Carmen (eds), *The Gender Gap in Psychotherapy: Social Realities and Psychological Processes*. New York, Plenum Press, 1984, pp. 17–39.

Chakravarti, Uma. *Rewriting History: The Life and Times of Pandita Ramabai*. Delhi, Kali for Women, 1998.

Chatterjee, Partha. 'The Nationalist Resolution of the Women's Question', in Kumkum Sangari and Sudesh Vaid (eds), *Recasting Women: Essays in Colonial History*. New Delhi, Kali for Women, 1989, pp. 233–253.

Chattopadhyay, Swati. 'Goods, Chattels and Sundry Items: Constructing 19th-Century Anglo-Indian Domestic Life', *Journal of Material Culture*, 7:3 (November 2002), pp. 243–271.

Chaudhuri, Nupur. 'Memsahibs and Motherhood in Nineteenth-Century Colonial India'. *Victorian Studies*. 31:4 (1988), pp. 517–535.

— 'Memsahibs and their Servants in Nineteenth-century India', *Women's History Review*, 3:4 (1994), pp. 549–562.

Chaudhuri, Nupur and Margaret Strobel (eds). *Western Women and Imperialism: Complicity and Resistance*. bloomington and Indianapolis, Indiana University Press, 1992.

Chesler, Phyllis. *Women and Madness*. Harmondsworth, Penguin Books, 1979.

Chowdhry, Prem. 'Customs in a Peasant Economy: Women in Colonial Haryana', in Kumkum Sangari and Sudesh Vaid (eds), *Recasting Women:*

Essays in Colonial History. New Delhi, Kali for Women, 1989, pp. 302–336.
— *The Veiled Women: Shifting Gender Equations in Rural Haryana, 1880–1990*. New Delhi, Oxford University Press, 1994.
Cleall, Esme. *Missionary Discourses of Difference: Negotiating Otherness in the British Empire, 1840–1900*. Cambridge Imperial and Postcolonial Studies, Basingstoke, Palgrave Macmillan, 2012.
Cohn, Bernard S. *Colonialism and Its Forms of Knowledge: The British in India*. Princeton, Princeton University Press, 1996.
Cox, Jeffrey. *Imperial Fault Lines: Christianity and Colonial Power in India, 1818–1940*. Stanford, Stanford University Press, 2002.
— *The British Missionary Enterprise since 1700*. London and New York, Routledge, 2008.
Curtin, Philip. *Death by Migration: Europe's Encounter with the Tropical World in the Nineteenth Century*. Cambridge, Cambridge University Press, 1988.
Davies, Philip. *Splendours of the Raj: British Architecture in India, 1660–1947*. London, J. Murray, 1985.
Davin, Anna. 'Imperialism and Motherhood'. *History Workshop Journal*, 5:1 (1978), pp. 9–66.
De Souza, Eunice. 'Recovering a Tradition: Forgotten Women's Voices'. *Economic and Political Weekly*, April 29 (2006), pp. 1642–1645.
Dyson, K. K. *A Various Universe: A Study of the Journals and Memoirs of British Men and Women in the Indian Sub-Continent, 1765–1856*. [1978], New Delhi, Oxford University Press, 2002.
Ernst, Waltraud. *Mad Tales from the Raj: The European Insane in British India, 1800–1858*. London and New York, Routledge, 1991.
— 'European Madness and Gender in Nineteenth-century British India'. *The Social History of Medicine*, 9:3 (1996), pp. 357–382.
Fhlathuin, Maire ni (ed.). *The Poetry of British India, 1780–1905*, vol 2. London, Pickering and Chatto, 2011.
Fischer-Tine, Harald. *Low and Licentious Europeans: Race, Class and 'White Subalternity' in Colonial India*. New Delhi, Orient BlackSwan, 2009.
— '"The Drinking Habits of Our Countrymen": European Alcohol Consumption and Colonial Power in British India'. *The Journal of Imperial and Commonwealth History*, 40:3 (September 2012), pp. 383–408.
Fitzgerald, Rosemary. '"Clinical Christianity": The Emergence of Medical Work as a Missionary Strategy in Colonial India, 1800–1914', in Biswamoy Pati and Mark Harrison (eds), *Health, Medicine and Empire: Perspectives on Colonial India*. New Delhi, Orient Longman, 2001, pp. 88–136
Forbes, Geraldine H. 'In Search of the "Pure Heathen": Missionary Women in Nineteenth Century India'. *Economic and Political Weekly*, 21:17, Review of Women's Studies, April 26 (1986), pp. WS2–WS8.
— *Women in Modern India*, The New Cambridge History of India, Vol. IV.2. Cambridge, Cambridge University Press, 2000.
George, Rosemary Marangoly. 'Homes in the Empire, Empires in the Home', *Cultural Critique*, 26 (Winter 1993–94), pp. 95–127.

Ghose, Indira. *Women Travellers in Colonial India: The Power of the Female Gaze*. Delhi, Oxford University Press, 1998.

Ghosh, Durba. 'Household Crimes and Domestic Order: Keeping the Peace in Colonial Calcutta, c.1770–c.1840', *Modern Asian Studies*, 38:2 (2004), pp. 599–623.

Gilbert, Sandra and Susan Gubar. *The Mad Woman in the Attic: The Woman Writer and the Nineteenth Century Literary Imagination*. New Haven, Yale University Press, 1978.

Glover, William J. '"A Feeling of Absence from Old England": The Colonial Bungalow', *Home Cultures*, 1:1 (2004), pp. 61–82.

Goldberg D. and P. Huxley, *Common Mental Disorders*. London, Routledge & Kegan Paul, 1992.

Goswami, Supriya. *Colonial India in Children's Literature*. London and New York, Routledge, 2012.

Gowans, Georgina. 'Imperial Geographies of Home: Memsahibs and Miss-Sahibs in India and Britain, 1915–1947', *Cultural Geographies*, 10 (2003), pp. 424–441.

Greenwood, Anna. 'Looking Back: The Strange History of Tropical Neurasthenia', *The Psychologist*, 24:3 (March 2011), pp. 226–227.

Grossman, Joyce. 'Ayahs, Dhayes, and Bearers: Mary Sherwood's Indian Experience and "Constructions of Subordinated Others"'. *South Atlantic Review*, 66:2 (Spring 2001), pp. 14–44.

Guha, Sumit. 'Nutrition, Sanitation, Hygiene, and the Likelihood of Death: The British Army in India *c.* 1870–1920'. *Population Studies: A Journal of Demography*, 47:3 (1993), pp. 385–401.

Guha, Supriya. 'The Unwanted Pregnancy in Colonial Bengal'. *Indian Economic and Social History Review*, 3:4 (1996), pp. 403–435.

Haggis, Jane. 'White Women and Colonialism: Towards a Non-recuperative History', in Clare Midgley (ed.), *Gender and Imperialism*. Manchester, Manchester University Press, 1998, pp. 45–75.

— 'A Heart that Has Felt the Love of God and Longs for Others to Know It': Conventions of Gender, Tensions of Self and Constructions of Difference in Offering to Be a Lady Missionary'. *Women's History Review*, 7:2 (1998), pp. 171–193.

— 'Ironies of Emancipation: Changing Configurations of "Women's Work" in the "Mission of Sisterhood" to Indian Women'. *Feminist Review*, 65 (2000), pp. 108–126.

Harrison, Mark. *Public Health in British India: Anglo-Indian Preventive Medicine, 1859–1914*. Cambridge, Cambridge University Press, 1994.

— *Climates and Constitutions: Health, Race, Environment and British Imperialism in India, 1600–1850*. New Delhi, Oxford University Press, 1999.

Haskins, Victoria K. and Claire Lowrie (eds). *Colonisation and Domestic Service: Colonial and Contemporary Perspectives*. London and New York, Routledge, 2014.

Hassan, Narin. *Diagnosing Empire: Women, Medical Knowledge, and Colonial Mobility*. London, Ashgate, 2011.

Headrick, Daniel R. *Tools of Empire: Technology and European Imperialism in the Nineteenth Century*. Oxford, Oxford University Press, 1981.

Hennessy Rosemary and Rajeswari Mohan, 'The Construction of Woman in Three Popular Texts of Empire: Towards a Critique of Materialist Feminism', *Textual Practice*, 3:3 (1989), pp. 323–359.

Hodges, Sarah (ed.). *Reproductive Health in India: History, Politics, Controversies*. New Delhi, Orient Longman, 2006.

Jackson, E. M. 'Glimpses of a Prominent Indian Christian family of Tirunelveli and Madras, 1863–1906: Perspectives on Caste, Culture and Conversion', in Robert E. Frykenberg and Alaine Low (eds), *Christians and Missionaries in India: Cross-cultural Communication since 1500*. London, Routledge Curzon, 2003, pp. 315–335.

Jayawardena, Kumari. *White Women's Other Burden: Western Women and South Asia during British Colonial Rule*. New York, Routledge, 1995.

Johnston, Anna. *Missionary Writing and Empire 1800–1860*. Cambridge, Cambridge University Press, 2003.

Kennedy, Dane. 'The Perils of the Mid-day Sun: Climatic Anxieties in the Colonial Tropics', in John M. Mackenzie (ed.), *Imperialism and the Natural World*. Manchester, Manchester University Press, 1990, pp. 118–140.

— 'Diagnosing the Colonial Dilemma: Tropical Neurasthenia and the Alienated Briton', in Durba Ghosh and Dane Kennedy (eds), *Decentring Empire: Britain, India and the Transcolonial World*. New Delhi, Orient Longman, 2006, pp. 157–181.

Kent, Eliza F. *Converting Women: Gender and Protestant Christianity in Colonial South India*. New York, Oxford University Press, 2004.

Kincaid, Dennis. *British Social Life in India: 1608–1937*. [1938], London, Routledge & Kegan Paul, 1973.

Kishwar, Madhu. 'The Daughters of Aryavarta', in Sumit Sarkar and Tanika Sarkar (eds), *Women and Social Reform in Modern India: A Reader*, Vol. I. New Delhi, Permanent Black, 2007.

Kosambi, Meera. 'Indian Response to Christianity, Church and Colonialism: The Case of Pandita Ramabai'. *Economic and Political Weekly*, 27: 43–44, 24–31 October (1992), pp. WS61–WS63.

— 'Life after Widowhood: Two Radical Reformist Options in Maharashtra', in Meera Kosambi (ed.), *Intersections: Socio-Cultural Trends in Maharashtra*. New Delhi, Orient Longman, 2000, pp. 92–119.

Lawrence, Dianne. *Genteel Women: Empire and Domestic Material Culture, 1840–1910*. Manchester, Manchester University Press, 2012.

Macmillan, Margaret. *Women of the Raj*. London, Thames and Hudson, 1988.

Malhotra, Anshu. *Gender, Caste and Religious Identities: Restructuring Class in Colonial Punjab*. New Delhi, Oxford University Press, 2002.

Manktelow, Emily J. *Missionary Families: Race, Gender and Generation on the Spiritual Frontier*. Manchester, Manchester University Press, 2013.

McClintock, Anne. *Imperial Leather: Race, Gender and Sexuality in the Colonial Contest*. London and New York, Routledge, 1995.

Mickelson Gaughan, Joan. *The 'Incumberances': British Women in India, 1615–1856*. New Delhi, Oxford University Press, 2013.

Midgley, Clare (ed.). *Gender and Imperialism*. Manchester, Manchester University Press, 1998.

— 'Can Women be Missionaries? Envisioning Female Agency in the Early Nineteenth-century British Empire'. *Journal of British Studies*, 45 (2006), pp. 335–358.

Mukherjee, Meenakshi. 'Mrs Mullens and Mrs Collins: Christianity's Gift to Indian Fiction'. *The Journal of Commonwealth Literature*, 16:65 (1981), pp. 65–75.

— *Realism and Reality: The Novel and Society in India.* New Delhi, Oxford University Press, 2010.

Oddie, Geoffrey A. *Imagined Hinduism: British Protestant Missionary Constructions of Hinduism, 1793–1900*. New Delhi, Sage, 2006.

O'Hanlon, Rosalind. *Caste, Conflict and Ideology: Mahatma Jotirao Phule and Low-caste Protest in Nineteenth Century Western India*. [1985], Cambridge, Cambridge University Press, 2002.

— 'Issues of Widowhood: Gender and Resistance in Colonial Western India', in Douglas Haynes and Gyan Prakash (eds), *Contesting Power: Resistance and Everyday Social Relations in South Asia*. Delhi, Oxford University Press, 1991, pp. 62–108.

— (ed.) *A Comparison Between Women and Men: Tarabai Shinde and the Critique of Gender Relations in Colonial India*. Delhi, Oxford University Press, 1994.

O'Malley, L. S. S. (ed.). *Modern India and the West: A Study of the Interactions of Civilisations*. [1941], London, Oxford University Press, 1968.

Pal-Lapinski, Piya. 'Infection as Resistance: Medical Discourse, Indian Courtesans and Flawed Memsahibs in Flora Annie Steel's Colonial Fiction'. *ARIEL: A Review of International English Literature*, 30:3 (July 1999), pp. 141–161.

— *The Exotic Woman in Nineteenth-century British Fiction and Culture: A Reconsideration.* New Hampshire, University of New Hampshire Press, 2004.

Pati, Biswamoy and Mark Harrison (eds). *The Social History of Health and Medicine in Colonial India*. London and New York, Routledge, 2009.

Pati, Biswamoy and Mark Harrison (eds). *Health, Medicine and Empire: Perspectives on Colonial India*. New Delhi, Orient Longman, 2001.

Patwardhan, Daya. *A Star of India: Flora Annie Steel, Her Works and Time*. Pune, Griha Prakashan, 1963.

Paxton, Nancy. *Writing under the Raj: Gender, Race and Rape in the British Colonial Imagination, 1830–1947*. New Brunswick, NJ, Rutgers University Press, 1999.

Peers, Douglas M. *Between Mars and Mammon: Colonial Armies and the Garrison State in Nineteenth Century India*. London, I. B. Tauris, 1995.

— 'Privates Off Parade: Regimenting Sexuality in the Nineteenth-century Indian Empire'. *The International History Review*, 20:4 (December 1998), pp. 823–854.

— 'Imperial Vice: Sex, Drink, and the Health of the British Troops in North Indian Cantonments, 1800–1858', in David Killingray and David Omissi (eds), *Guardians of Empire: The Armed Forces of the Colonial Powers, 1700–1964*. Manchester, Manchester University Press, 1999, pp. 25–52.

Powell, Violet. *Flora Annie Steel: Novelist of India*. London, Heinemann, 1981.

Pratt, Mary Louise. *Imperial Eyes: Travel Writing and Transculturation*. London and New York, Routledge, 1992.

Procida, Mary A. *Married to the Empire: Gender, Politics and Imperialism in India, 1883–1947*. Manchester, Manchester University Press, 2002.

— 'Feeding the Imperial Appetite: Imperial Knowledge and Anglo-Indian Discourse'. *Journal of Women's History*, 15:2 (Summer 2003), pp. 123–149.

Ramusack, Barbara N. 'Cultural Missionaries, Maternal Imperialists, Feminist Allies: British Women Activists in India, 1865–1945', in Nupur Chaudhuri and Margaret Strobel (eds), *Western Women and Imperialism: Complicity and Resistance*. Bloomington and Indianapolis, Indiana University Press, 1992, pp. 119–136.

Rao, Parimala. *Foundations of Tilak's Nationalism: Discrimination, Education and Hindutva*. New Delhi, Orient Blackswan, 2010.

Raza, Rosemary. *In their Own Words: British Women Writers and India, 1740–1857*. New Delhi, Oxford University Press, 2006.

Rowbotham, Judith. '"Hear an Indian Sister's Plea": Reporting the Work of 19th-century British Female Missionaries'. *Women's Studies International Forum*, 21:3 (1998), pp. 247–261.

— '"Only When Drunk": The Stereotyping of Violence in England, c. 1850–1900', in Shani D'Cruze (ed.), *Everyday Violence in Britain, 1850–1950, Class and Gender*. Harlow, Longman-Pearson Education, 2000, pp. 155–169.

Roy, Benoy Bhushan and Pranati Roy. *Zenana Mission: The Role of Christian Missionaries for the Education of Women in Nineteenth Century Bengal*. Delhi, Indian Society for Promoting Christian Knowledge, 1998.

Roye, Susmita and Rajeshwar Mittapalli (eds). *The Male Empire under the Female Gaze: The British Raj and the Memsahib*. Amherst, Cambria, 2013.

Sangari, Kumkum and Sudesh Vaid (eds). *Recasting Women: Essays in Colonial History*. New Delhi, Kali for Women, 1989.

Sarkar, Tanika (ed.). *Words to Win: The Making of 'Amar Jiban': A Modern Autobiography*. New Delhi, Kali for Women, 1999.

— *Hindu Wife, Hindu Nation: Community, Religion, and Cultural Nationalism*. New Delhi, Permanent Black, 2001.

Savage, David. 'Missionaries and the Development of a Colonial Ideology of Female Education in India'. *Gender and History*, 9:2 (1997), pp. 201–221.

Sehrawat, Samiksha. *Colonial Medical Care in North India: Gender, State and Society, c. 1840–1920*. New Delhi, Oxford University Press, 2013.

Semple, Rhonda. *Missionary Women: Gender, Professionalism and the Victorian Idea of Christian Mission.* Suffolk, Boydell Press, 2003.

— 'Christian Model, Mission Realities: The Business of Regularizing Family in Mission Communities in Late Nineteenth-century North India'. *Journal of Colonialism and Colonial History*, 14:1 (2013), DOI: 10.1353/cch.2013.0003.

Sen, Indrani. 'The White Woman's Burden: The Dilemmas of Social Reform in the Fiction of Flora Annie Steel', *Studies in Humanities and Social Sciences* (Journal of the Indian Institute of Advanced Study, Shimla), 3:1 (Summer 1996), pp. 89–100.

— 'Between Power and "Purdah"': The White Woman in British India, 1858–1900'. *The Indian Economic and Social History Review*, 34:3 (1997), pp. 355–376.

— *Woman and Empire: Representations in the Writings of British India, 1858–1900.* New Delhi, Orient Blackswan, 2002.

— 'The Memsahib's "Madness"': The European Woman's Mental Health in Late Nineteenth Century India'. *Social Scientist*, 33: 5/6 (May–June, 2005), pp. 26–48.

— (ed.) *Memsahibs' Writings: Colonial Narratives on Indian Women.* New Delhi, Orient Blackswan, 2008.

— 'Discourses of "Gendered Loyalty"': Indian Women in Nineteenth century "Mutiny" Fiction', in Biswamoy Pati (ed.), *The Great Rebellion of 1857 in India: Exploring Transgressions, Contests and Diversities.* London, Routledge, 2010, pp. 111–128.

— 'Memsahibs and Health in Colonial Medical Writings, c.1840–1930'. *South Asia Research*, 30:3 (2010), pp. 253–274.

Seton, Rosemary. *Western Daughters in Eastern Lands: British Missionary Women in Asia.* Oxford, Praeger, 2013.

Sharpe, Jenny. *Allegories of Empire: The Figure of Woman in the Colonial Text.* Minneapolis and London, University of Minnesota Press, 1993.

Showalter, Elaine. *The Female Malady: Women, Madness and English Culture, 1830–1980.* London, Virago, 1987.

Sinha, Mrinalini. *Colonial Masculinity: The 'Manly Englishman' and the 'Effeminate Bengali' in the Late Nineteenth Century.* Manchester and New York, Manchester University Press, 1995.

Stoler, Ann Laura. *Race and the Education of Desire: Foucault's 'History of Sexuality' and the Colonial Order of Things.* Durham, Duke University Press, 1995.

— 'Carnal Knowledge and Imperial Power: Gender, Race and Morality in Colonial Asia', in Roger N. Lancaster and Michaela Di Leonardo (eds). *The Gender/Sexuality Reader: Culture, History, Political Economy.* New York, Routledge, 1997, pp. 13–36.

— *Carnal Knowledge and Imperial Power: Race and the Intimate in Colonial Rule.* Berkeley, University of California Press, 2002.

Sutcliffe, Rebecca J. 'Feminizing the Professional: The Government Reports of

Flora Annie Steel'. *Technical Communication Quarterly*, 7:2 (Spring 1998), pp. 153–173.

Swenson, Kristine. *Medical Women and Victorian Fiction*. Missouri, University of Missouri Press, 2005.

Taylor, Ruth E. 'Death of Neurasthenia and its Psychological Reincarnation: A Study of Neurasthenia at the National Hospital for the Relief and Care of the Paralysed and Epileptic, Queen Square, London, 1870–1932'. *The British Journal of Psychiatry*, 179 (2001), pp. 550–557.

Teltscher, Kate. *India Inscribed: European and British Writing on India, 1600–1800*. Oxford, Oxford University Press, 1995.

Thompson, Andrew S. (ed.). *Writing Imperial Histories*. Manchester, Manchester University Press, 2013.

Trollope, Joanna. *Britannia's Daughters: Women of the British Empire*. London, Hutchinson, 1984.

Trustram, Myna. *Women of the Regiment: Marriage and the Victorian Army*. Cambridge, Cambridge University Press, 1984.

Ussher, Jane. *Women's Madness: Misogyny or Mental Illness?* London, Harvester Wheatsheaf, 1991.

Vishwanathan, Gauri. *Outside the Fold: Conversion, Modernity and Belief*. New Delhi, Oxford University Press, 2001.

Wald, Erica. 'Health, Discipline and Appropriate Behaviour: The Body of the Soldier and Space of the Cantonment', *Modern Asian Studies*, 46:4 (July 2012), pp. 815–856.

— *Vice in the Barracks: Medicine, the Military and the Making of Colonial India, 1780–1868*. London, Palgrave Macmillan, 2014.

Ware, Vron. *Beyond the Pale: Women, Racism and History*. London and New York, Verso, 1992.

PhD theses

Haggis, Jane, 'Professional Ladies and Working Wives: Female Missionaries in the London Missionary Society and Its South Travancore District, South India in the Nineteenth Century', University of Manchester, 1991.

Johnston, Anna. 'Adams' Ribs: Gender, Colonialism and the Missionaries, 1800–1860', University of Queensland, 1999.

Procida, Mary A. 'Married to the Empire: British Wives and British Imperialism in India, 1883–1947', University of Pennsylvania, 1997.

Web resource

Letter of Lance-Corporal David Banham of the 94th Regiment of Foot, Moulmein, Burma, to a friend in England, dated 1 August, 1845: National Army Museum, London, www.nam.ac.uk/exhibitions/online-exhibitions/wives-sweethearts/women-regiment/lives-misery-transcript-1 (accessed 26 August 2016).

INDEX

EU authorised representative for GPSR:
Easy Access System Europe, Mustamäe tee 50,
10621 Tallinn, Estonia
gpsr.requests@easproject.com